Langford
Starting
Photography

A guide to better pictures for film and digital camera users

Fourth Edition

Michael Langford
Philip Andrews

AMSTERDAM • BOSTON • HEIDELBERG • LONDON • NEW YORK • OXFORD
PARIS • SAN DIEGO • SAN FRANCISCO • SINGAPORE • SYDNEY • TOKYO
Focal Press is an imprint of Elsevier

ELSEVIER

Focal
Press

Focal Press
An imprint of Elsevier
Linacre House, Jordan Hill, Oxford OX2 8DP
30 Corporate Drive, Burlington MA 01803

First published 1976
Second edition 1993
Reprinted 1994, 1997, 1998
Third edition 1999
Reprinted 2000, 2001, 2002, 2003, 2004
Fourth edition 2005

Permissions may be sought directly from Elsevier's Science and Technology Rights Department in
Oxford, UK: phone: (+44) (0) 1865 843830; fax: (+44) (0) 1865 853333; e-mail:
permissions@elsevier.co.uk. You may also complete your request on-line via the Elsevier homepage
(www.elsevier.com), by selecting 'Customer Support' and then 'Obtaining Permissions'

British Library Cataloguing in Publication Data
A catalogue record for this book is available from the British Library

Library of Congress Cataloguing in Publication Data
A catalogue record for this book is available from the Library of Congress

ISBN 0 240 51967 1

For information on all Focal Press publications visit our website at:
www.focalpress.com

Printed and bound in Italy

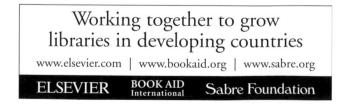

Contents

Part 4

Part 5

Part 6

Part 7

Part 8

Part 9

Part 10

Introduction

Langford's *Starting Photography* is a hands-on book for those photographers just starting their love affair with photography. It equally suits shooters with entry and mid-priced level film and digital cameras, students at school or college using photography as part of art courses as well as those involved in other formal studies, such as the City & Guilds Certificate in Photography. The skills and knowledge presented in the book show you how to take and make great photographs using a highly visual step-by-step approach. *Langford's Starting Photography* gently guides new photographers from tentative beginnings through wobbly first steps to a level where they can confidently create their own great pictures. The photographic examples scattered throughout the text are chosen to encourage and challenge the reader, as they are all within the technical capabilities of beginners with modest gear, such as compact or single lens reflex (SLR) cameras (preferably with manual controls), and the knowledge and skill provided within.

Taking photographs is enjoyable and challenging in all sorts of ways. After all, it's a method of creating pictures which does not demand that you have drawing skills. It's a powerful means of storing memories, showing situations or expressing views which does not insist that you be good at words. But don't fall into the trap of thinking you must have the latest, expensive 'gee whiz' camera to get the most telling shots. What photography demands of you are skills of a different sort that are independent of the technology used to capture the picture. Of these, the most important is the ability to observe – sharpen up your 'seeing' of surroundings, people and simple everyday objects in the world around you. Avoid taking these things for granted just because they are familiar. Develop your awareness of the way lighting and viewpoint can transform appearances, and be quick thinking enough to capture an expression or sum up a fast-changing situation by selecting the right moment to shoot. Become skilled in these areas and you will be a good photographer.

Don't get the wrong idea. I'm not saying that technical abilities and the latest digital equipment do not contribute to the making of great pictures – they do. It is just that you should keep in the forefront of your mind that the techniques and ideas presented in this text serve only one purpose. That is, to support the creation of images that you see with your eye first and capture with your camera second. This seems a funny way to start a book that, let's face it, is about learning the techniques of photography, but seeing is the foundation skill upon which all good photography is built and so I think that it is essential to remind you of its importance right from the start.

Although not primarily a school text, *Langford's Starting Photography* covers most of the core content and practical work for National Curriculum studies. It is also intended for City & Guilds 'Starting Photography', 'Introduction to Black and White Photography', 'Introduction to Color Photography' and Part 2 modules such as 'Landscape Photography'. Above all, the book is planned to help every beginner expand their photography and increase their enjoyment of picture making with today's cameras.

Michael Langford was a major influence on British photographic education. He was a fellow and Course Director in Photography at the Royal College of Art and was renowned for producing a string of 24 books, translated into many languages, which have remained the standard reference works for students and professionals alike across the world.

Michael started his career at the age of 16, as a photographer's apprentice in Bournemouth. Two years later he was assigned to the RAF Photographic Section. After his national service, he had a brief spell with a press photography firm, moving on to work as an industrial photographer while teaching evening classes. Michael continued as a professional photographer throughout his life and his work has appeared in a range of mediums, from postage stamps and book covers to TV commercials.

Michael went on to teach full-time at Ealing Technical College (now Thames Valley University), whilst teaching evening classes at the London College of Printing, after which he moved to become Head of the School of Photography at Birmingham College for Art and Design. He served as an external assessor for several BA courses, as well as an adviser to national examination boards for photography at school and college levels. He moved to the RCA in 1967, became a senior tutor in 1973, departmental head 12 years later and from 1994 to 1997 he suitably held the position as course director.

As a result of his intimate involvement with photography courses and examination syllabuses at all levels he fully understood what a student needed from a textbook. One of his most successful books, *Basic Photography*, was first published in 1965 and the work for the seventh edition was completed just a few days before he died aged 67, bringing it right up to date with the inclusion of information on digital photography. Other works include a companion volume *Advanced Photography*, *The Darkroom Handbook*, *Langford's Starting Photography* and the *Story of Photography*. Many of his books have been adapted as standard texts, bibles for generations of photographers who owe their careers to his work and are still used today for courses from high school to university.

As a writer, teacher and practitioner Michael Langford was a legend in the world of British photography. 'His enormous skill in balancing the art and technique of photography has helped to both inspire and educate an extraordinary number of people, and this will continue for many years to come', Jenny Ridout, former Publishing Director, Focal Press. Along with Michael's other titles, this fourth edition of *Langford's Starting Photography* will ensure that he lives on through his work, providing guidance to everyone who shares his great passion for photography and wants to develop and learn more.

Michael Langford, photographer, teacher and writer
28 February 1933–28 April 2000

1 Picture Making

This first section of the book is mainly concerned with developing your skills of observation – and how to select the interesting and unusual from what you see around you. It is concerned with picture-composing devices such as: framing up your shot in the camera viewfinder or LCD monitor; choice of viewpoint and moment to shoot; and picking appropriate lighting. It also discusses how to recognize pattern, line, color and tone in the subject you intend to photograph, and how to use such features to good effect. These are visual rather than technical aspects of photography and most stem from drawing and painting. They apply no matter what camera you own – cheap or expensive, digital or film, auto-everything or covered in dials and controls.

1 Seeing and photographing

All the world's cameras, sensors, desktop printers, scanners, films, enlargers and other photographic paraphernalia are no more than tools for making pictures. They may be very sophisticated technically, but they cannot see or think for themselves. Of course, it's quite enjoyable playing around with the machinery and testing it out, but this is like polishing up your bicycle and only ever riding it around the block to see how well it goes. Bicycles enable you to get out and explore the world; cameras challenge you to make successful pictures out of what you see around you, in perceptive and interesting ways.

Anyone who starts photography seriously quickly discovers how it develops their ability to see. In other words, not just taking familiar scenes for granted but noticing with much greater intensity all the visual elements – shapes, textures, colors and human situations – they contain. This is an exciting and rewarding activity in itself. The second challenge is how to put that mindless machine (the camera) in the right place at the right time, to make a really effective photographic image out of any of these subjects. Seeing and organizing your picture making is just as important as technical 'know-how' and it comes with practice.

To begin with, it is helpful to consider the ways seeing differs from photographing. You don't necessarily have to regard differences as a barrier. The point is that by understanding how the scene in front of you will appear on a final print you will start to 'pre-visualize' your results. This makes it much easier to work through your camera.

Pictures have edges

Our eyes look out on the world without being conscious of any 'frame' hemming in what we see. Stop a moment and check – your nose, eyebrows, glasses (if you wear them) do form a sort of frame, but this is so out of focus and vague that you are not really aware of any definite 'edge' to your vision. However, immediately you look through a camera viewfinder the world is cut down into a small rectangle with sharply defined edges and corners. Instead of freely scanning your surroundings, you have to compose their essence within this artificial boundary.

Original scene

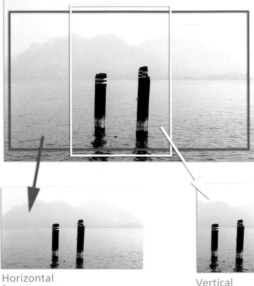

Horizontal framing

Vertical framing

Figure 1.1 The same scene can be framed in a variety of ways, producing photographs that emphasize different parts of the picture. Try turning your camera from the horizontal to the vertical to produce a different point of view. Image courtesy of www.ablestock.com.

The hard edges and their height-to-width proportions have a strong effect on a photograph. Look how the same scene in Figure 1.1 is changed by using a different shooting format. Long, low pictures tend to emphasize the flow of horizontal lines and space left to right. Turning the camera to form an upright picture of the same scene tends to make more of its depth and distance, as the scale between foreground and furthest detail is greater and more interactive.

Framing up pictures is a powerful way to include or exclude – for example, deciding whether the horizon in a landscape should appear high or low, or how much of an expanse of color to leave in or crop out. The edge of the frame can crop into the outline of something and effectively present it as a new shape too. Remember, though, that nothing you leave outside the viewfinder can be added later!

The camera does not select

When we look at something we have an

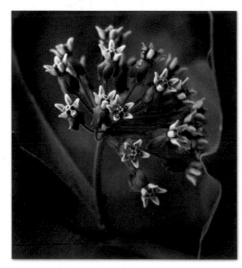

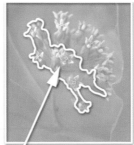

Small zone of focus used to add emphasis

extraordinary ability to concentrate on the main item of interest, despite cluttered surroundings. Our natural 'homing device' includes turning the head, focusing the eyes and generally disregarding any part of the scene considered unimportant. Talking to a friend outside their house, you hardly register details of the building behind, but the camera has no brain to tell it what is important and unimportant. It cannot discriminate and usually records too much – the unwanted detail along

Figure 1.2 Because the camera is not as selective as the human eye, photographers use a range of techniques to add emphasis to their pictures and to direct the attention of the viewer. Here a small zone of focus (sometimes called depth of field) is used to emphasize the flowers and de-emphasize the surrounding leaves. Image courtesy of www.ablestock.com.

with the wanted. This becomes all too apparent when you study the resulting photograph. Drainpipes and brickwork in the background may appear just as strongly as your friend's face . . . and how did that dustbin appear in the foreground?

You therefore have to help the camera along, perhaps by changing your viewpoint or filling up the frame (if your camera will focus close enough). Perhaps you should wait for a change in lighting to pick out your main item from the rest by making it the brightest or the most contrasting color in the picture. Or you might control your zone of sharp focus (a device called depth of field or DOF, discussed further on page 58) in order to limit detail to one chosen spot, as is the case in Figure 1.2. Other forms of emphasis are discussed on page 9.

You have to train your eyes to search the scene for distractions. When looking through the viewfinder, check the background, midground and foreground detail. Above all, always make a quick scan of everything in the viewfinder before pressing the button.

Sensors and films cannot cope with the same contrast as the eye

Our eyes are so sophisticated that we can make out details both in the dark shadows and brightly lit parts of a scene (provided they are not right next to each other). This is an ability that is beyond the capabilities of a photograph. Photography generally makes darkest areas record darker and lightest areas lighter than they appeared to the eye, so that the whole image becomes more contrasty. It is important to remember that your eyes will always see the contrast of a scene differently to how the camera will record it. With practice this will mean that you can anticipate the differences and therefore be able to predict more accurately

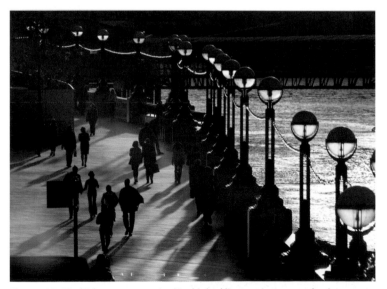

Figure 1.3 The high contrast contained in this backlit scene is too great for the camera to record clear detail in both the highlight and shadow areas. Instead, the result is a silhouette. Image courtesy of www.ablestock.com.

how your pictures will turn out (see Figure 1.3).

The camera has one 'eye'

Unlike humans, the cameras we use do not have binocular vision. Their pictures are not three-dimensional. They do not photograph from two points of view. So when we want to show depth in a scene we are photographing we have to imply it through devices such as the use of converging lines (see Figure 1.4), changes in scale or changes in tones aided by lighting. To help you see more like the camera does, close one eye to forecast the camera's two-dimensional way of imaging.

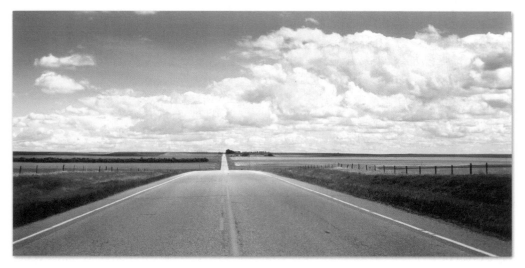

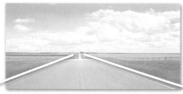

Converging lines
showing depth

Figure 1.4 Because the camera only provides a 'single-eye' view of the world, photographers have to rely on devices like converging lines to portray distance and depth in their pictures. Image courtesy of www.ablestock.com.

Most photographs capture just one moment in time

When things are active in front of the camera your choice of when to take the picture often 'sets' someone's momentary expression or the brief juxtaposition of one person to another or their surroundings. Capturing the peak of the action often produces photographs that are frozen moments of time (see Figure 1.5). There is often a decisive moment for pressing the button that best sums up a situation or simply gives a good design. You need to be alert and able to make quick decisions if you are going for this type of picture. Once again, the camera cannot think for you.

Color translated into monochrome

When you are shooting or printing out results in black and white ('monochrome'), the multicolored world becomes simplified into different shades or tones of gray. A scarlet racing car against green bushes may reproduce as two grays that very nearly match. Try not to shoot monochrome pictures

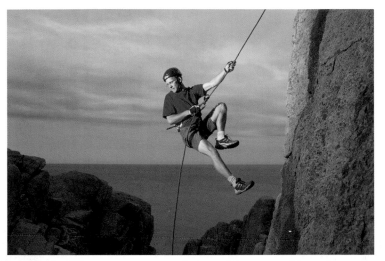

Figure 1.5 The camera has the ability to capture a moment in time and then preserve it frozen for ever. Image courtesy of www.ablestock.com.

that rely a great deal on contrast of colors unless this will also reproduce as contrasty tones. Look at colors as 'darks' and 'lights'. Remember too that an unimportant part of your subject visually much too strong and assertive (such as an orange door in a street scene) can probably be ignored because it will merge with its surroundings in black and white (see Figure 1.6).

Occasionally, you might want to adjust the way colors translate into monochrome. This can be done with the aid of a colored filter over the camera lens (page 216).

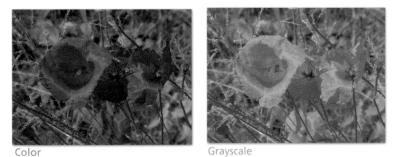

Color   Grayscale

Figure 1.6 Contrasting colors can become similar shades of gray when they are recorded in monochrome. If you are shooting black and white, you will need to train yourself to see your subject in terms of light and dark rather than color. Image courtesy of the author.

2 Using the viewfinder – framing up

Experienced photographers often make a rough 'frame' shape with their hands to exclude surroundings when first looking and deciding how a scene will photograph (see Figure 2.1). Similarly, you can carry a slide mount, or a cardboard cut-out, to look through and practice ways of framing up your subject. When you come to

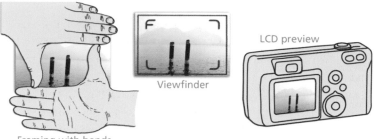

Figure 2.1 You can practice framing a scene in several ways – using your hands, the viewfinder in the camera or the LCD screen on the back of your digital camera.

buying a camera, it is most important to choose one which has a viewfinding system you find clear and 'comfortable' to use, especially if you wear glasses. After all, the viewfinder is a kind of magic drawing pad on which the world moves about as you point the camera – including or cropping out something here; causing an item to appear in front of, or alongside, another item there. Digital cameras have the added advantage of often allowing you to frame your pictures on the camera's inbuilt LCD screen as well as through the viewfinder.

Precise and accurate viewfinder work is needed to position strong shapes close to the camera, as in Figure 2.2, to symmetrically fill up the frame. Or alternatively you might frame up your main subject off-center, perhaps to relate it to another element or just to add a sense of space. With practice you will start to notice how moving the camera viewpoint a few feet left or right, or raising or lowering it, can make a big difference to the way near and distant elements in, say, a landscape appear to relate to one another. This is even more critical when you are shooting close-ups, where tiny alterations of a few centimeters often make huge changes to the picture.

The way you frame up something which is on the move across your picture also has interesting effects. You can make it seem to be entering or leaving a scene by positioning it facing either close towards or away from one side of your picture. A camera with a large, easy-to-use viewfinder will encourage you to creatively explore all these aspects of viewpoint and framing before every shot, instead of just crudely acting as an aiming device 'to get it all in'.

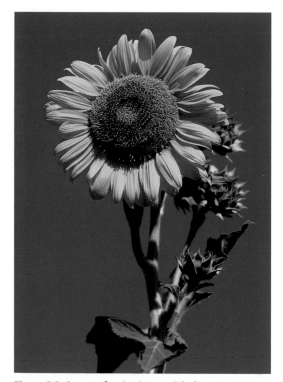

Figure 2.2 Accurate framing is essential when you are filling the frame with subjects close to the camera. Image courtesy of www.ablestock.com.

Using foregrounds and backgrounds

Foreground and background details cause problems when you are a beginner, for in the heat of the moment they are easily overlooked – especially when you are concentrating on an animated subject. And yet far from being distracting, what lies in front of or behind your main subject can often be used to make a positive contribution to your picture.

Sometimes, for example, you are forced to shoot from somewhere so distant that even with the lens zoomed to its longest setting your key element occupies only a tiny area in the frame. It then pays to seek out a viewpoint where other, much closer, items will fill in the foreground and help to create a 'frame within a frame'. They may even make the small size of the main element an asset that adds a sense of depth and distance. With landscape subject matter you can often use nearby foliage, rock or other appropriate elements to frame a distant subject.

Even simply photographing from a low viewpoint so that the background shows only sky and very distant detail (Figure 2.3) often eliminates unwanted assertive material in the foreground. Equally, by picking a high viewpoint you can fill up your background with grass or similar plain ground – or you may find an angle from which the background is seen shrouded in shadow. On the other hand, always try to make use of background details when these will add interesting information to a shot. This is also a way of making some visual comment through comparisons between like objects, perhaps parodying one element against another – for example, people passing by giant figures on a billboard. Statues and monuments also offer good opportunities.

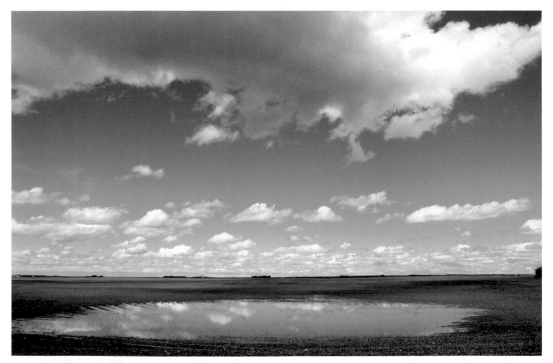

Figure 2.3 Tilting the camera upwards and filling the frame with an interesting sky can remove the problem of unwanted details in the foreground. Image courtesy of www.ablestock.com.

When framing, always try to fill up the picture area, but don't let your camera's fixed height-to-width picture proportions restrict you (2:3 ratio is standard for 35 mm film cameras). Some subjects will look better framed up in square format; others need a more extreme oblong shape. You may be able to get around this by again using a 'frames within frames' arrangement. You can also trim the picture after it has been taken. You can hide the unwanted details or change the picture's shape by using L-shaped cards for prints or the Crop tool for digital files (see Figures 2.4 and 2.5). Some digital cameras provide the ability to select several different formats for your photographs. This is true

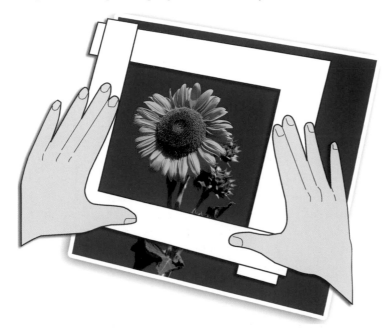

Figure 2.4 Don't think that the shape of your pictures is restricted to the format of the film that you are using. At the print stage you can crop out unwanted details or even change the format of the picture.

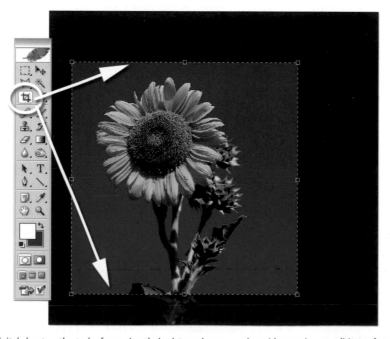

Figure 2.5 For digital shooters the task of cropping their pictures is even easier, with most image editing software containing specific Crop tools that can be used to interactively trim your images.

also for APS cameras, allowing you to choose between three format ratios before each shot. The setting you make alters frame lines in the viewfinder and also informs the processing lab to print your picture the required shape.

3 Creating a point of emphasis

Most photographs are strengthened and simplified by having one main subject or 'center of interest'. In a picture of a crowd, for example, this might be one figure waving a flag; a landscape might center on a cottage or a group of trees. Having first decided your main element, you can help to bring it into prominence and at the same time improve the structure of your shot by calling on a range of long-established visual devices used in picture composition.

In some situations you will be able to create emphasis through making the chosen item stand out relative to its surroundings because it appears to break the horizon, or perhaps is placed where lines within your picture converge. You can also give it prominence through its contrasting color or tone, or by the way the subject is shown within some eye-catching shape either in front or behind it. To achieve these results, it is once again important to learn to seek out the right camera viewpoint and compose your pictures in the viewfinder with thought and care.

Using lines

Lines are formed in a picture wherever lengthy, distinct boundaries occur between tones or colors. A line need not be the actual outline of an object but it could be a whole chain of shapes – clouds, roads and hedges, shadows, movement, blur – which together form a strong linear element through a picture. Clear-cut lines steeply radiating from, or converging to, a particular spot (as in Figure 3.1, for instance) achieve the most dramatic lead-in effects.

At the same time, their shape (curved, straight) and general pattern (short and jagged, long and parallel) can strongly influence the mood of your shot too.

You can best control the appearance of lines in your picture by where you position the camera – high, low, near, far, square-on or oblique to them. As you try each of these different viewpoints, observe carefully in the viewfinder how objects overlap or appear to join up with others in front or

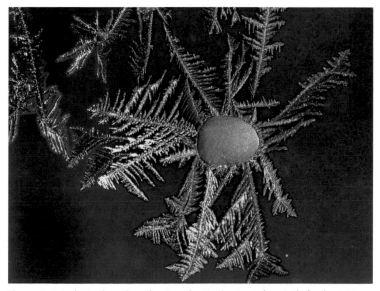

Figure 3.1 Radiating lines draw the viewer's attention towards a single focal point in the picture. Image courtesy of www.ablestock.com.

behind them to create useful shapes and lines. Then change focal length (zoom in or out, page 70) if necessary to frame up exactly the area you need.

Positioning within the picture format

Most beginners position the main subject they want to emphasize centrally in the picture. This may work well for a strictly symmetrical composition with a child's face centered in the middle of whirling concentric circles, but it easily becomes repetitive and boring. There is, however, a viewer-researched classical guide to placing the principal element called the 'golden mean', which artists have favored in composition over the centuries. The concept is that the strongest, most 'pleasing' position for points of interest is at one of the intersection lines dividing vertical and horizontal zones in an 8:5 ratio. A simple interpretation of this idea is often called the 'rule of thirds'. Figure 3.2 shows the four so-called 'strong' positions this gives within a 35 mm camera's

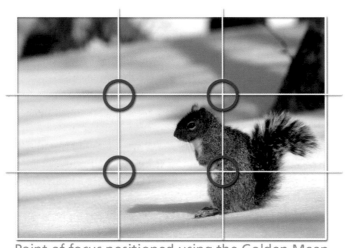

Point of focus positioned using the Golden Mean

Figure 3.2 You can add a sense of balance to an off-center composition by using the rule of thirds as a guide. Simply place the points of interest from your picture at the intersection of the grid lines. Image courtesy of www.ablestock.com.

picture format ratio. Many cameras have a viewfinder that displays these grid points to help aid with composing your pictures.

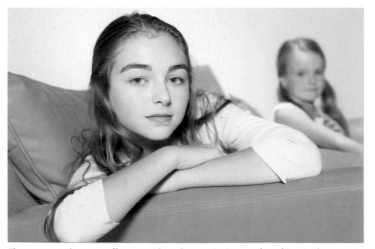

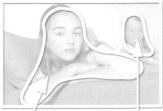

Off-center   Balancing
subject   subject

Figure 3.3 Balance an off-center subject by positioning another object in the opposite part of the frame.

The golden mean is an interesting guide in photography but, as with other forms of picture making, it is something that should never be slavishly adopted. Lines and tones elsewhere in pictures all contribute to photographs with unified balance and strong structure. Pictures with their main element placed very off-center against plain surroundings tend to look unstable, but they can be lively and have a spacious, open-air feel. Off-centring can work very well where another secondary element (typically on the opposite side of the frame) relates to it and gives your picture balance (see Figure 3.3).

Contrasting with surroundings

Making your main element the lightest or darkest tone, or the only item of a particular color included in the picture, will pick it out strongly. This is also a good way to emphasize an interesting shape and help set mood. For maximum emphasis pick a camera position that shows your chosen item against, or surrounded by, the most contrasting background. Bear in mind that the eye is most attracted to where strong darks and lights are adjacent, so make sure the emphasis really is where you want it to be. Often, you can use the fact that the background has much less, or more, lighting than your main subject and then expose correctly for what is the important part (make sure your camera's exposure settings are not over-influenced by the darker or brighter areas around it).

Remembering how photographs step up the appearance of contrast in a scene, preview roughly how it will record by half-closing your eyes and looking through your eyelashes. Shadows now look much darker and contain less detail. In a really high-contrast situation – like Figure 3.4 – you can expect a silhouette effect when exposure is correct for most of the surrounding scene. Having dark figures against the lightest part of the environment gives their shapes great emphasis.

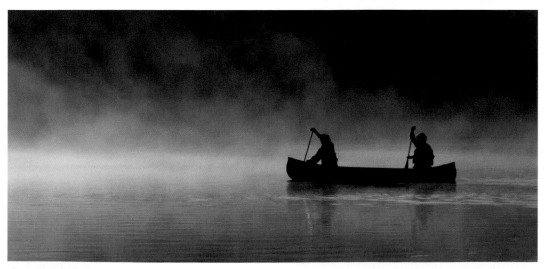

Figure 3.4 By backlighting your main subjects, it is easy to create silhouette effects. In this type of image the shape of the subjects is paramount, as texture and color are kept to a minimum. Image courtesy of www.ablestock.com.

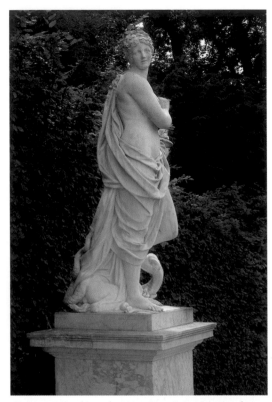

Figure 3.5 Tonal interchange: using existing contrast of tone.

The same device, known as tonal interchange, is used in the statue picture (Figure 3.5). Here, however, lighting is soft and even, and plays a minor role. Tonal differences between objects in the picture (the statue being the only white item amongst almost uniformly dark foliage) create their own tonal interchange. Contrast of tone is an especially important emphasizing device when you are shooting something in black and white.

Tonal interchange is a device worth remembering when you are taking a portrait, where you have some control over arrangement of the lighting. Showing the lightest side of a face against the darkest part of the background and vice versa, as in Figure 3.6, picks out the shape of the head. Often, this lighting is achievable by just part closing a curtain or having someone shade the background with a card from one side.

Don't forget the value of seeking out a handy frame within a frame as the means of isolating your main subject by color or tone from otherwise confusing surroundings. Windows and doors are particularly useful – a figure photographed outside a building can be isolated by picking a viewpoint from where they appear framed in front of the dark shape of an open entrance behind them (preferably some way back, and out of focus). Similarly, a closed door may give a patch of colored background. Take care, however – this local surround should never

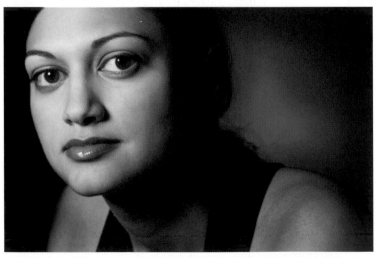

Figure 3.6 Tonal interchange: manipulating light sources to create contrast of tone.

contain color or patterning in such a strong manner that it overwhelms or camouflages your main subject.

Choice of moment

Of course, if you are photographing someone you know, or a largely 'still life' subject or landscape, you often have sufficient time to pick some means of emphasis, such as the use of line, or tone, or positioning in the frame. But in a fast-changing, active situation, often the best you can do is choose the most promising viewpoint and wait for the right moment. Sometimes this will mean first framing up a background shape or foreground lead-in, and then waiting patiently for someone to enter the picture space. On the other hand, your picture may be full of people surrounding some relatively static element. Having framed up the scene, the moment to shoot is dependent on the the various subjects in the picture. You will need to wait until the expressions and positions of your subjects are just right before releasing the shutter.

Always be on the lookout for fleeting comparisons which support and draw attention to one element – your main subject. Perhaps you can do this by showing two different 'compartments' in your picture. For example, comparing people framed in adjacent windows of a crowded bus or row of telephone booths. A mirror on the wall or some other reflective surface is another useful way of bringing two quite separate components together into your picture.

4 Picking lighting conditions

Most photographs (especially when you begin) are taken under 'existing light' conditions. This term means natural or artificial lighting as it exists for your subject at the time, rather than flash or lamps in the studio, which are used to provide a fully controlled lighting set-up (see pages 133 and 136). It's easy to regard the lighting by which you see the world around you simply as illumination – something taken for granted. But as well as giving the eye the basic ability to see, it can be responsible for communicating strong emotional, subjective responses too. In fact, the effect of lighting on a subject is often the reason for taking a picture as much as the subject itself.

We have all experienced the way the appearance of something is transformed under different weather conditions or at different times of the day, due to changes in the direction, color, quality (e.g. overcast or direct sunlight) and contrast-producing effect of the light. You may not be able to exert control over these existing light conditions, but excellent pictures often result from you recognizing the right time and best camera position, choices which greatly influence the whole mood of a picture.

Quality and direction

The quality of the light falling on your subjects is often defined with terms such as 'hard' or 'soft'. Hardest natural light comes direct from the sun in a clear sky; objects then cast well-defined, hard-edged shadow shapes and these may contribute strong lines and patterns to a picture, as well as stark, dramatic contrast. Figure 4.1 is an example where well-defined shadow shapes on a sunny day become a key part of the picture.

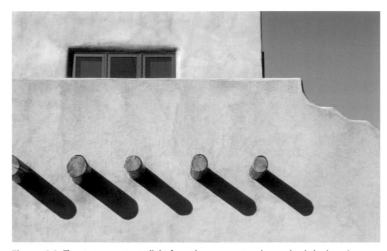

Figure 4.1 The strong, contrasty light from the sun creates sharp-edged shadows in your pictures. The shadows' dark tone and graphic shape mean that they play an important part in the balance and design of the photograph. Image courtesy of www.ablestock.com.

In Figure 4.2, sunlight from one side, 90° to the subject, gives a strongly three-dimensional effect. Lit parts are well defined, forming a strong pattern especially where picked out against an area of solid dark shadow areas. In addition to defining shape well, side lighting also creates strong texture. However, you must be careful when photographing very contrasty pictures like this. It is important to expose accurately because even a slight error either 'burns out' the lightest detail or turns wanted shadow detail impenetrably dark. Beware too of shadows being cast by one subject onto another, as this may give confusing results.

Softest quality light comes from a totally overcast sky. Shadows are ill-defined or more often non-existent, so that lines and shapes in your picture are created by the forms of the subject itself. Pictures that are full of varied shapes and colors are best shot in soft, even lighting to reveal maximum overall information without complications of shadow. Even on a clear, sunlit day you can still find soft lighting by positioning your subject totally in shadow – for instance, in the shade of a large building, where it only receives light scattered from sky alone. Results in color may show a blue cast, however, unless carefully corrected via the editing software or when printing.

In Figure 4.3 you will notice how hazy sunlight gives an intermediate, semi-diffused lighting effect to the scene. Shadows are discernible but have ill-defined, well-graduated edges and there is less

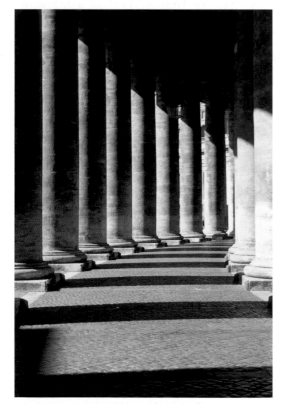

Figure 4.2 Side lighting creates pictures with strong, well-defined shapes and striking texture. Here the shadow area of one column is contrasted against the highlight area of the next, producing a pattern of alternating shades. Image courtesy of www.ablestock.com.

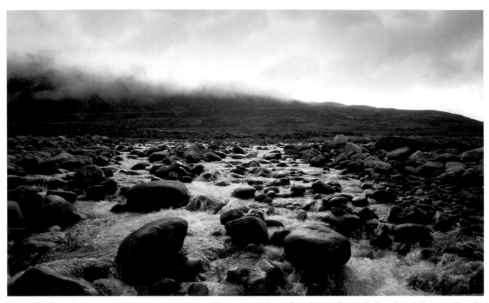

Figure 4.3 The hazy lighting produced by the low cloud has provided a soft and even, but still directional, light to the whole of this scene. Highlights and shadows are clearly present on the rocks in the foreground, but they are not as strong and distinct as they would be if the same location was photographed in midday sun. Image courtesy of www.ablestock.com.

contrast than given by sunlight direct. Intermediate lighting conditions like this are excellent for many photographic subjects, and are especially 'kind' to portraits.

Time of day

Throughout the day, the sun moves its position around the sky; the color of its light reaching us also changes at dawn and dusk. Combined with the effects of weather and other atmospheric conditions like haze or smoke, you have a tremendously wide range of lighting opportunities. If possible, forward plan to ensure that you are in the right place at a time when a fixed subject such as a landscape receives lighting that brings out the features and creates the mood you want to show.

Photography at dusk is often very rewarding because, as the daylight fades, the scene's appearance changes minute by minute. It is good to shoot landscape pictures during the brief period when there is enough daylight in the sky to still just make out the horizon, yet most of the buildings have switched on their lighting – not difficult to judge by eye. A firmly mounted camera with automatic exposure measurement can adjust settings as daylight dims (see Figure 4.4).

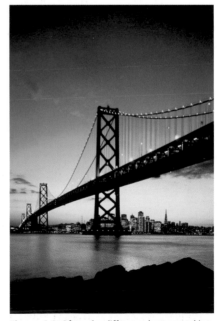

Figure 4.4 Often, the difference between taking an okay picture and one that really suits the subject is the time of day that the photograph is captured. City night scenes are often taken just on dusk when the landscape is lit by both the city lights and the remaining daylight. Image courtesy of www.ablestock.com.

Mixed lighting

Pictures lit with, or containing, a mixture of light sources – daylight, domestic lamps, fluorescent tubes, street lighting, etc. – will not photograph all the same color. Most color films are designed to be accurate in daylight. Many digital cameras have an auto white balance setting that interactively adjusts the capture to suit the light source. Alternatively, some models allow the user to change the setting to suit specific light sources such as daylight, domestic lamps and fluorescent tubes. When your digital camera is set to the daylight white balance setting, it will create pictures with similar color to those captured on daylight balanced film.

Looking at a distant scene with mixed lighting you notice and accept differences of color, even though they are exaggerated when photographed. But it would be a mistake to shoot a portrait lit by the pink light of dusk, or by the floodlighting on the foreground terrace. Skin rendered pink by one and yellow by the other looks odd in isolation, and is probably beyond the ability of your processing lab to normalize in printing. Keep to using a lighting source that your film or camera 'white balance' setting is suited for.

Problems can also occur when photographing people, food, flowers and similar 'color-sensitive' subjects in surroundings with strongly tinted daylight. The greenery of sunlit grass and foliage in an enclosed garden or woods may do this, or it may be a nearby strongly colored wall or vehicle – particularly with subject close-ups. Oddly enough, wrong color becomes much more acceptable if your picture actually shows the environment which was its cause.

5 Pattern, texture and shape

Most photographs are 'subject orientated', meaning that who, or what, is featured in the shot is of the greatest interest. Others are more 'structure orientated' – enjoyed not necessarily so much for the subject as for the way the picture has been seen and constructed. In practice, both aspects should be present if you want a unified picture rather than a random snap.

The pattern and shapes used in photographs are like notes and phrases used to structure music. But in visual image form they are linked with texture too – each one of the three often contributing to the others. Pattern, for example, may be formed by the position of multiple three-dimensional shapes,

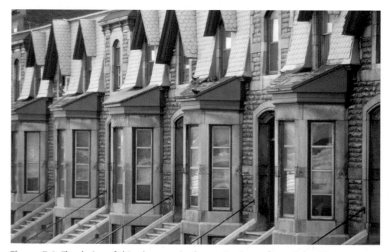

Figure 5.1 The design of this photograph of repeating house fronts is based on the structure of the image rather than its content. It is the pattern of regular shapes, repeating colors and textures that forms the core of the picture's interest. Image courtesy of www.ablestock.com.

like the house fronts in Figure 5.1. Or it might be no more than marks of differing tones on an otherwise smooth, flat surface. Then again, pattern can be revealed on an even-toned textured surface through the effect of light – as with the weatherboard on an old barn. Pattern, texture and shape should be sought out and used as basic elements of composition, provided they support and strengthen rather than confuse your picture.

Pattern

Be wary of filling up your picture with pattern alone – the result is usually monotonous like wallpaper, and without any core or center of interest. You can help matters by breaking the pattern in some way, perhaps having one or two elements a different shape or color. Another way to create variety in a regular pattern is to photograph it from a steeply oblique viewpoint, in order to get a difference in size.

Shadows frequently form interesting patterns, especially when the surface receiving the shadow is undulating rather than flat. You can see this, for instance, when the shadow of a window frame falls on pleated white curtaining.

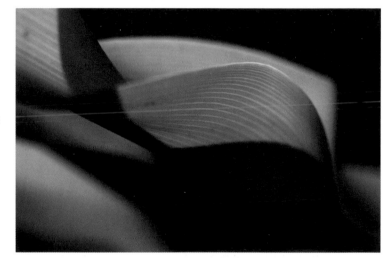

Figure 5.2 The abstract mixture of shadow and shape keeps the audience interested in this photograph. Here the shadow has become more than just a by-product of the lighting – it is an integral part of the photograph's design. Image courtesy of www.ablestock.com.

Texture

Revealing the texture in the surface or surfaces of your subject helps to make a two-dimensional photograph look three-dimensional. Texture also adds character to what might otherwise be just flat-looking slabs of tone and color, helping to give your subject form and substance. A multitude of different and interesting textures exist all around us. Rough wood (Figure 5.3) or stone comes immediately to mind, but look also at the texture of ploughed earth, plants, ageing people's faces, even the (ephemeral) texture of wind-blown water. Or even in rugged landscapes, distant hills and mountains, as these represent texture on a giant scale.

There are two essentials for emphasizing texture. One is appropriate lighting, the other is the ability to resolve fine detail (e.g. accuracy of focusing, no camera shake, or a light recording material without a pattern of its own). Where the subject's textured surface is all on one plane, direct sunlight from one side will separate out the raised and hollowed parts. The more the angled light just grazes the surface, the greater the exaggeration of texture.

Such extreme lighting also tends to leave empty black shadows – if these are large and unacceptable, pick a time when white cloud is present in other parts of the sky, and so able to add some soft 'fill-in' light. When your subject contains several textured surfaces shown at

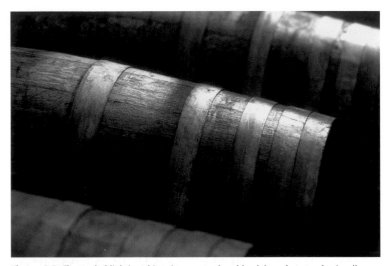

different angles, the use of harsh lighting from one direction may suit one surface but lights others flat-on or puts them totally in shadow. More diffused, hazy sunlight (but still steeply directed from above or one side) will then give the best results. What you can learn from sunlight can also be applied on a smaller scale, working with a lamp or camera flash, in the studio (see page 132).

Figure 5.3 The angled lighting skimming across the old oak barrels not only visually describes the form of the barrels, but also shows off the wood's texture. Image courtesy of www.ablestock.com.

Shape

A strong shape is a bold attraction to the eye, something that you can use to structure your whole picture. It might consist of one object, or several items seen together in a way that forms a combined shape. Shape is also a good means of relating two otherwise dissimilar elements in your picture, one shape echoing another, perhaps in a humorous way. Bear in mind too that shapes are often made stronger when repeated into a pattern – like the informal

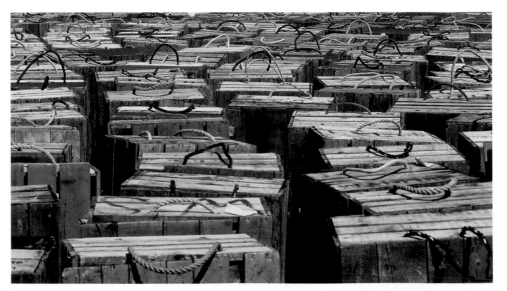

Figure 5.4 The repeated design of the crates in this photograph has produced an informal pattern of texture, shape and color. Image courtesy of www.ablestock.com.

rows of crates in Figure 5.4 or (very differently) the irregular pattern of similarly shaped boats in Figure 5.5.

The best way to emphasize shape is by careful choice of viewpoint and the use of contrast. Check through the viewfinder that you are in the exact position to see the best shape. Small camera shifts can make big changes in edge junctures, especially when several things at different distances need to align and combine. If this position then leaves your subject too big or small in the frame, remain where you are, but zoom the lens until it fits your picture.

Shape will also gain strength and emphasis through contrast with its surroundings – difference in tone or color of background and lighting. A good example of this is the contrast of shape and color of the group of women in front of the Taj Mahal in Figure 5.6. Their repeating shapes add an extra dimension to the picture by providing a patterning effect. Sometimes you will find it possible to fill up a shape with pattern.

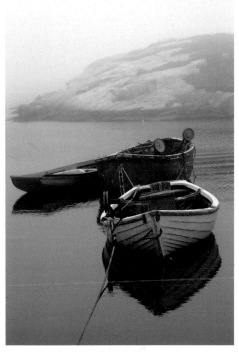

Figure 5.5 Though not identical, there are enough similarities between the boats in this group to provide a visual echo of each other's design. Image courtesy of www.ablestock.com.

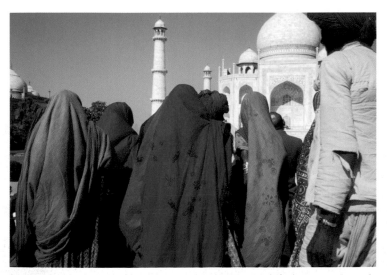

Figure 5.6 Though not identical, the shapes and colors of the clothed women in front of the Taj Mahal form an irregular pattern that adds interest to the picture's foreground. Image courtesy of www.ablestock.com.

6 Using color

Like shape and pattern, it may be the colour in a scene that first attracts your eye and becomes a dominant feature in your picture. (Just switch your TV or computer screen between color and black and white settings to prove how much color contributes to an image.) Color can help create harmony or discord. It may pick out and emphasize one important element against all others, or link things together as in Figure 6.1, by repeating the shape of the chairs and then contrasting them with different colors. A more varied pair of colors will interact and gain contrast from one another, especially if they are strong hues, well separated and 'complementary' in the spectrum. The resulting effect may then shout for attention and be lively and exciting or perhaps just garish.

It is interesting to notice, in pictures that combine contrasting colors, that the reds often seem to advance or 'come forward' while greens and blues 'stand back'. Even black or white is influential. Areas of black surrounding small areas of color can make them seem luminous and bright, as in Figure 6.2, whereas colors against white make the hues look darker.

Once again, the key to practical success is selection – mainly through tightly controlled framing and viewpoint. You should rigorously exclude from your picture any elements that confuse or work against its color scheme. Where possible, select lighting conditions that help to present colors in the way you need. For example, have you noticed how a car that looked brilliant red in hard sunlight appears a diluted color in overcast weather conditions as it reflects light from the white sky in its polished surface? Similarly, atmospheric haze or mist in

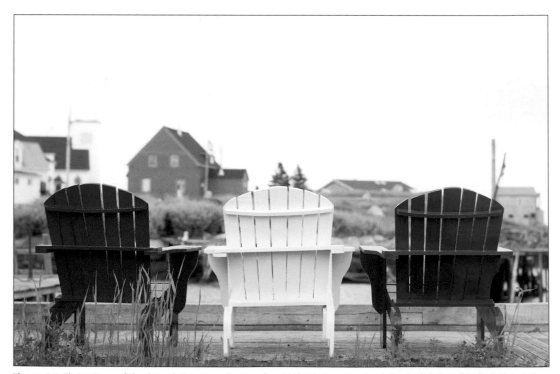

Figure 6.1 The patterns of the three chairs are made more dynamic by their contrasting colors and their positioning against the relatively muted tones of the background. Image courtesy of www.ablestock.com.

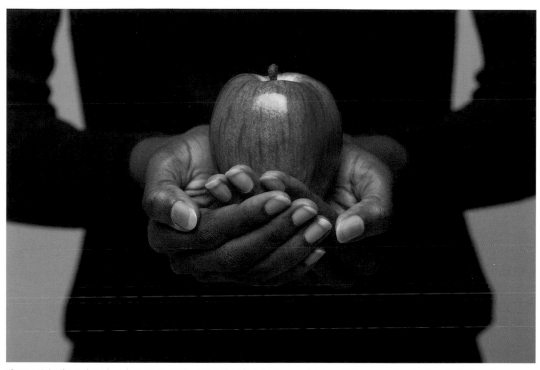

Figure 6.2 The red apple, when contrasted against the black background, seems to be more vibrant, almost glowing, than if the fruit was photographed with a brighter backdrop. Image courtesy of www.ablestock.com.

a landscape scatters and mixes white light with the colored light reaching you from distant objects, so that they appear less rich and saturated. Then, if dull overcast conditions change to direct sunlight (especially immediately after rain), clear visibility enriches and transforms all the colors present in your photographs.

Color of the light

The actual color of the light that falls on your subject at different times of the day and from different light sources – domestic lamps or candles, for instance – can make big differences to the emotional effect of your picture. The comfortable mood of a cottage interior may be intensified by a warm color cast from domestic lights and firelight. Bare tree branches in winter can appear cold and bleak in light from a clear blue sky, or be transformed in the orangey light of sunset.

It is important to realize that subject color is never completely constant and need not always be strictly accurate. This is especially true when atmosphere and mood are your main priorities. Contrast the cold blue of the ice scene in Figure 6.3 with the warm desert rocks in Figure 6.4. An empty ruined building can seem more mysterious in a photograph with a dominant color scheme of blues and gray – greens, especially when the overall tone of the picture is dark (low key) too. A 'cold' color filter over the lens (page 214) may help to achieve this effect.

Other macabre results – inhuman-looking portraits, for example – are possible using offbeat but easily found light sources such as sodium street lighting, at night. You can judge by

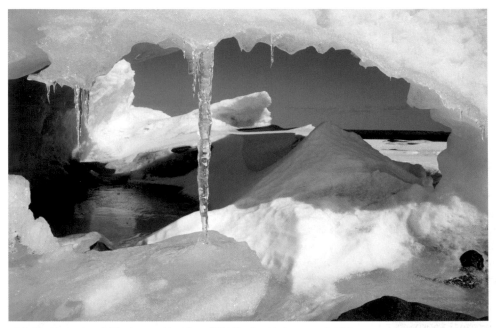

Figure 6.3 The blue tones of this picture add to the cold feeling for this icy scene. Don't be too quick to dismiss the emotive power of color to help communicate through your pictures. Image courtesy of www.ablestock.com.

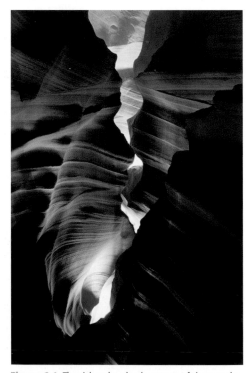

Figure 6.4 The rich red and ochre tones of these rocks seem to emit the very heat of the desert that surrounds them. Image courtesy of www.ablestock.com.

eye when lighting of this kind makes familiar colors such as red look just dark gray, and skin seem an unholy greenish yellow. The distortion is even stronger when your digital camera is set to 'daylight' white balance or you are using regular daylight-type color film.

Finally, don't overlook the value of blurred and 'stretched out' semi-abstract shapes and streaks of color for making pictures depicting action and movement in dynamic ways. At night, fairgrounds or just roads with busy traffic lanes will provide you with fruitful subject matter (see page 204).

Developing a personal approach

This first part has been concerned with 'seeing' – with not taking simple everyday objects for granted but observing them as mixtures of shapes and forms, with various color and pattern characteristics and set against a background. Over-familiarization as to what things are actually for (or who people are) easily blunts your visual sense. Looking and photographing in a completely unfamiliar environment like a strange town or country is often more productive because newly seen things trigger perception strongly. The more you begin to see objects as potential picture subjects, the less your photography will be limited to cliché like postcard-type views or the conventional family group.

At the same time, the various structures of picture making itself allow plenty of scope for a personal approach. For convenience, ways of composing pictures have been discussed here under framing, lighting, color, etc., but in practice almost all photographs (including most of the ones reproduced here) use a mixture of devices. One may be more effectively used for a particular set of circumstances than another, but rarely to the exclusion of all others. You have to decide your priorities and seize opportunities on the spot.

A good way to develop awareness of picture possibilities is to set yourself projects. These can be applied to subjects which interest you – family, locations, sport, etc. The example projects that follow are similar to assignments and tests in photography course programmes. You will probably be able to find subjects in your locality for most of them, even though they differ somewhat from the suggestions made. Don't slavishly copy pictures in this and other books. Approach each project as a chance to make your own discoveries – sometimes these come from producing

unexpected images (including mistakes!) that are worth following up later.

'Developing your eye' in this way will also provide a powerful incentive for learning technical aspects of photography in order to get what you want into final picture form. The way cameras work and how their controls can contribute to results are the themes of the next sections of the text.

1 Select five letters of the alphabet and then go and photograph objects or parts of objects in your local environment that look like your chosen letters. Make sure that the shapes of your objects suggest the letter shapes and where possible use contrast (in color, texture, lighting or tone) to make the letter shape obvious in your picture.

2 Often, photojournalists are required to submit two versions of the same picture – one vertical and one horizontal. This gives the paper or magazine more choice when laying out the story. Select a landscape, still-life or portrait as your subject and practice making two versions (horizontal and vertical) of each photograph you take.

3 Most cameras record their pictures in a rectangular format, but for this project I want you to imagine that your camera shoots in a square format (rectangle minus the edges). Compose five different pictures using the square format and then check the success of your results by cropping the resultant pictures as squares in your image editing program (or use L-shaped cardboard cut-outs to frame your print – see Figure 2.4).

4 The majority of cameras are used at eye level, so most photographs show the world from this height. Take six pictures of familiar subjects using your camera only below waist height or above normal head height.

5 Making appropriate use of color, lighting, composition and expression, take two portraits

(continued)

of the same person. One should show your subject as gentle and friendly, the other as sinister and frightening. Keep clothing and setting the same in each picture.

6 Make a series of three pictures of one of the following subjects: wheels, doorsteps or trees. One photograph should emphasize shape, another pattern, and the third color.

7 Shoot three transiently textured surfaces. Suggestions: rippled water; clouds; billowing fabric; smoke. Remember choice of moment here, as well as lighting.

8 Find yourself a static subject in a landscape – an interesting building, a statue, even a telephone box or tree – and see in how many ways you can vary your viewpoint and still make it the center of interest. Utilize line, tone and color.

9 Take four pictures which each include a cast shadow. Use your own shadow, or one cast by a variety of objects shown or unshown.

10 Using your camera as a notebook, analyze shapes found in your local architecture. Do not show buildings as they appear to the casual eye, but select areas that are strong in design.

11 Produce three interesting pictures of people in surroundings that can be made to provide strong lead-in lines, e.g. road and roof lines, steps, corridors, areas of sunshine and shadow. Make sure your subject is well placed to achieve maximum emphasis.

12 Machinery often has a regularity of form. Produce a set of four differing images that make this point, either through four separate mechanical subjects or using only one of them but photographed in a variety of ways.

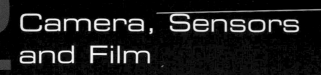

2 Camera, Sensors and Film

7 Camera principles

The word photography means drawing (or writing) with light. It's a good description because every time you take a photograph you are really allowing light from the subject to draw its own picture on the sensor or film. But just how does this 'automatic drawing' take place? Have you ever been lying in bed in the morning watching patterns formed on walls or ceiling by sunlight coming through gaps in the curtains? Sometimes the shadowy shapes of trees and buildings can be made out, especially if the curtains are dark with only one narrow space between them. If you can use a room with a window small enough, cover the window completely with black paper or opaque kitchen foil. Pierce a small clean hole through the blackout with a ball-point pen. Provided the daylight is bright and sunny you should be able to see the dim outlines of the scene outside projected on a piece of thin paper held about 30 cm (1 ft) from the hole (Figure 7.1). Various shapes should be visible although everything will be upside down.

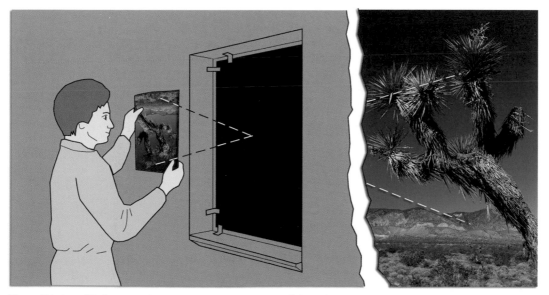

Figure 7.1 A small hole in a window blackout forms a dim image of the sunlit tree on the tracing paper.

This arrangement for making images is called a *camera obscura*, meaning 'darkened chamber'. It has been known for centuries, and all sorts of portable camera obscuras about the size of boxes were made which also allowed people to trace over the image, and so help them draw scenes. Figure 7.2 shows a camera obscura you can make yourself out of an old cardboard cylinder and tracing paper. The image is upside down because light always travels in straight

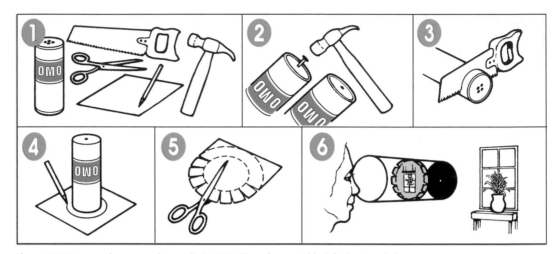

Figure 7.2 Home-made camera obscura. (Paint its inside surface matt black for best results.)

lines. Light from the top of the window passing through the small hole reaches the bottom of the image on the paper viewing screen.

Enlarging the hole makes the image brighter but much more blurred. However, you can greatly improve clarity and brightness by using a magnifying glass instead of just an empty hole. A magnifier is a piece of glass polished so that its edges are thinner than its center. This forms a converging lens, which is able to give a brighter and more detailed image of the scene, provided it is the correct distance from the screen. Try fitting a lens of this kind to the hole in your camera obscura. You will find that you now need some way of altering the distance between lens and screen ('focusing') until the best position is found to give a clearly defined image. All properly made camera lenses are made up of several lenses together in a single housing. In this way, the faults, or 'aberrations', of individual lens elements cancel out to give clearer, 'sharper' images.

Light-sensitive films and sensors

We have now almost invented the photographic camera, but need some way of recording the image without actually having to trace it by hand. There are many materials that are sensitive to light. Curtains and carpets and paintwork of all kinds gradually fade under strong illumination. Newspaper yellows if left out in the sun. The trouble with these sorts of materials is that they are much too slow in their reaction – exposure times measured in years would be needed to record a visible picture in the camera. For many years, most cameras used film coated with chemical compounds of silver called silver halides to record the scene. The silver halides are extremely light sensitive and change from a creamy color to black when exposed to light. To construct a film, the silver halides are mixed with gelatine and coated onto plastic backing, giving it a pale yellowish/orange appearance called a 'light-sensitive emulsion'.

Scientists also discovered that it is not even necessary to wait until the silver halides darken in the camera. You can just let the image light act on it for a fraction of a second, keep the film in the dark and then later place it in a solution of chemicals that develops the silver until the recorded image is strong enough to be visible.

With most films, processing gives us a negative picture on film. Subjects that were white appear as black metallic silver, and dark subjects as clear film. Parts of the subjects that were neither light nor dark are represented as intermediate gray density. The negative is then printed in the darkroom onto paper coated with a similar emulsion containing silver halides. After development, the image on the paper is 'a negative of the negative', i.e. the paper appears white where the original subject was light, black where it was dark and (assuming you are using monochrome materials) a suitable gray tone where it was in bctween. We have a positive print. The advantage of using negative and positive stages is that many prints can be run off one camera exposure. And by putting the negative in an enlarger (which is rather like a slide projector), enlarged prints can be made. So you don't have to have a big camera to make big photographs.

Figure 7.3 shows, in basic form, the optical and chemical steps in making a black and white photograph. Most pictures of course are shot in color, but the same principles apply. Color films are coated with several emulsion layers, sensitive to blue, green and red. After appropriate processing, color negative film carries images that are reversed in color (blues appear yellow, greens magenta, etc.) as well as in tone. When such a negative is enlarged onto multi-coated color paper the paper responds in a similar way to give a positive print with colors brought back to their original subject hues.

The change to digital

More recently, photography has undergone a massive change in the way that we record images. Film cameras, though still readily available, are being outsold by their digital equivalents. With these cameras, the film is replaced as the light-sensitive part of the photographic process with an electronic sensor, or more accurately, a grid of sensors

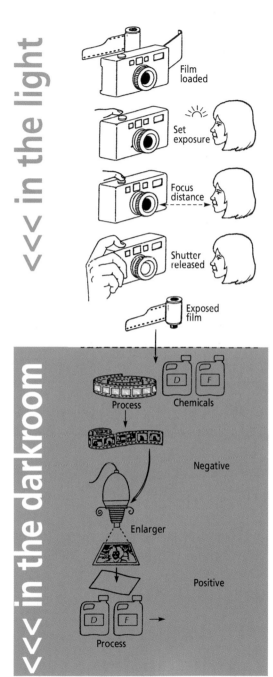

Figure 7.3 Basic stages in making a traditional black and white photograph – from loading and using the camera (top) to processing and printing the film.

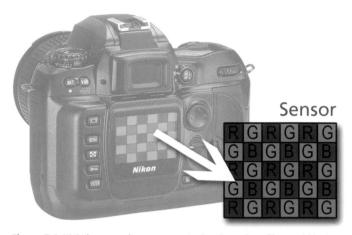

Figure 7.4 Digital cameras have a sensor in the place where film would be in traditional cameras.

(see Figure 7.4). Instead of the light in a scene being recorded by silver halide grains, it is captured with small electronic sensors. Each of the individual sensors provides a small portion of the full description of the scene that makes up the digital file. After photographing the file is stored on a memory card held within the camera. For more details on how sensors work, see page 41.

Unlike with film, there are no chemical steps involved in using your digital files to make prints. The camera is connected to your computer and all the digital photographs stored on your camera's memory card are transferred into the memory of the computer. This process is called downloading. Once on the computer, the pictures can be displayed on screen, enhanced and edited using a software program called an image editor, such as Adobe Photoshop or Photoshop Elements. After all the picture changes have been made, the image is then printed using a desktop color printer or taken to a photo-laboratory for printing. Figure 7.5 shows the basic steps involved in producing a simple digital photograph.

8 The camera

There are so many cameras you can buy that, to begin with, it is quite confusing. Remember though, every camera is basically just a light-tight box with a lens at one end and a light-sensitive surface (e.g. sensor or film) at the other. Film and digital cameras vary a great deal in detail, but they all possess the basic features shown in Figure 8.1 in some form. These are, first and foremost, a lens positioned the correct focusing distance from the

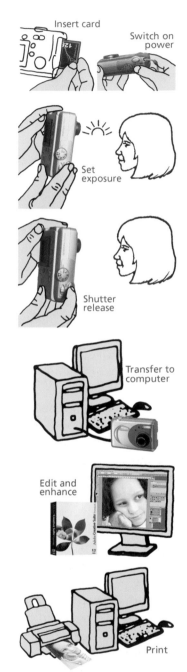

Figure 7.5 The basic steps in taking and making a digital photograph – from exposing (top) through editing on a computer to printing.

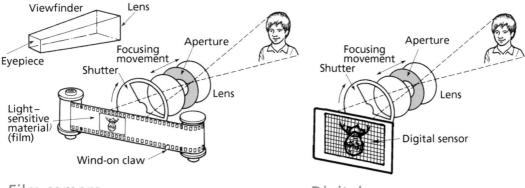

Film camera

Digital camera

Figure 8.1 The basic elements of a simple 35 mm film camera and its digital equivalent.

film/sensor; a shutter; a lens aperture; a viewfinder; a means of moving to the next picture or advancing the film; and an indicator to show how many pictures you have taken.

The lens is the most important part of the whole camera. It must be protected from finger-marks and scratches, otherwise images resemble what you see when your eyes are watering. The spacing of the lens from the sensor/film has to change for subjects at different distances. Cheapest cameras have the lens 'focus-free', meaning it is fixed for what the makers regard as the subject distance for average snaps. Some have a ring or lever with a scale of distances

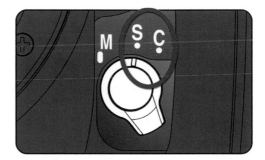

Figure 8.2 Most modern cameras have automatic focusing systems built in, with some SLR models containing features that allow the user to switch between manual and auto-focus modes.

(or symbols for 'groups', 'portraits', etc.). Operating this focusing control moves the lens slightly further from the film the nearer your subject distance setting. Most modern cameras have lenses with an auto-focusing mechanism able to alter focusing to suit the distance of whatever the camera is pointing at in the central area of your picture (see Figure 8.2). In all cases though, anything nearer than the closest subject setting the camera allows will not appear sharp, unless you switch to macro mode, fit an extra close-up lens or extension ring (see page 40).

The shutter prevents light from the lens reaching the sensor/film until you press the release button, so it allows you to decide exactly when the picture will be taken. On simplest beginners' cameras it may function at one speed only, typically opening for about 1/25 second, although this may not be marked. Shutters on more advanced cameras offer a range of ten or so speed settings, from several whole seconds down to 1/1000 second or less. Having a choice allows you to 'freeze' or 'blur' moving subjects, and also compensate for dim or bright lighting (see Figure 8.3). On fully automatic cameras, such as most compacts, the shutter speed is selected by the camera mechanism itself, according to the brightness of the scene and light sensitivity of your sensor/film.

The aperture (also known as the diaphragm or stop) is a circular hole positioned within or just behind the lens. It is usually adjustable in size like the iris of the eye – changing to a smaller or

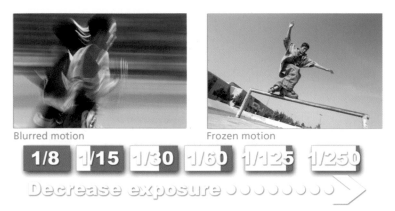

Blurred motion   Frozen motion

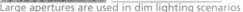

1/8   1/15   1/30   1/60   1/125   1/250

Decrease exposure

Figure 8.3 The shutter speed controls both the amount of light entering the camera and the way that action or movement is captured. Fast shutter speeds freeze the action, whereas slower settings blur the movement.

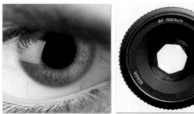

Large apertures are used in dim lighting scenarios

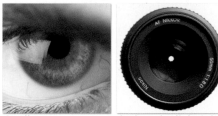
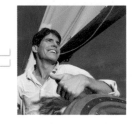

Small apertures are used when the light is bright

Figure 8.4 The aperture of the camera works like the iris in our eyes. Changing the aperture size (hole size) alters the amount of light entering the camera. Typically, small aperture holes (large f-numbers) are used for bright days and larger ones (small f-numbers) when the light is low.

larger diameter makes the image dimmer or brighter, so again this is a means of compensating for strong or weak lighting conditions (see Figure 8.4). The shutter therefore controls the time the image is allowed to act on the film, and the aperture controls the brightness of the image. Together, they allow you to control the total exposure to light the film receives. The aperture also has a very important effect on whether parts of scenes closer and further away than the subject on which the lens is focused also appear sharp. The smaller the aperture, the greater this foreground-to-background sharpness or 'depth of field' (see Figure 8.5).

Very basic cameras have one fixed aperture, or two to three settings simply marked in weather symbols – 'clouds' for dull light conditions and 'sun' for bright lights. Most advanced or single lens reflex cameras offer half a dozen aperture settings, which are given 'f-numbers'. Each change of f-number lets in half or double the light; this is explained further on page 60. Automatic cameras have an aperture setting selected by the camera mechanism in response to the brightness of your subject lighting, and often display no settings at all.

The viewfinder allows you to aim the camera and preview how much of your subject will be included in the picture. Some cameras (non-reflex types) have a direct viewfinder, which you can recognize by its own separate window above the lens (Figure 8.6). SLR (single lens reflex) cameras allow you to look inside the camera itself and view the actual image formed by the lens.

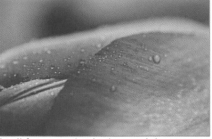
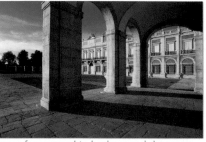

Small foreground to background sharpness   Large foreground to background sharpness

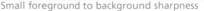
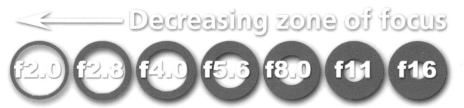

Figure 8.5 The aperture setting also controls the depth of sharpness in the picture. Smaller holes are used to create pictures where sharpness extends further into the image. Large apertures tend to restrict sharpness to just the subject that is focused.

This is the same for both digital and film SLR cameras (Figures 8.7a and b). Digital cameras which look like compacts often use a combination of a direct viewfinder and a small flat display screen (LCD monitor) on the back. Since this screen is wired direct from the CCD it shows your picture when you are framing up your subject, offering the same parallax-free accuracy as an SLR film camera. An added advantage is that, after shooting, it displays the picture you have just taken so that you can check your results.

Direct viewfinders are bright and clear, but less accurate than SLR or LCD monitor systems for composing pictures, particularly close-ups. You have to follow correction lines denoting the true top edge of your picture at the camera's closest focusable distance.

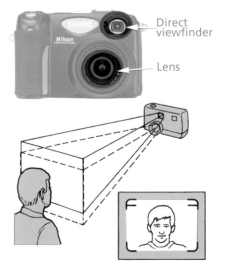

Figure 8.6 Direct viewfinder cameras allow the user to compose the picture via a viewing window that is separate to the lens.

Shot advance or film wind-on mechanisms

Cameras that accept 35 mm wide film in cassettes use a roller with teeth to engage in the film's two rows of perforations. Winding on after you have taken a picture (by hand or motorized) moves the film onto a built-in take-up spool. At the same time a frame number, displayed in a window on the camera body, shows how many shots you have taken and the shutter is made ready for the next picture. As digital cameras have no film to advance, the process involves storing the picture just taken onto the camera's memory card and preparing the shutter for a new exposure.

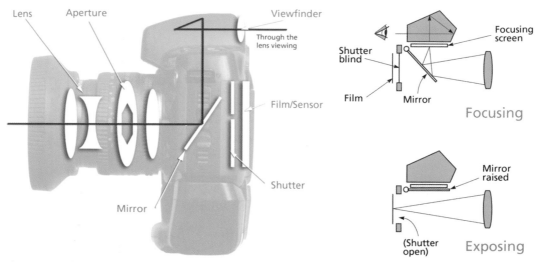

Figure 8.7a When you look through the viewfinder of an SLR or single lens reflex camera you are looking through the actual lens that will be used to take the picture. For this reason focusing and composition are more accurate when using SLR cameras rather than direct viewfinder compacts.

Figure 8.7b Viewing through the lens in an SLR camera is accomplished with the aid of a mirror positioned in front of the shutter and film. When you press the shutter of most SLR cameras, the mirror raises to allow the light to pass through to the film stored at the back of the camera. After the exposure, the mirror returns to its original position to allow viewing again.

Although all the features above are found in every camera, the way they are presented to you to use (or arranged to function automatically) varies from one brand to another. Cameras fall into two main 'families':

- Compact cameras, which often have a direct viewfinder, limited focusing, shutter and aperture control, and tend to be all-in-one models with no add-on extras.
- Single lens reflex cameras, which are slightly larger and heavier, and allow you to see through the taking lens. These are often the nucleus of a kit comprising a whole range of interchangeable lenses and other attachments.

Both are made in manual and automated forms. Their parts and features can be summarized as follows (see Figure 8.8):

1 *Built-in flash* – designed for night-time and inside photography to add extra light to a scene when needed.
2 *Video out connection* – to connect your camera to a television so that your pictures can be viewed on screen.
3 *USB connector* – used to connect your camera to a computer for downloading of pictures.
4 *Lens* – to focus the image in front of the camera onto the sensor. On some cameras, the lenses are interchangeable. Almost all models, both digital and film based, are now supplied with a zoom lens.
5 *Battery compartment* – to hold the batteries used by your camera to power its different functions.
6 *Mode or command dial* – switches the camera between different shooting modes, such as night-time, portrait and landscape.
7 *Shutter release button* – captures the photograph when pressed.
8 *Eyelet for camera strap* – used to secure a carrying strap to your camera.
9 *Power switch* – to turn the camera on and off.
10 *Zoom buttons or controls* – adjust the lens of the camera to bring distant scenes closer (to zoom in) or capture a wider view (to zoom out).
11 *Flash mode button* – turns flash on and off, and switches between flash functions such as red eye reduction and flash with long exposure.

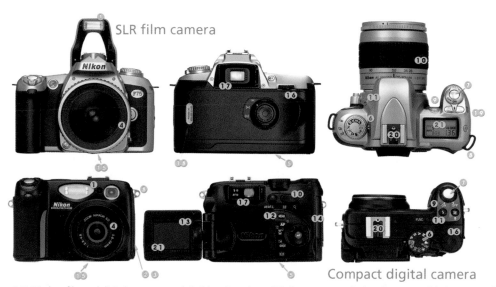

SLR film camera

Compact digital camera

Figure 8.8 Modern film and digital cameras are full of functions that will help you capture the best image possible in a range of different shooting scenarios. Getting to know your camera's various parts and features will help you make the most of these shooting functions and the creative opportunities they afford. See text for explanation of numbered items.

12 *Menu button* – used to display the camera's settings in menu form on the monitor or LCD screen.

13 *Monitor or preview screen* – a screen used to play the pictures stored in your camera or preview the scene you are about to photograph.

14 *Memory card chamber* – insert the memory card here that will be used to store your photographs.

15 *Tripod socket* – screw a tripod to this socket when taking pictures with a long shutter speed.

16 *Multi selector button* – used to change camera or picture options or settings.

17 *Viewfinder* – used to compose the scene before capturing the photograph.

18 *Film chamber* – used to house the film whilst it is being exposed.

19 *Film release/rewind button* – press here before rewinding the film into the canister.

20 *Flash hot shoe* – a connector used to hold and control an additional external flash.

21 *LCD information panel* – displays your camera's current settings and functions.

Beginners' cameras

New, or young, photographers often start with a low-cost compact camera – maybe a disposable type, or one which you can reload with film. Disposable or 'single use' basic cameras come with film already loaded and sealed in. After shooting the last picture, you hand the camera in to the photo-lab, where it is broken open and the film processed. The cost of a disposable camera is only about twice the cost of a film, so it can be treated as a fun camera on the beach or even in the rain.

Also included in this category is the simplest reloadable compact cameras (see Figure 8.9). They are the next step up and, like disposables, have a viewfinder window (with eyepiece at the back of the camera) that gives you a direct view of the subject. You see your subject clear and bright, and apparently with everything always in focus. Most settings are 'fixed', so all you have to do after loading the film is to point the camera, press the shutter and wind on. This sounds ideal, but with many models the lens has a fixed setting to focus subjects from infinity (the far horizon) through to about 2.5 m (8 ft) away. You cannot get sharp images any closer, nor can you take shots with foreground detail sharp and background unsharp.

The fixed shutter speed of about 1/125 second avoids camera shake effects when you shoot hand-held, but is too slow to freeze fast subject movement. The fixed (or very limited range) aperture means that you cannot adjust for correct exposure for varying lighting conditions, nor choose between deep or limited depth of field to suit your picture. The viewfinder, being an inch or so from the taking lens, 'sees'

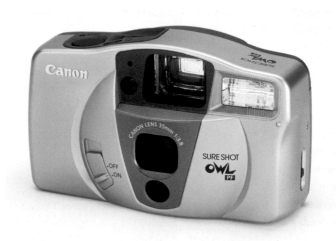

Figure 8.9 Low-cost, entry-level film cameras are a good place for kids and new photographers to start. Though there is little control over the shutter speed, aperture and focus, good images can still be taken in well-lit situations.

your subject from a slightly different position. This difference of viewpoint or parallax error becomes greater the nearer your subject. Remember to use the correction lines.

Nevertheless, with care reasonable photographs can be taken with a simple compact provided you understand and work within its limitations. (Otherwise, you may start with a simple camera, expect too much of it and end up disheartened.) Load fast (ISO 400) film for correct exposure in cloudy conditions and slow (ISO 100) film for bright sunshine, and use flash indoors.

Simple compact digital cameras have many of the same limitations of their film equivalents, including limited focus and exposure control. In addition, some models do not contain a preview monitor on the back of the camera and do not have the ability to increase the amount of memory available for picture storage via removable memory cards. The cheapest cameras have a relatively small number of sensors and therefore produce pictures that are only suitable for viewing on screen or producing small prints. For example, a sensor grid having 640 × 480 pixels gives a just acceptable image viewed on a small computer monitor, but to get 6 in × 4 in photo-quality color pictures out of your computer printer the camera must have several million pixels. Since, unlike film, you can't change the camera's sensor, pixel (number of sensors) count has to be considered when you buy the camera and is very much linked to price.

Advanced compacts

Top-of-the-range compact cameras are much more expensive. They are fitted with lenses giving higher resolution images (noticeable when you make bigger enlargements) and wider apertures (to cope with dimmer light). Advanced compacts are still designed to handle most things automatically, but more and more models are being released with manual override for features such as aperture and shutter speed. This is especially true in the area of digital cameras, where good quality compact cameras hold most of the market. Whether used manually or in automatic mode, these units give technically good results over a wide range of lighting conditions and subject distances.

Such control is gained through sophisticated electronic automation. For example, a camera as shown in Figure 8.10 will sense whether the film you have loaded is fast or slow in sensitivity, together with its length. A sensor behind a small window near the lens measures the brightness of your subject. The camera uses this film and subject information to set an appropriate aperture and shutter speed – ranging from smallest aperture and fastest speed in brilliant lighting, to widest aperture and slowest holdable speed in dim light.

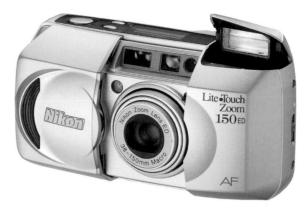

Figure 8.10 Fully automatic advanced compacts with zoom lenses and built-in flashes are the most popular of all film and digital cameras. More and more models are now offering manual and semi-manual modes to cater for those photographers who want to regain a little more control of the process.

Two further windows near the camera top sense the distance to whatever you have composed centrally in the viewfinder. As you press the release button, the lens adjusts its focusing position to suit this distance. If the subject is too close, the camera signals a warning in the viewfinder; if lighting is too dim, another signal warns you and may automatically switch on the camera's built-in flash or even activate the flash automatically. When the flash is in use it will sense how much light to give out, according to subject distance, and whether other lighting is present. For the film-based models, a motor winds on the film one frame after each shot and once you have taken the last picture on the film it winds it all back into the cassette ready to unload.

Despite this level of sophistication internally, often the only external control offered to the photographer, apart from the shutter release, is a focal length changing 'zoom' button, which makes the image bigger or smaller. In this way you get more (or less) of a scene to fill your picture without having to move further back (or closer) – see page 70. The camera's viewfinder automatically zooms too, adjusting to match these focal length changes. It may also tilt slightly according to the distance of your auto-focused subject, to help to compensate for parallax error and so more accurately show what you are getting in.

Between completely 'fixed' and completely automatic models you will find a whole range of compact cameras at intermediate prices. Some are cheaper because they omit completely one of the features described. They may lack a zoom lens, or the range of shutter speeds and apertures. They may also have a smaller set of automated and manual features, which in turn will limit the range of conditions you can shoot under. Bear in mind that having a camera with settable controls is often an advantage, as you will see in Part 3 of this book.

Single lens reflex (SLR) cameras

All SLR cameras have a clever optical system (as shown in Figure 8.7b), which allows you to view an image of the subject formed by the lens. It is a true 'what you see is what you get' (WYSIWYG) system. Unlike a compact camera, the shutter is not in the lens but in the back of the camera just in front of the film or sensor.

Looking into an eyepiece at the back of an SLR you observe a small, ground-glass focusing screen, onto which the scene is reflected by a mirror. So you see what the lens sees, and as you focus the lens it is easy to examine which parts of the subject are in focus and sharp and which areas are blurry. When you are satisfied that the picture is correctly composed, you press the shutter release button. The mirror then rises out of the way, blocking out the focusing screen briefly and allowing the image to reach the back of the camera, where the shutter opens to expose the sensor or film. As the distance from lens to film is the same as lens to screen (via the mirror), what was focused in the viewfinder will also be sharp on the film/sensor. In addition, because we view through the lens there is no viewfinder parallax error no matter how close the subject.

Since the shutter is at the back of the camera body, you can remove the lens and fit others of different focal length, even in the middle of a film roll or when the camera card is half empty. In fact, single lens reflexes are 'system cameras', meaning that the makers offer a wide variety of lenses and accessories, ranging from close-up rings (page 38) to special dedicated flashguns. So, starting off with a camera body and regular lens, you can gradually build up quite an elaborate camera outfit bit by bit as you become more experienced.

Cameras of SLR design include manual types, where you set most of the controls, automatic models that work with built-in programs and those that combine both systems. Both manual and automatic approaches have their advantages and limitations, so let's take a closer look at each design.

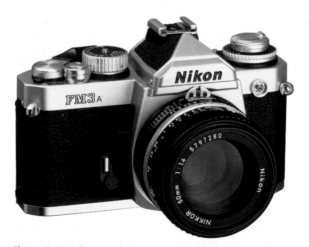

Figure 8.11 Fully manual SLR cameras provide the photographer complete control over all aspects of focus and exposure.

Manual SLRs

A typical manual-only camera, like the one shown in Figure 8.11, has setting dials for shutter, aperture and focus, and also a film wind-on lever and a rewind knob. Having loaded and set the speed of your film, you look through the eyepiece and turn the lens focusing ring until the most important part of your picture appears sharp. Typically, you then set a shutter speed such as 1/125 second if you are hand-holding the camera (see page 55). Look through the eyepiece, half depress the shutter release and turn the aperture control until a signal light or needle next to the focusing screen indicates that the exposure set is correct. Alternatively, you can first make an aperture setting because depth of field is important (see page 58) and then alter the shutter setting until correct exposure is signalled. Pressing fully on the release then takes your picture, and you must use the wind-on to advance the film by one frame ready for the next shot.

As you can see from this sequence of steps, a manual SLR camera requires you to know something about choice of technical settings, but it will tackle a wider range of lighting conditions and subject distances than all but the most advanced compacts. Since it only uses electronics for its exposure meter, the camera will still take photographs with its (tiny internal) batteries flat.

Fully manual cameras are film only. Though most digital SLR cameras have a manual mode that allows you to set you camera as above, there are no manual-only digital SLR cameras on the market. All models contain at least some automatic modes along with their manual options.

Advanced SLRs

A technologically advanced SLR (Figure 8.12) has features such as auto-focusing, film speed sensing, built-in flash, the ability to take a sequence of pictures with rates of five pictures per second and more, and what is known as 'multi-mode' functioning. Multi-mode means that by selecting one mode you can have the camera function as if it were manual, or by selecting another have it totally auto-programmed (just point and shoot). Yet another mode will allow you to choose and set shutter speed, but makes every other setting automatically, whilst a fourth mode allows you to make the aperture your priority choice instead.

An SLR camera like this may also offer you five or six modes covering different ways of

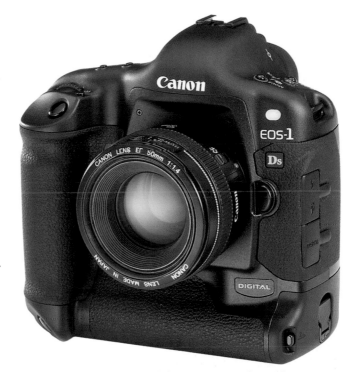

Figure 8.12 Advanced multi-mode (auto, semi-auto and manual) SLR cameras contain many features and controls. These cameras are available for both film-based and digital photography.

exposure reading and making settings, plus an almost overwhelming range of other options. You can even programme the camera to take a rapid 'burst' of three pictures when you press the button, each one giving a slightly different exposure. Virtually all the camera actions are battery powered – from its internal focus sensor, motor drive for film advancement, to the electronically timed shutter providing a much wider setting range (typically 1/8000–30 seconds) than a manual camera. The digital version of these cameras also includes the ability to change the sensitivity of the sensor frame by frame, adjust the camera to suit shooting under different colored lighting conditions and even alter the contrast or color saturation of specific photographs.

Typically, all the information concerning the chosen mode, shutter and aperture settings made and number of pictures left appears on a display panel on top of the camera body or on the LCD monitor on the back of the camera. Some of this data is also shown alongside the focusing screen when you look through the eyepiece. Digital cameras often record this information along with details about the picture itself in the digital file. These settings can be displayed by calling up the information (sometimes called metadata) in an image editing program such as Photoshop.

Figure 8.13 Portrait mode.

Figure 8.14 Party/Indoor mode.

Figure 8.15 Night Portrait mode.

Figure 8.16 Beach/Snow mode.

Figure 8.17 Landscape mode.

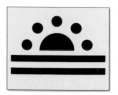

Figure 8.18 Sunset mode.

Specialist shooting modes

Some cameras contain a range of shooting modes designed to take the guesswork out of adjusting camera settings to suit different shooting scenarios. Selecting these modes will automatically change your camera's functions to the most appropriate setting for the photographic task at hand. The guide below will give you an idea of when best to use which mode.

N.B. Not all modes will be available on all cameras and some modes are digital-only options. Check you manuals for details of what specialist modes your camera contains.

Portrait. Designed for portraits producing a picture where the main is sharply focused whilst other details in the background are softened or left unsharp. The degree to which the background is unsharp will depend on the amount of light that is available (see Figure 8.13).

Party/Indoor. This mode is designed for use in low light situations, where detail is required both in the foreground and background. This setting uses a slow shutter speed, so be sure to hold your camera very still or use a tripod (see Figure 8.14).

Night Portrait. You should use this mode if you want to create a good balance of lighting between the foreground subject and the background lights. It is great for photographing portraits against a background of night scenery. With this setting the flash is activated to light the foreground and a long shutter speed is used to capture the night lights. When using this mode be careful of camera shake (see Figure 8.15).

Beach/Snow. Brightly lit, lightly colored subjects often fool your camera, resulting in dark muddy images. This mode rectifies this problem by adjusting the camera so that light tones in beach and snow scenes are recorded correctly (see Figure 8.16).

Landscape. Designed to enhance the color and detail of distant scenes, this mode is great for making landscape pictures. With this setting the flash is turned off automatically and the camera's focusing system is locked at the most distant setting (see Figure 8.17).

Sunset. Designed to preserve the strong colors often found in sunsets, this mode automatically turns off the flash for the camera. This means that foreground objects appear silhouetted against the sunset sky. Use a tripod or hold your camera very still to stop camera shake when using this mode (see Figure 8.18).

Night Landscape. As a slow shutter speed is in this mode to capture the dimly lit tones of a night landscape, a tripod is recommended when shooting with this setting. In addition, the flash is automatically turned off and the focus set to the most distant setting (see Figure 8.19).

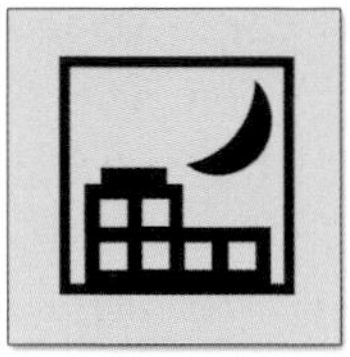

Museum. For use indoors when flash is not permitted, this setting is perfect for capturing pictures in museums or art galleries. The flash is turned off automatically and, where available, a function like the Best Shot Selector (BSS) is activated to ensure that only the finest quality photograph is saved (see Figure 8.20).

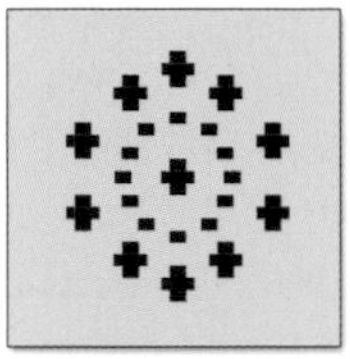

Figure 8.19 Night Landscape mode.

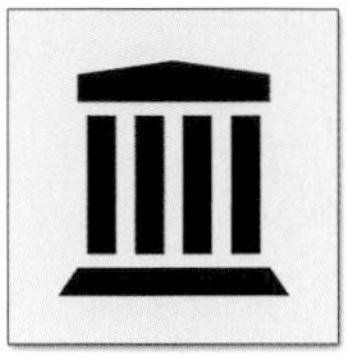

Figure 8.20 Museum mode.

Figure 8.21 Fireworks Show mode.

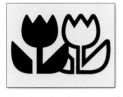

Figure 8.22 Close Up mode.

Fireworks Show. This mode fixes the focus at the most distant setting, turns off the flash and uses a slow shutter speed to capture the expanding burst of light from a firework. For best effect follow the trail of the ascending firework, releasing the button at the start of the burst (see Figure 8.21).

Close Up. The camera is set to focus on subjects very near to the lens (10 cm or less). This setting is also called 'macro' mode. Be sure to hold the camera steady or use a tripod to reduce camera shake when capturing these close-up photographs (see Figure 8.22).

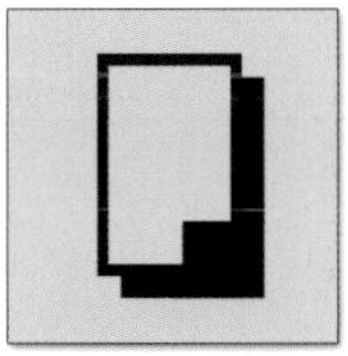

Figure 8.23 Copy mode.

Copy. This setting is designed to provide clear photographs of maps, documents or business cards. The mode works best with black and white type or printed documents with high contrast (see Figure 8.23).

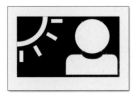

Figure 8.24 Back Light mode.

Back Light. Use this mode when light is coming from behind your subject. The camera's flash is turned on automatically and fills in the shadows in the foreground of the picture (see Figure 8.24).

Off. Turns off all preselected camera mode settings, allowing the photographer to choose how the camera is set up.

Accessories

A great range of accessories is available for cameras – although almost all are designed for SLR types. Figure 8.25 shows the most useful items.

- *Extra lenses*. Provided your camera body accepts interchangeable or supplementary lenses, you can fit a wide angle or telephoto type in place of its standard focal length or zoom lens (the advantages of doing this are explained on page 70).
- *Extension tubes*. Fitted between the lens and body, these allow you to work very close up to your subject (see page 110). Digital cameras often contain a specialist macro shooting mode that changes the way that the camera lens works, so that you can get in closer to your subject. Some models can focus down to 1 cm (0.4 in).
- *Tripod with tilting top*. A firm support when you want to use exposure times that don't allow the camera to be steadily held by hand (longer than 1/60 second, for instance). Most compact cameras as well as SLRs have a threaded baseplate to accept a tripod.

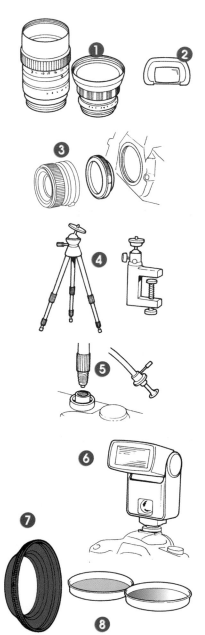

Figure 8.25 Useful camera accessories. (1) Extra lenses. (2) SLR eyepiece corrector. (3) Extension tube (close-up ring) between SLR body and lens. (4) Tripod and camera clamp. (5) Cable release or remote release. (6) Flashgun, fits on the hot shoe connector. (7) Lens hood. (8) Lens filters.

- *Shutter release extension*. As long as your camera's shutter button is either threaded for a cable release or has connections for a cable switch, this accessory minimizes risk of camera shake when you give a long exposure. For some cameras not accepting either form of release it may be possible to fit an adapter or you can use the self-timer option to allow the camera to settle before the shutter is released.
- *Flashgun*. Even if your camera has a built-in flash, a separate, more powerful, unit that can be attached and used instead will allow far more interesting lighting opportunities (see page 76).
- *Lens hood*. A much underrated accessory, the lens hood not only shades the lens from flare created by strong back or side light on your subject, but it also helps protect it from knocks. For sharp, well-saturated pictures, always use a lens hood wherever possible.
- *Filters*. Push-on or screw-on color filters can be helpful in black and white photography (see pages 106 and 212), and color correcting filters help neutralize color photographs taken under unusual lighting. There is also a whole range of lens attachments designed for creating special effects.

So which camera is best?

There is no ideal camera, which is why so many variations exist even within the types discussed here (for cameras using film other than 35 mm wide, see pages 27 and 263). Even if money is no object and you buy the most expensive multi-mode SLR, just having so many options available can be confusing, overwhelming your picture making. And yet keeping it set to 'auto-program' is wasteful if you then never use its other possibilities.

A modern, automatic-only compact camera is easy to carry and quick to bring into use. It is a truly pocketable camera, lightweight and small. You don't have to carry accessories either, which encourages you to take the camera everywhere. Without the delays caused by you having to adjust your camera's settings, you can concentrate on composition, viewpoint and people's expressions when taking pictures, knowing that technicalities like focus and exposure are taken care of.

If you want a bit more image control, without having to understand any technicalities, a compact with zoom lens gives you helpful image size adjustment. The wider the zoom range though, the more a camera increases in size and price. If you buy a low-cost compact camera, remember that poorly lit or fast-moving subjects will be generally beyond its capabilities, as well as accurate and sharp close-ups. Digital compacts with LCD preview or monitor screens and SLR cameras are unrivalled for framing accuracy and close working, but they are more expensive and, in the case of SLR equipment, definitely generally heavier and more bulky.

Automatic modes or automatic-only cameras work using programs that ensure a high level of technical success (e.g. sharp focus, correct exposure) under most conditions. The trouble is that, when using these modes, you are unable to make individual settings – such as distance, shutter speed and aperture – which means that you deprive yourself of many of the creative visual possibilities, as shown here in the next parts of this book. For someone who wants to understand photography and is prepared to learn to set the controls, it is still difficult to beat an advanced compact with a manual mode or a manual SLR. Such cameras generally accept a great range of accessories. For SLRs in particular, this includes the same high-quality lenses used on the makers' most expensive models. Again, if you buy an SLR with a choice of modes, make sure one of these is 'manual'. Then, having really learnt the controls, you are in an informed position to know whether changing to a semi-automatic or fully programmed mode offers a short cut for particular subject conditions, but will still give the result you want.

9 Sensors

For most new digital camera owners it comes as a bit of surprise when they find out that their beautifully colored and delicately textured photographic prints are in fact constructed of a grid of rectangular colored boxes. These boxes are the basic building ingredient of any digital photography and were originally called 'picture elements'.

These days, most readers will know them by their common title – pixels – but their original description as elements from which a picture is made still holds true. Traditional film-based photography has a similar image component called grain, and for this reason some writers have also started to call pixels 'digital grain'. Whatever the terminology you use, you cannot escape the importance of pixels when creating great pictures.

Each pixel represents both color and tone. Together, many pixels create the shapes and details in your images in much the same way that the great mosaics of Roman times depicted scenes using small pieces of tile. But unlike the mosaics, the grid-like structure of the digital image is not noticeable when the picture is seen from a distance, or the pixels are printed very small. Our eyes mix the colors and tones so that what we see is a photographic image containing smooth graduations and sharp details, and not a collection of discrete blocks arranged in rows and columns (see Figure 9.1).

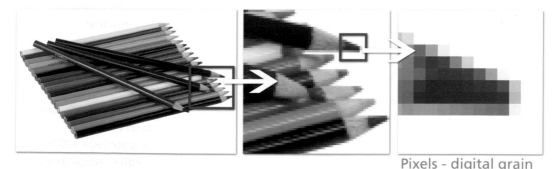

Pixels - digital grain

Figure 9.1 Digital photographs are constructed from a grid of colored rectangles called pixels (picture elements).

Creating pixels

Creating images in this form is essential if they are to be edited or enhanced by computers. There is no doubt that computers are amazing machines. Their strength is in being able to perform millions of mathematical calculations per second. To apply this ability to working with images, we must start with a description of pictures that the computer can understand. This means that the images must be in a digital form. This is quite different from the way our eyes, or any film-based camera, see the world.

With these devices we record pictures as a series of 'continuous tones' that blend seamlessly with each other. To make a version of the image the computer can use, the tones need to be converted to a digital form. The process involves sampling the image at regular intervals and assigning a specific color and brightness to each sample. Each of these areas, or samples, becomes a pixel in the resultant digital file, and in this way the pixel grid is constructed.

The grid can be made by taking pictures with a digital camera or by using a scanner to convert existing prints or negatives into pixel-based form. Most digital cameras have a grid of sensors, called CCDs (charge-coupled devices), in the place where traditional cameras would have film. Each sensor measures the brightness and color of the light that hits it. When the values from all sensors are collected and collated, a digital picture made up of a grid of pixels results (see Figure 9.2).

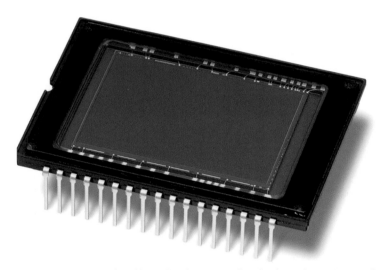

Figure 9.2 Sensors replace film in digital cameras. When the shutter button is pressed, the image (color and tone) is captured by each cell of the sensor and a digital photograph results.

Scanners work in a similar way, except that these devices use rows of CCD sensors that move slowly over the original, sampling the picture as they go. Generally, different scanners are needed for converting film and print originals; however, some companies are now making products that can be used for both.

What is all this fuss about megapixels?

With the rapid rate of change in the development of digital cameras, photographers and manufacturers alike have been searching for ways to compare the many different models that fill the marketplace. To this end, the number of 'megapixels', or millions of pixels, contained in the camera's sensor is often used as a means of comparison.

The general consensus from most quarters is that the 'more megapixels the better', and as a general rule this is probably true. This is certainly the case if your goal is to produce the

Table 9.1

Chip dimensions (pixels)	Chip resolution (megapixels) (1 million = 1 megapixel)	Maximum print size at 200 dpi (inches) (e.g. photo print)	Maximum image size at 72 dpi (inches) (e.g. web use)
640 × 480	0.30	3.2 × 2.4	8.8 × 6.6
1440 × 960	1.38	7.4 × 4.8	20 × 13.2
1600 × 1200	1.90	8 × 6	22 × 16
2048 × 1536	3.21	10.2 × 7.58	28.4 × 21.3
2304 × 1536	3.40	11.5 × 7.5	32 × 21.3
2560 × 1920	4.92	12.8 × 9.6	35.5 × 26.6

biggest photographic quality prints possible. In this scenario, more pixels from the sensor translates into bigger print sizes. But this is certainly not the whole story.

It is worth thinking about what you are going to use your digital files for. If we can identify the 'end use' of our image files first, then we can relate this back to camera sensor sizes. For example, if you intend to produce web pages exclusively, there is little reason for you to have a 6 or 8 megapixel camera. You simply will never use this number of pixels for screen-based presentations. Similarly, if you intend to print your pictures from an A4 desktop printer only, then a 3.4 megapixel camera will be sufficient to guarantee you fantastic photo-quality images.

It pays to remember the old adage 'horses for courses' when selecting the right sensors for your shooting requirements. Too few pixels and your prints will not be photo-quality at the size you want, too many and you will pay for image detail you don't need (see Table 9.1).

Sensor sensitivity (ISO equivalence)

Like film, digital sensors have an amount of light that is optimum for making well-exposed pictures. Films are rated with an ISO value according to their sensitivity – the higher the value, the greater the film's sensitivity to light (see Section 10 for more details). With digital cameras the restrictions of being locked into shooting with a single film with all its particular abilities and flaws have been lifted. The ISO idea still remains, though strictly we should refer to it as 'ISO equivalence', as the original ISO scale was designed specifically for film not sensors. Most digital cameras have the ability to change the ISO equivalent setting for the sensor, with a growing number offering settings ranging from 100 to 800. Each frame can be exposed at a different 'ISO' value, releasing the digital shooter from being stuck with a single sensitivity through the whole shooting session.

Entry-level digital cameras usually contain chip sensitivity that is fixed by the manufacturer and can't be altered by the user, but as you start to pay a little more, the level of sophistication and control of the camera's ISO begins to increase. Most middle-of-the-range and prosumer cameras now contain a variety of sensitivity settings. Changing the ISO is usually a simple matter of holding down the ISO button whilst turning a command dial. The changed setting is reflected in the LCD screen at the back of the camera and, in some cases, in the viewfinder as well (see Figure 9.3).

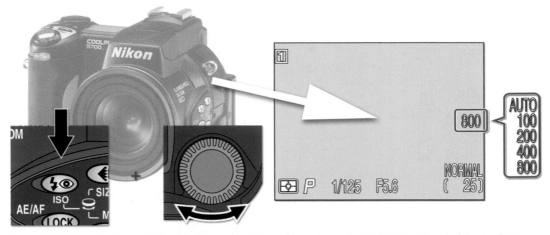

Figure 9.3 With most mid- to high-level digital cameras, it is possible to change the ISO (ISO equivalence) of the chip from frame to frame.

Some digital cameras also contain an Auto ISO setting that can be selected instead of specific sensitivity values. This feature keeps the camera at the best quality option, usually 100, when the photographer is shooting under normal conditions, but will change the setting to a higher value automatically if the light starts to fade. It's a good idea to select and use this option as your camera's default setting. It's good for most situations and you can always change to manual when specific action or low light scenarios arise.

Sensor size compared to film

Most digital sensors are smaller in size than their 35 mm film equivalents. When contained in a compact camera there is little way for the photographer to discern that.

10 Films (see Figure 10.1)

Film records the image exposed onto it in your camera, using light-sensitive chemicals (silver halide crystals) coated as a gelatine emulsion on a plastic base. The size, shape and how tightly packed these silver halides are, basically determines the speed of a film – from fine-grained and relatively 'slow' in reaction to light, to coarser grained and 'fast' in sensitivity.

Color negative films

These are the most popular and are made in the widest range of types and speeds, particularly in 35 mm size. From color negatives it is possible to have enlargements made cheaply in color or (in some labs) in black and white. Labs can also scan negatives and slides and save them to a CD ready for input into a home computer system.

Black and white films

Black and white films make a refreshing change. Pictures are simplified into monochrome without the realism (and sometimes distraction) of color. However, few labs offer a black and

(a)
(b)

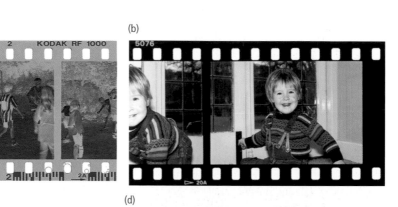

(c)
(d)

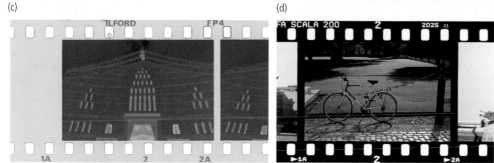

(e)

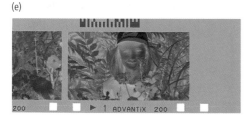

Figure 10.1 A range of film types. From the top: (a) 35 mm color negative; (b) color slide; (c) black and white negative; (d) black and white slide; (e) APS color negative. All actual size.

white processing service. One solution is to use the type of monochrome negative film – Kodak TMAX-TCN or Ilford XP2, for example – which labs can process in their regular color chemicals and produce black and white results. Black and white is also your best choice to start your own processing and printing (see Part 8, page 178).

Color slide films

Color slide films are designed to be 'reversal' processed so that positive color images are formed in the film instead of negatives. You can then project these pictures as slides. It is possible to have color prints made off 35 mm slides, but (as with the purchase and processing of the film itself) this is more expensive than making the same prints from color negatives. You must be more accurate with exposure when shooting slides and, where necessary, have a filter to correct the lighting (see page 134).

Film information

The film box gives you all the important information. Apart from type, brand and size, it shows the number of pictures, film speed, type and the 'use by' date.

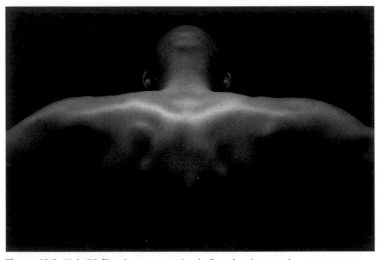

Figure 10.2 High ISO films (or sensor settings) allow the photographer to capture pictures under low light, but contain large and sometimes distracting grain (or noise in the case of digital).

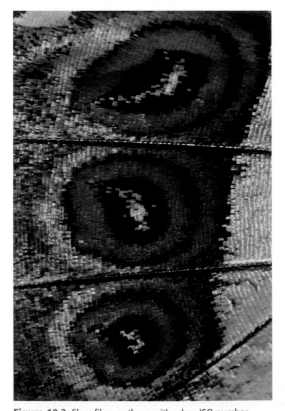

Figure 10.3 Slow films or those with a low ISO number (or sensor setting) record the finest detail and the smoothest gradation of tone and color.

Film speed

Light sensitivity is shown by your film's ISO (International Standards Organisation) speed rating. Every doubling of the ISO number means that a film is twice as fast. Regard films of about ISO 100 or less as slow in speed, ISO 200 and 400 as medium, and ISO 800 upwards as fast.

Choose a fast film if all your pictures will be shot under dim lighting conditions with a simple camera, or when you don't want to have to use a slow shutter speed or wide lens aperture. However, expect resulting prints – especially big enlargements – to show a more visible granular pattern. Sometimes 'graininess' suits a subject, as in Figure 10.2. But since it destroys fine detail and coarsens tones, it would not be the best choice for the fine pattern and texture in Figure 10.3. Fast film is also more expensive.

A slow film suits bright light conditions, where you don't want to be forced into using a fast shutter speed or small lens aperture. It's clearly the best choice if you want prints with the highest image resolution. For most situations though, a medium-speed film offers the best compromise. Always check that your camera is properly set for the ISO rating of the film it contains.

Table 10.1 summarizes the benefits and disadvantages of different ISO settings. Use it as a guide when selecting which value to use for your own work.

Expiry date

The expiry date is the 'use before' date on the film box. It assumes average storage conditions away from fumes, heat and humidity. Outdated

Table 10.1 Benefits and disadvantages of different ISO settings

	ISO and ISO equivalent setting		
	100	**200**	**800**
Benefits	• Low noise (fine grain) • Good color saturation • Good tonal gradation	• Good noise/sensitivity balance • Good sharpness, color and tone • Can be used with a good range of apertures and shutter speeds	• Very sensitive • Can be used with fast shutter speeds, large aperture numbers or long lenses • Good depth of field
Disadvantages	• Not very sensitive • Needs to be used with fast lens or tripod	• Not the absolute best quality capable by the camera • May not be fast enough for some low-light or action scenarios	• Obvious noise (grain) throughout the picture • Poor picture quality
Best uses	• Studio • Still life with tripod • Outdoors on bright day	• General hand-held shooting	• Sports • Low light situations with no flash • Indoors

film becomes less light sensitive, and colors may suffer. To extend shelf-life, store your films (sealed) in the main compartment of your refrigerator.

35 mm film

The biggest range of film is made for 35 mm cameras. Double perforated 35 mm wide film comes in a light-tight cassette you load into your camera's empty film compartment with its paler, light-sensitive surface facing the back of the lens. As you take pictures, the

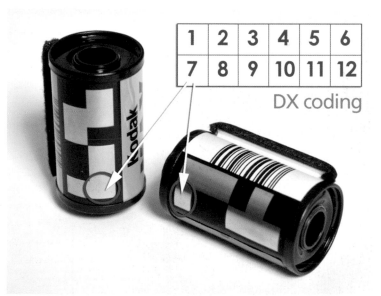

Figure 10.4 The DX coding on the outside of film canisters informs the camera about the characteristics of the film. The characteristics conveyed by each conductive position are: positions 1 and 7 always set; positions 2–6 used for ISO value; 8–10 for number of exposures per film; 11 and 12 for exposure latitude of the film.

film winds onto an open take-up spool within the camera. It therefore has to be rewound back safely into the cassette before you open the camera and remove your exposed film. Never load or remove film in bright light – especially direct sunlight. (The slot in the cassette through which the film protrudes has a velvet lining, but intense light may still penetrate.) Always find a shady area or at least turn away from the sun. Speed, length and type are also encoded in a chequer-board silver pattern on the side of the cassette (Figure 10.4). Electrical contacts inside the film compartment press against this pattern and so read and programme the camera's exposure measuring circuit for film speed, etc.

Number of pictures

The standard picture format given by a 35 mm camera is 24 mm × 36 mm, and you can buy cassettes containing sufficient length of film for either 24 or 36 pictures. A few come in 12 exposure lengths.

APS films and cameras

The Advanced Photo System (APS) is a film format introduced in 1996. APS films are only 24 mm wide, giving negatives slightly over half the area of pictures on 35 mm film (see page 45). They do not fit 35 mm cameras, and so a whole range of scaled down cameras from compacts to single lens reflex designs have been introduced for APS photography. They are similar in price to 35 mm equipment.

APS film comes in an oval-shaped cartridge (Figure 10.5) that, when inside the camera, opens and pushes out the leading edge of the film to automatically load it. After the last shot is taken the film rewinds automatically and you hand in the cassette for processing. APS film carries a transparent magnetic coating used to record information from your camera to instruct the processing laboratory machinery. For example, a picture shape setting on your camera allows selection of either full 'H' format (9:16 ratio), 'classic' format (2:3, the same height-to-width ratio as 35 mm) or a longer, narrower 'panoramic' 1:3 ratio. This causes the lab printer to crop the particular picture to the shape you selected when framing up your shot.

Other information passed from an APS camera via the film to the lab can also cover the lighting used for each individual shot, and time and date of shooting (ink printed on the back of your photo). APS films and equipment therefore offer many conveniences, but for large prints they do not match 35 mm in final image quality. There is a much wider choice of film types

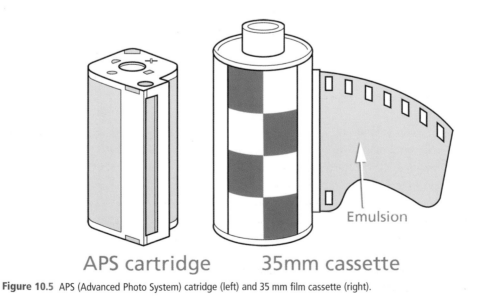

APS cartridge   35mm cassette

Figure 10.5 APS (Advanced Photo System) catridge (left) and 35 mm film cassette (right).

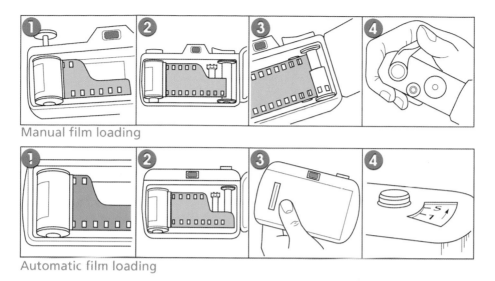

Manual film loading

Automatic film loading

Figure 10.6 Inserting and loading a 35 mm film into a manual or auto-loading camera. Manual loading instructions: (1) Pull out rewind knob and lay cassette in film chamber. Replace knob. (2) Push film tip fully into take-up spool slot. (3) Wind over enough film to bring both sets of perforations onto teeth. (4) Close camera and wind on two frames before starting to shoot. Auto-loading instructions: (1) Insert film cassette (motor-driven cameras have no rewind knob). (2) Pull out enough film to lay across and touch far end. (3) Close the camera back. The window in the back allows you to read film data off the cassette. (4) Closing triggers film advance and the counter moves from S to 1.

available in 35 mm size, and this larger format is also less costly to have processed than APS (see Figure 10.6).

11 Scanners

Though much of the big hype surrounding digital photography is concentrated on the new camera technologies, the humble desktop scanner is still the most cost-effective way to capture high-quality digital images. In this module we will look at the features and functions that make a good scanner, as well as the steps involved in making your first scan.

Film and print scanners

For the most part, scanners can be divided into two distinct varieties – print and film.

Print scanners, which are sometimes also called flatbed or reflection scanners, are designed to convert standard photographs into digital images by reflecting light from the surface of the picture onto a sensor. The film variety captures digital information from negative or slide originals. With these machines the image is scanned by passing light through the film to a high-resolution sensor. This process is the reason why these types of devices are sometimes referred to as 'transmission' scanners. The capture process involves recording the color and brightness of the image, converting these values to digital form and then saving the file to computer (see Figures 11.1 and 11.2).

As most negative and slide originals are smaller than their print counterparts, film scanners generally have higher specifications and are therefore more expensive than flatbeds.

Reflective scanning

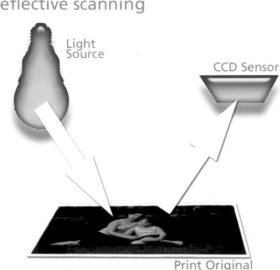

Figure 11.1 Reflective scanners, sometimes called 'flatbeds', are used for prints and documents.

Transmission scanning

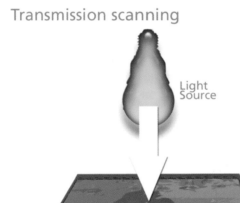

Figure 11.2 Transmission scanners are specially designed for use with negatives and transparencies, and are usually referred to as film scanners.

Scanner types

Up until a few years ago, the technology needed to capture each of the photographic media types meant that photographers had to buy two completely different pieces of equipment to handle their prints and negatives/slides. Though it is still possible to buy dedicated print and film scanners, many manufacturers are now producing combination or hybrid products that are capable of capturing both media.

Dedicated film. This device is set up specifically for negative or slide capture and is usually restricted to a single format (135 mm × 120 mm/5 in × 4 in). The hardware is not capable of reflective scanning. If your business involves the repeated capture of images of the one film type, a dedicated scanner is a good investment (see Figure 11.3).

Hybrid. These scanners are capable of both reflective and transmission scanning. This means that both film and print images can be captured by the one device. Starting life as flatbeds with added transparency adapters, these scanners have developed into multi-function devices that are capable of producing quality files from both types of originals (see Figure 11.4).

Dedicated print. The scanners in this category are the most affordable and easily obtainable of the three types. If you can't afford a digital camera of the quality that you desire and you have loads of prints in boxes lying around the house, then spending a couple of hundred dollars here will have you enhancing high-quality digital versions of your pictures in no time (see Figure 11.5).

Scanner parts

Getting to know you way around your scanner will help you make digital versions of your treasured prints and negatives more quickly and easily. Many companies provide a printed instruction manual as well as online help files that will introduce you to your scanner's particular functions and features, but here we provide a visual guide to the most common scanner parts and features (see Figure 11.6):

1 *Power button* – used to switch the scanner on and off. Some models do not have a power button, with the unit being turned on and off via the computer.

2 *Quick scan button* – many newer scanners have several one-step buttons at the front of the unit. These are designed to help make the job of everyday scanning quick and easy. The quick scan button creates a scan with a single click.

3 *Copy button* – used to provide a one-step copy or 'scan and print' option for those users who want to make 'photocopies' of documents or papers.

4 *E-mail button* – used to provide a one-step scan and e-mail option for those users who regularly want to send pictures to friends via the web. After the picture is scanned, your e-mail program will open automatically and the picture will be inserted as an attachment to a new message. Simply address and add a few words of explanation and mail away.

5 *Photocopy or direct print button* – a single-step process that scans a picture and then prints it with the press of one button. Some companies provide a little pop-up window, which looks very much like the key pad of a photocopier to be used with this feature.

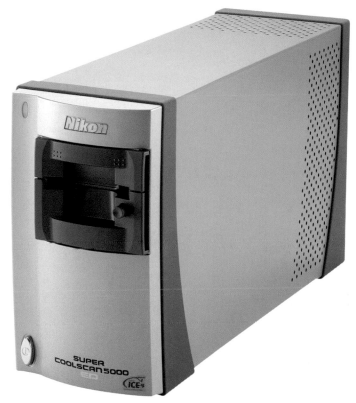

Figure 11.3 Dedicated film scanners can obtain very good quality results from negative and slide originals.

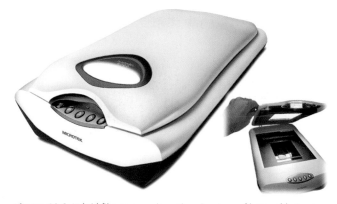

Figure 11.4 Hybrid film scanners have the advantage of being able to scan prints as well as negatives or slides.

6 *Scanning area* – the part of the scanner where your original is placed. This usually takes the form of a glass plate for print scanners or a negative holder for film scanners.

7 *Negative holder* – supports the film as it is scanned. These devices are hinged, with the film inserted and sandwiched between two plastic supports. Care has to be taken so the edges of the holder match up with each of the negative frames.

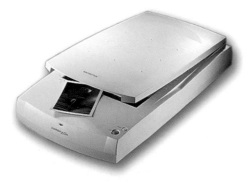

Figure 11.5 Print scanners are the most economical way to generate high-quality digital images.

8 *Power light* – indicates that the scanner is turned on. Some models also use a blinking version of this light as a way to show that a scan is in progress.

9 *Scanning light* – the light source that illuminates the surface of the print. In film scanners the negative is positioned between the light source and the sensor.

10 *Power socket* – used to connect power to the scanner. Some units combine the power and computer (data) connection in the one cable and so don't contain a separate power socket.

11 *Computer socket* – connects the scanner to the computer and is used for transferring the picture data. Depending on the scanner model, this connection might be in the form of a USB, Firewire, SCSI or Parallel port socket.

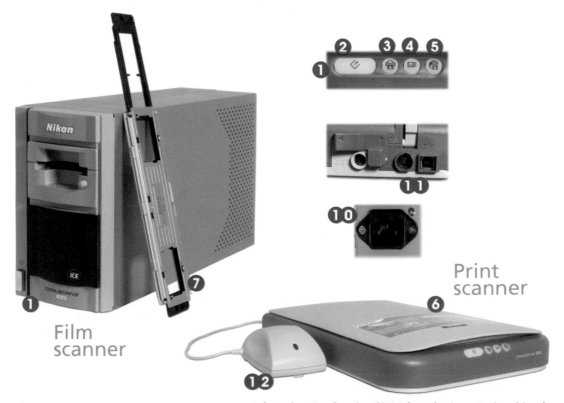

Figure 11.6 Common scanner parts and features. See text for explanation of numbered items (note that items numbered 8 and 9 in text are not shown here).

12 *Transparency adapter –
provides a way to scan your
negatives using a flatbed or
print scanner. These
adapters are usually
purchased separately as an
optional extra. If you have
a varied collection of
photographs, in both print
and negative forms, this
type of scanner might be
a good option.*

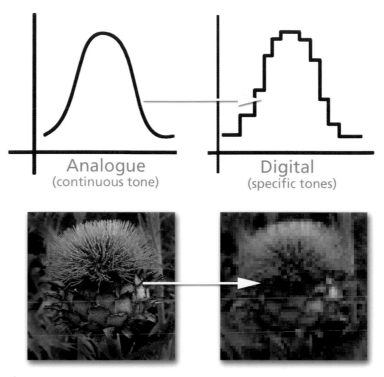

Analogue
(continuous tone)

Digital
(specific tones)

Analog to digital

The act of scanning, be it
using a flatbed model or
one designed for film
stock, involves converting
continuous tone images
into digital files.
Photographs in either
print or negative (or slide)
form contain a range of

Figure 11.7 Scanners convert continuous tone images such as prints or negatives into
the same pixel-based files that we obtain from digital cameras.

subtle tones and colors that blend smoothly into each other. These are referred to as continuous
tone images. For instance, in a black and white image it is difficult to see where one shade of
gray starts and another one finishes. The effect is a smooth transition from the deepest shadows
through to delicate highlights.

Computers are clever machines but they have difficulty handling images in this form. So, in
order for the photograph to be used in an image manipulation program like Photoshop Elements
or Paint Shop Pro, it must be changed to a digital file. The file describes the image as a series of
discrete colors and tones. When we scan a negative or slide we make this conversion by
sampling the picture at regular intervals. At each sample point, a specific color is chosen to
represent the hue found in the original. In this way, a grid of colors is put together to form a
digital version of the continuous tone original (see Figure 11.7).

Film scanners versus flatbed scanners

The current crop of print or reflection scanners are quality machines that are capable of creating
good quality, high-resolution images containing millions of colors. Most mid-range and even some
entry-level devices are more than capable of capturing the full range of image content and picture
details present in your photographic prints. New, and perhaps tentative, scanner users might find
it useful to cut their teeth using economical flatbed technology. This option provides the cheapest
way to gain access to the world of digital photography. Despite my comments in the next few
sentences, very good results can be obtained from files captured using this type of technology.

Until recently, the cost of most film scanners was out of the range of most desktop imaging budgets, but new technology advancements and more competition in the market now mean that these pieces of kit are more affordable. This fact should have serious digital image makers dancing in the aisles.

Why? Because scanning from film gives you the chance to capture more of what your camera saw when you pressed the button. This is for the simple reason that the information contained in a negative or slide is greater than what can be printed. Some of the detail and spread of tones that was initially captured on your film is lost when it is converted to print.

If you carefully compare a negative and its print you will probably be able to see details in the shadows and highlights that have failed to make it to the print. With careful printing, using techniques like burning-in and dodging, or split grade filtration, these details can be made more evident, but they will never be recorded as well as they were in the film original. It follows then that a quality film scan will capture more information than the flatbed version made from the print.

Dedicated film scanners have the advantage of being specifically designed for the job of transmission scanning. These units generally can capture high resolution, large numbers of different colors and detail in both highlight and shadow areas. Early hybrid systems were basically flatbed scanners with a transparency adapter placed on top. In most cases, these devices didn't provide the quality needed for photographic work. The scanned file was usually low resolution with muted colors and often contained banding across the image.

I am happy to say that this is no longer the case. The new range of hybrids have been designed from the ground up as two separate scanners that are then built into the one box. Sure, they use the same scanning head but they are a lot more than a reflective model with an add-on. In this way, manufacturers such as Microtek have been able to provide a single solution for both transmission and reflective needs.

Choosing which of type of scanner to buy will be largely dependent on the way that you work, your budget and your existing equipment.

If you don't own a scanner, then a flatbed is a cheap and easy way to get your digital hands dirty. If, on the other hand, you already own a flatbed and regularly shoot one film size such as 35 mm, then a dedicated scanner might be a good investment.

For the photographer with a little more to spend, who is looking to buy a first scanner, likes to photograph with a range of film stock (35 mm, 6 cm × 6 cm, 5 in × 4 in) and wants to scan prints as well, then a good quality hybrid scanner will provide a one-unit solution for all scanning needs.

3 Creative Use of Camera Controls

Each of the camera's technical features introduced in the previous part – lens focusing, shutter, aperture, etc. – is there for two purposes. Firstly, it helps you to get clear, accurately framed and properly exposed pictures of subjects – distant or close, under dim or bright lighting conditions. But each control also has its own creative effect on the image. This allows you some interesting options – in other words, you can choose a particular setting for its creative influence, and then adjust the other controls if necessary to still maintain correct exposure. Clearly, the more controls your camera offers and the wider their range, the more choices you will be able to make. Fully automatic-only cameras work from set programs based on choices set by the manufacturer, but as you will see, even here a measure of control is possible – for example, by loading fast or slow film.

12 Shutter speeds and movement

A shutter set for 1/125 second should safely avoid overall blur due to camera movement when you are trying to hold it stationary in the hand. This setting will also overcome any blurring of slower moving subjects, particularly if some distance away.

If you want to 'freeze' action subjects you will need a camera offering faster shutter speeds. The movements of athletes in most sporting activities can be frozen using a shutter speed of 1/250 second or faster. Cycle races and autocar events will probably need 1/1000 or 1/2000 second to lose all blur, but much depends on the direction of movement and how big the moving subject appears in your picture, as well as its actual speed. Someone running across your picture will record more blurred than the same runner moving directly towards you. Filling up your picture with just part of the figure – by shooting close or using a telephoto lens – again exaggerates movement and needs a shorter shutter speed to freeze detail.

With a manually set camera select a fast shutter setting, then alter the lens aperture until the meter signals that the exposure is correct. On a semi-automatic or multi-mode camera choose 'shutter priority' ('Tv' or 'S'), pick a fast shutter speed and the camera will do the aperture setting for you. An auto-only camera loaded with fast film will set its briefest shutter speed, in strong light. In fact, shooting on film of ISO 400 or 1000, or equivalent setting for digital cameras, is advisable with all cameras using briefest shutter settings, to avoid underexposing.

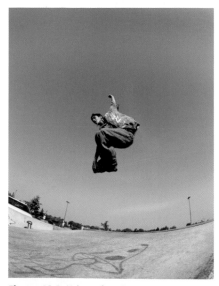

Figure 12.1 Using a fast shutter speed can freeze the movement of subjects in your photographs. Image courtesy of www.ablestock.com.

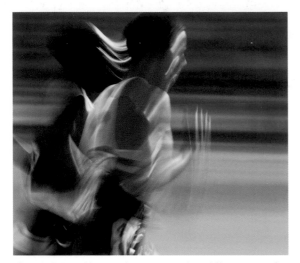

Figure 12.2 In this example you can see how different parts of the runners are more blurred than others, depending on how much they moved during the long shutter speed used for exposure. Image courtesy of www.ablestock.com.

If you have a simple, one-fixed-shutter-speed camera, try instead to swing ('pan') the camera in the same direction as the moving subject (see page 208). This can give you a reasonably sharp picture of your subject against a blurred background. Another alternative is to freeze the motion using a short burst of light, such as a flash (see page 76).

Slow shutter speeds, say 1/30 second, or as long as several whole seconds may be necessary just to get a correctly exposed result in dim light, especially with slow film. These longer times also allow you to show moving objects abstracted by different degrees of blur. Look at the blurred runners in Figure 12.2. Notice that different parts of the body show different amounts of blur depending on how much these areas moved during the long exposure. Often, action can be suggested more strongly this way than by recording everything in frozen detail.

Working with these longer exposures, however, means taking extra care to steady the camera, or camera shake will blur everything instead of just those parts of your subject on the move. Figure 12.3 suggests several ways of improving steadiness when using your camera hand-held. Learn to squeeze the shutter release button gently – don't jab it. Even then, if you use settings of 1/30 second or longer, find a table, doorway or post and press the camera firmly against this. With some models your camera may display a 'shake' warning when it automatically selects a slow shutter speed. Be careful too when using a telephoto lens, because the larger image it gives magnifies camera movement, like looking through binoculars. A tripod, or even a clamp, which will secure your camera to the back of a chair, will allow steady

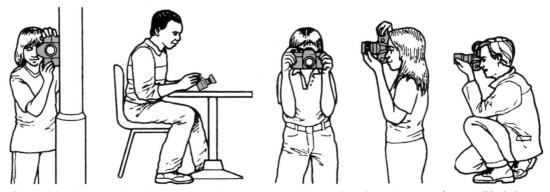

Figure 12.3 When using slow shutter speeds it is important to ensure that you keep the camera as steady as possible during the exposure. Here are a few techniques that you can use to make sure that you obtain blur-free photographs.

exposures of unlimited length. Make sure that the tripod has a pivoting head so you can angle the camera freely before locking it in place (see page 39).

The range of slow shutter speeds offered on many compacts and manually set SLR cameras only goes down to about 1 or 2 seconds. For exposures longer than this, SLRs (and a few compacts) offer a 'B' or time setting. With this feature the shutter stays open for as long as the release button remains pressed, and you time your exposure with a watch.

In practice, it is best to use an extension shutter release (Figure 8.25) to avoid camera shake. Advanced SLR cameras may set timed exposures of 30 seconds or longer. Exposure times of several seconds open up a whole range of blur effects that you can first experiment with and then increasingly control – although results always have an element of the unexpected. Pick something light and sparkling against a dark background. At night fairgrounds, fireworks, or simply street lights and moving traffic, make good subjects. Use slow film and a small lens aperture so that you can give a long exposure time without overexposing. (Some manual SLR camera meters will not measure exposure for B settings, in which case 'cheat' the meter as described on page 206.)

13 Focus and aperture

Selectively focusing your camera lens for a chosen part of the subject is a powerful way of drawing attention to it, subduing unwanted details at other distances, and helping to give your picture a sense of depth. In Figures 13.1 and 13.2, for example, emphasis has been switched from the flowers to the background simply by changing the focus setting. Think carefully about where your location of greatest sharpness should be. In portraits, it is best to focus on the eyes; with sports events you might pre-focus on the crossbar of the high jump or just the sports track line a runner will use.

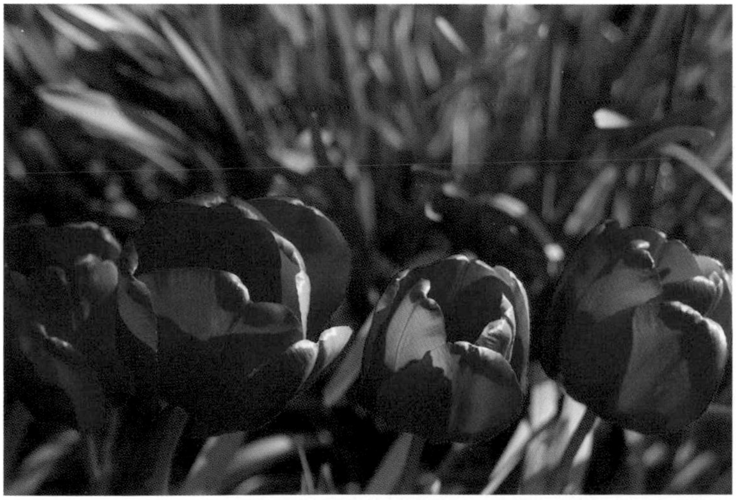

A manually focused SLR

Figure 13.1 Focusing on the flowers only draws the viewer's attention towards this part of the frame. In this way, the photographer can direct the way that his or her audience looks at their pictures.

camera allows most scope to actually observe how a particular point of focus makes the whole picture look. With an auto-focusing (AF) camera you will probably need your point of focus filling the tiny auto-focus frame line in the center of your viewfinder (see Figure 13.3). Then, if you want to compose this point off-center, operate the camera's AF lock (often half pressure on the release) to maintain the same focus while you reframe the picture before shooting.

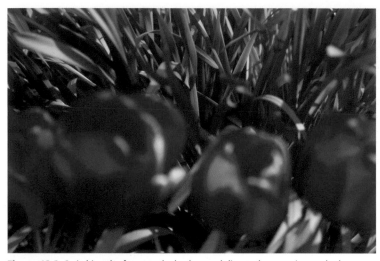

Figure 13.2 Switching the focus to the background directs the attention to the leaves first, as they are the sharpest part of the picture. This is despite the fact that the flowers are a vibrant color and, for this reason, would usually attract our attention first.

The degree of auto-focusing accuracy your camera will give depends upon the number of 'steps' (settings) it moves through between nearest and furthest focusing positions. Fewer than ten is relatively crude; some have over 100. Where a good AF scores most is when faced with a moving target. Here it will adjust continually to maintain your subject in focus as subject distance changes. However, most auto-focusing SLR cameras allow you to change to manual focusing if you prefer to work this way.

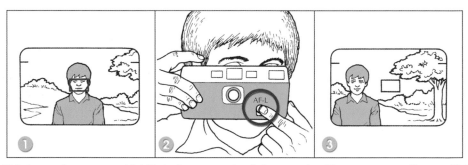

Figure 13.3 An auto-focus camera with AF lock allows you to sharply focus a main subject you compose off-center. (1) First, center the subject in the auto-focus rectangle. (2) Half depress the shutter release to make the lens focus, then operate the AF-L control. (3) Now you can compose the subject anywhere within the frame before shooting.

Aperture and depth of field

The adjustable size aperture in your lens has an effect on how much of your picture appears sharply focused (see Figure 13.4). The smaller the diameter of the hole (large f-stop number), the greater the range of items, at distances closer or further away, that will appear sharply focused (along with the specific subject that you actually focused on). A photograph with objects spread over a wide range of distances, where all are clearly focused, is said to have a large depth of field.

The opposite to large depth of field, small or shallow depth of field, is created when you photograph a scene using an aperture with a large-diameter hole (small f-stop number). These images generally have a single object sharply focused, with the rest of the image blurry or unsharp. Using a shallow depth of field is a great way to ensure that your audience is concentrating on the part of the picture that you, as the photographer, deem as important.

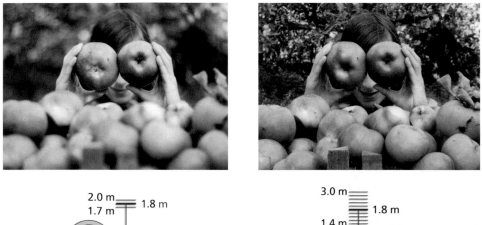

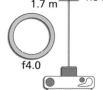

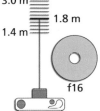

Figure 13.4 The effect of aperture. In both pictures, the lens focus setting remained the same, but changing from f4 to f16 greatly increases depth of field.

Aperture size is described by an 'f-number', and if your camera lens has manual control this will carry a scale of f-numbers as set out in Figure 13.5. Digital, advance compacts and most new SLR cameras also display the aperture setting on a small readout screen located on the top of the camera. Unlike the numbers marked on the lens barrel, which represent full f-stop changes, the settings displayed on the small LCD screen often change in quarter or third of an f-stop jumps.

Notice how the wider the aperture, the lower the f-number. To see this in action, look at the picture of the girl with apples (Figure 13.4). In both shots the lens was focused on the girl's

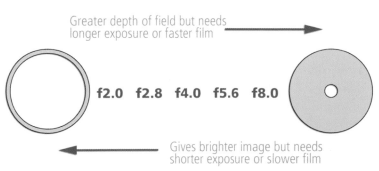

Figure 13.5 F-number aperture settings.

hands. But whereas one picture was taken at a wide aperture (an f-number of f4), the other was taken at a small aperture (f16). The f4 result has a very shallow depth of field. Only where the lens was focused is really sharp – apples in the foreground and trees in the background are very fuzzy. The other version shows much greater depth of field. Almost everything nearer and further away than the point of focus, the hands, now appears sharp.

Of the two versions, the one on the left works best for this subject because it concentrates your attention on the two apple 'eyes'. The same applies to the edges of the flower's petals

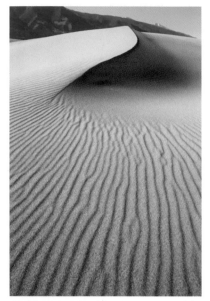

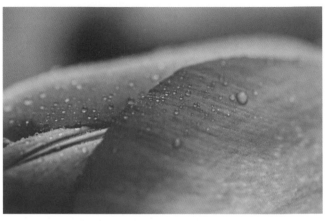

Figure 13.7 In contrast, a shallow or small depth of field is employed in this image to ensure that only a portion of the whole photograph is sharp. Image courtesy of www.ablestock.com.

Figure 13.6 Using the aperture to control the amount of the picture that appears sharp is a great way to control the look of your image and to direct your viewer's attention to the important parts of the picture. In this photograph, a large depth of field has been used to ensure that detail is sharp from the foreground right into the distance. Image courtesy of www.ablestock.com.

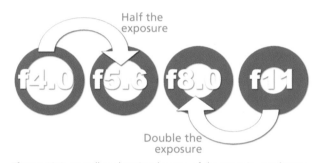

Figure 13.8 As well as changing the zone of sharpness in our pictures, the aperture also controls the amount of light entering the camera. Each full f-number change represents a halving or doubling of light.

shown in Figure 13.7. But on other occasions – the sand dunes shown in Figure 13.6, for example – you may want to show all the pattern and detail clearly from just in front of the camera to the far horizon. So controlling depth of field in a picture by means of the lens aperture setting is a useful creative tool.

As well as changing the zone of sharpness in a picture, each f-number in the series also doubles, or halves, the brightness of the image (see Figure 13.8). The wider the maximum aperture provided by a lens, the more expensive and bulky the lens becomes (see Figure 13.9).

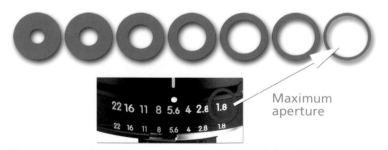

A simple fixed-aperture camera may only offer a single aperture of f5.6; many compacts have lenses which 'open up' to f4.5 and 'stop down' to f16. SLR standard lenses may offer a longer range of f-numbers – from f1.7 or f1.4, through to f16 or f22.

Figure 13.9 Most lenses display the available apertures on the barrel of the lens, with the widest aperture (biggest hole) being represented by the smallest f-number.

SLR cameras are designed so that you always see the image on the focusing screen with the lens held open at the widest aperture, which is brightest to view and most sensitive to focus. This situation is deceptive, though, if you have set a small aperture – just as you release the shutter the aperture changes to the size you set, so the picture is recorded with far more depth of field than you originally saw on the screen. Some single lens reflex cameras have a depth of field preview or 'stop-down lever'. Pressing this while you are looking through the viewfinder reduces the aperture size to whatever you have set, so you can visually check exactly which parts of a scene will be sharply recorded. (Although, at the same time, the smaller aperture makes the image on the screen become darker.)

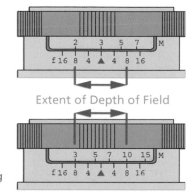

Extent of Depth of Field

Another way of working, if you have time, is to use the depth of field scale shown on some SLR camera lenses (Figure 13.10). First, sharply focus the nearest important detail – in the example shown, this reads as 3 m on the focusing scale. Next, refocus for the furthest part you also want sharp, which might be 10 m. Then, refer to the depth of field scale to see where to set focus between the two, and what f-number to use in order to embrace both 3 and 10 m – in this case f8.

Figure 13.10 Depth of field scale on SLR lens. (Top) Lens focus at 3 m; lower scale shows that f8 gives sharpness from 2 m to nearly 6 m. (Bottom) Focus 5.5 m, depth 3–10 m at f8.

Many digital camera users have the advantage of being able to preview the results of their aperture selection on the LCD screen immediately after the image is taken. Unlike film users, they have the advantage of being able to check their zone of sharpness straight away. Using this preview technique it is possible to shoot a range of images at different aperture settings and, after reviewing the depth of field results in each picture, make a final aperture selection.

Maximum depth of field (see Figure 13.11)

Pictures taken with an automatic-only camera will show greater depth of field the brighter the light and/or when fast film is loaded. This is because, in these conditions, the camera automatically sets a small aperture (along with brief shutter speed) to avoid overexposure. A simple fixed-focus compact camera is likely to have its lens set for about 4 m with a fixed aperture of about f8. In this way, you

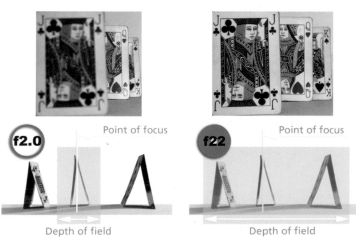

Figure 13.11 To achieve the maximum zone of focus in a picture using your aperture only, select the highest f-number available (i.e. f22, f32). In contrast, select the smallest f-number for shallow depth of field effects.

get depth of field from about 2 m to the far horizon. But remember that it remains unchangeable in every shot.

To adjust the depth of field when using a manually focused lens, you should first set the lens for the key element in your picture or, if there is not one, then focus for a distance of about one-third of the way into the scene. So, if the nearest important details are about 2 m (7 ft) and furthest detail 7.5 m (25 ft) from the camera, a difference of 5.5 m (18 ft), set your focus at about 4 m (13 ft). Select your smallest lens aperture (such as f16 or f22), then alter the shutter speed until the meter reads correct exposure.

Using a semi-automatic or multi-mode camera, choose 'aperture priority' ('Av' or 'A'), set the smallest aperture your lens offers and the camera will adjust the shutter speed to suit. In poor light, unless you are using fast film, this may lead you to a slow shutter speed – so be prepared to use a tripod or some other means to steady the camera when you are trying to capture large depth of field images.

Minimum depth of field

To get minimum depth of field you need a camera with wide aperture lens and a really accurate method of focusing. But remember, using apertures such as f2 means that a fast shutter speed will probably have to be set, to avoid overexposure. In bright lighting, such as a summer's day, it will be helpful to load slow film (for digital users set a low ISO number) into your camera to account for the big aperture hole.

There are two other methods for creating a shallow depth of field – use a longer focal length lens or move closer to your subject. Changing to a telephoto lens (or setting your zoom control to the longest setting, sometimes marked as 'T') gives less depth of field even if you keep to the same f-number. Remember, however, that this use of shallow, selective focus means there is no margin for error in setting the lens for your chosen subject distance. This is especially true with close-ups or macro subjects, where the depth of field is often measured in millimeters (fractions of an inch).

Use Table 13.1 as a quick guide for setting up your camera for either shallow or large depth of field effects.

Table 13.1 Create pictures with shallow or large depth of field effects using the following camera setups

DOF effect required	Best aperture numbers	Best focal lengths	Best subject-to-camera distance
Shallow	Low (e.g. f2.0, f2.8)	Longer than standard (e.g. 120 mm)	Close
Large	High (e.g. f22, f32)	Shorter than standard (e.g. 28 mm)	Distant

14 Choice of exposure

Essentially, giving 'correct' exposure means letting the image formed by the camera lens act sufficiently on your light-sensitive film or digital sensor to give a good quality picture. Good exposure, then, is a balance of neither too much nor too little light falling on the film or sensor. Remember, setting your aperture and shutter speed controls the amount of light entering your camera and therefore the degree of exposure that the film or sensor receives.

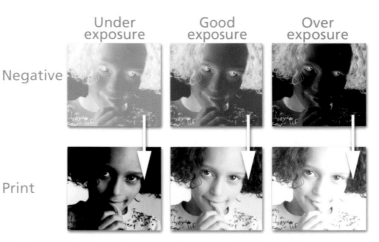

Notice in the image series in Figure 14.1 that the picture that is correctly exposed has plenty of detail recorded in both the darkest shadows and the brightest parts of the picture. The picture on the left, however, has been seriously underexposed (received too little light).

Figure 14.1 Correct or good exposure produces good prints. Images that are overexposed (too much light) or underexposed (too little light) result in prints with poorer image quality. Overexposure causes the highlights in the print to be clogged and lose detail. Underexposure produces the reverse effect, losing detail in the shadow area. Image courtesy of www.ablestock.com.

Dark parts of the picture have been recorded as detail-free black – and appear heavy and featureless when printed. Only the very lightest parts of the image, such as the girl's blouse (on the right), could be said to show as much detail as the correctly exposed version.

In contrast, the picture on the right has been overexposed. So much light has recorded in the highlight (lightest) parts of the subject they appear white and 'burnt out' on the print. Only the hair area shows the same detail that was evident in the correctly exposed shot.

To summarize, too much exposure and delicate light shades or highlight details in the image are lost, too little light and subtle shadow tones are converted to pure black. This is true for both digital and film-based images. When you are shooting slides the same final differences apply, although there are no negatives involved.

The exposure controls

Most cameras make settings that will give correctly exposed results by:

1 Sensing the ISO speed rating of the film you have loaded.
2 Measuring the brightness of the subject you are photographing.
3 Setting a suitable combination of shutter speed and aperture, either directly or by signalling when you have manually made the right settings.

The simplest cameras have no exposure adjustments and they expect you to load an appropriately fast or slow film for your lighting conditions (page 47), then rely on the ability of modern films to give prints of fair quality even when slightly over- or underexposed.

If you are using a manual SLR, you point the camera at your subject and alter either the shutter speed or lens aperture until a 'correct exposure' signal is shown in the viewfinder. Being able to choose aperture and/or shutter speed is like filling a bowl of water either by using a fully open tap (big aperture hole) for a short time (fast shutter speed) or a dribbling tap

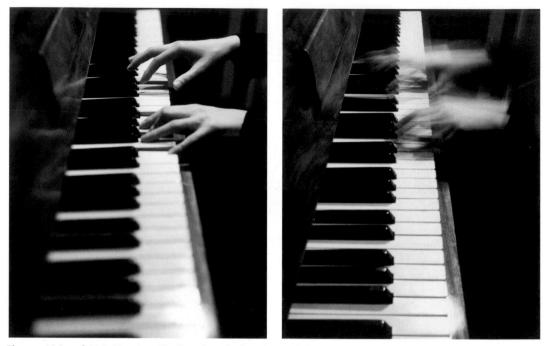

Figures 14.2 and 14.3 Metering will tell you how the f-numbers and shutter speeds line up. Left picture: 1/30 second at f2.8. Right picture: 1 second at f16. Both are correctly exposed but very different in appearance.

(small aperture hole) for a long time (slow shutter speed). Figures 14.2 and 14.3, for example, are both correctly exposed although one had 1/30 second at f2.8 and the other 1 second at f16.

The f-numbers associated with aperture sizes on your lens are set out in a special series, where each change in number represents a doubling or halving of the light entering the camera. Each change to a higher f-number halves the light, so f16 lets in only one-thirtieth of the light let in by f2.8, five settings up the scale. The pictures differ greatly, though, in other ways. Figure 14.2 has very little depth of field but frozen hand movements; Figure 14.3 shows nearly all the keys in focus but the moving hands have blurred during the slow exposure.

A fully automatic camera makes settings according to a built-in program or mode. This might start at 1/1000 second at f16 for a very brightly lit scene then, if the light progressively dims, changes to 1/500 second at f16, and 1/500 second at f11, 1/250 second at f11 . . . and so on, alternating shutter speed and aperture changes to account for the changing light conditions. Such an automatic program would never give results like either Figure 14.2 or Figure 14.3. It is more likely to set 1/8 second at f5.6.

If your camera, like most compacts, is fully automatic only you will always get maximum depth of field (combined with freezing of movement) in brightest light, especially if fast film is loaded. This is why multi-mode cameras, mainly SLRs and advanced compacts, also offer aperture priority mode, allowing you to set the f-number and so control depth of field. Alternatively, by selecting shutter priority mode you can choose and set shutter speed to control blur.

Standard shooting modes (see Figure 14.4)

These basic modes can be found on all but the most basic or entry-level film and digital cameras, and determine how the camera sets the correct aperture and shutter speed settings from the light available in the scene.

- *Auto or program* – the camera determines the shutter and aperture settings automatically based on the light in the scene.

- *Shutter priority* – the shutter speed is set by the photographer and the camera adjusts the aperture automatically to suit the light in the scene.

- *Aperture priority* – the aperture is set by the photographer and the camera adjusts the shutter speed automatically to suit the light in the scene.

- *Manual* – both the shutter speed and the aperture are set by the photographer.

Advanced cameras may contain more than one fully automatic program designed to make intelligent exposure setting decisions for you. For example, when you change to a telephoto lens the program alters to a set-up using the aperture mostly to adjust exposure, leaving the shutter working at its faster speed to counteract the extra camera shake risk from a long focal length. Other models contain specialist shooting modes that alter the camera's set-up to suit a range of photographic situations – portrait, sunset, landscape, etc.

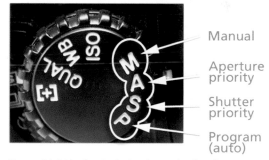

Manual
Aperture priority
Shutter priority
Program (auto)

Figure 14.4 The four basic shooting modes, found on many cameras as standard, provide different approaches for the setting of the camera's aperture and shutter speed to suit the light in the scene.

Measuring the light

Most compact cameras have a small, separate window next to the viewfinder. This window holds a sensor that responds to light reaching it from the whole of the scene you can see in the camera viewfinder. This so-called 'general' light reading is accurate enough for average subjects, such as those in Figures 14.5 and 14.6. In both photographs, the areas taken up by dark parts are roughly equal to the areas occupied by the brightest parts, with the rest of the scene in tones approximately halfway between the two. A general

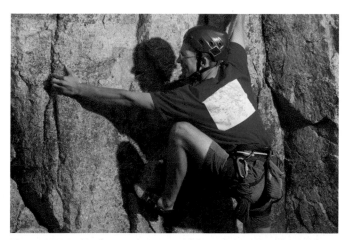

Figure 14.5 In this photograph, a general light reading works well as all the elements included in the scene combine to form a balance of light and dark tones. Image courtesy of www.ablestock.com.

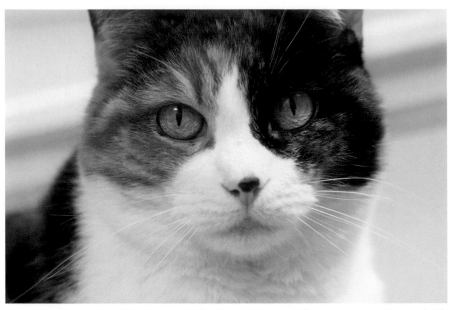

Figure 14.6 Despite the light background in this photograph, when all the picture parts are averaged with a general light reading, detail is held throughout. Image courtesy of www.ablestock.com.

reading of the whole lot averages out all these differences, and the camera settings that are made have produced an exposure that is a good compromise for everything in the picture.

Contrasty subjects

Simply averaging the whole subject area in this way is not suitable for all subjects. Sometimes this approach can let you down, especially when the subject is full of mainly dark or light subjects.

For instance, an overall reading of the scene will not work. If you want to shoot a picture, such as Figure 14.7, where the majority of the picture is filled with the light background. A general reading here would have been over-influenced by the (unimportant) lighter

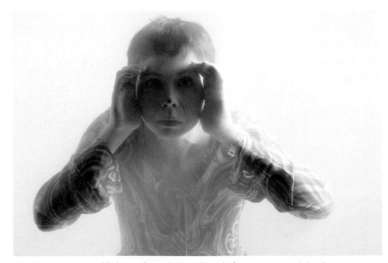

Figure 14.7 General light readings are not suitable for scenes containing large areas of light or dark tones, as these picture parts will overly influence the final exposure settings. To maintain detail in the face in this photograph, you need to alter the aperture and shutter speed selected by the camera to add extra exposure. Image courtesy of www.ablestock.com.

background, averaging out the scene as quite bright, and so providing settings which underexpose the girl's face. The result might even be a black, featureless silhouette such as Figure 14.8, as the camera does not know that detail in the girl's face is vital. Much the same thing can happen if you are photographing a room interior by existing light, and include a bright window.

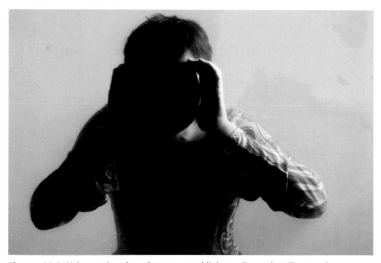

Figure 14.8 Using settings based on a general light reading only will cause the important face detail in this example to be too dark in the final photograph. Here we see how the camera's meter has overcompensated for the bright white background, making the whole photograph too dark.

In pictures like Figure 14.9, you meet the opposite problem. A general reading here would be influenced by the large shadowy dark areas that form the majority of the picture. It would cause the camera to select settings that would render the lighter areas, and the delicate details they contain, overexposed and bleached out. With the correct exposure, the camera indicated exposure less 1.5 stops, the picture maintains the original feeling of the lighting whilst keeping detail throughout all the important areas.

If your automatic camera has an exposure lock, you can first tilt the camera towards the area that you want to expose correctly so that the entire frame is filled. Then, by pressing the shutter halfway down or pushing the exposure lock button, the light reading is memorized and does not change when you compose the shot as you originally intended (see Figure 14.10).

With a camera set to manual mode you should use the same frame-filling procedure, adjust aperture or shutter speed to get a 'correct exposure' signal, and keep to these

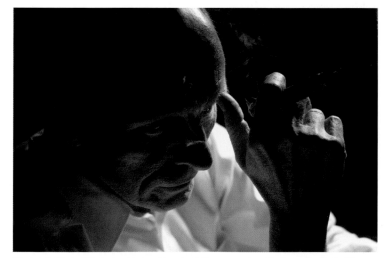

Figure 14.9 In this dark and moody portrait, the camera's meter is confronted with the opposite problem. A general light reading will cause the resultant photograph to be recorded as too light. Adjusting the camera settings so that it uses 1.5 stops less exposure maintains the dark and moody feel. Image courtesy of www.ablestock.com.

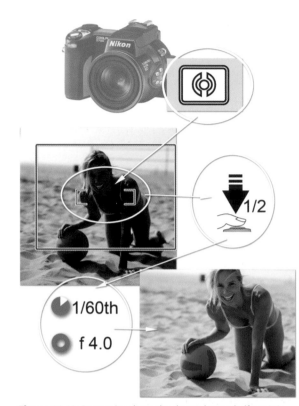

Figure 14.10 By pressing down the shutter button halfway it is possible, with many cameras, to lock the exposure settings used to capture a scene. As the metering system will try to average the scene's tones to match a mid-gray, photographers should carefully choose the parts of the picture that they use as exposure references. Pick a subject that is too dark and the picture will be overexposed. Use a section of the scene that is too light and the image will be underexposed. Image courtesy of www.ablestock.com.

settings (even though over- or underexposure may be indicated when you recompose).

Automatic cameras with an 'exposure compensation' control will also allow you to override the aperture or shutter speed values and allow an increase or decrease of the overall exposure from that suggested by the camera's meter. To double the exposure, for scenes with predominantly light subjects, you change the setting to '+1'. To reduce the exposure by half for scenes filled with dark objects, adjust the feature to '−1'.

Most entry-level cameras use a so-called 'center-weighted' light measurement, designed to take more account of the broad central part of the picture, where the majority of main subjects are deemed to be placed. Advanced compacts and many SLRs offer a 'multi-pattern' form of metering light. Measurements are taken from several parts of the picture and the camera then calculates the exposure from the variety of brightnesses in the scene. The more sophisticated versions of this system also take into account which segments should most influence the exposure for a given scene. This 'matrix' metering mode provides the most accurate exposure measurements for the majority of scenes and should be the mode that you keep as the default on your camera.

Some models also contain a 'spot' reading mode, whereby just a tiny area, shown centrally in the focusing screen, measures the light. You can position this over any key part, such as a face, even when some way off. A spot reading is very accurate and convenient, provided you don't let it stray to a completely wrong part of the scene.

Deciding priorities

It is important to learn to recognize situations where special care over the way the light is read will greatly improve a shot. For instance, in situations where the sun is lighting a small but important portion of a distant scene, you can overcome the meter's tendency to suit the exposure for the general view by temporarily filling the viewfinder with a similarly lit subject close at hand. Using a similar approach, you can measure the exposure for people's faces by reading off the back of your own hand (as long as both subjects have the same lighting). If your camera is equipped with a zoom lens, then it may also be possible to zoom in to take a reading from the important area of the scene and then zoom back to take the photograph.

Sunsets against tree shapes are often disappointingly colorless when exposure is measured by a general reading. For Figure 14.11, the camera was first angled so only sky filled the frame to make the exposure reading. Even when you make use of an exposure technique like this, it is best to take several shots of contrasty situations, 'bracketing' your exposure settings, i.e. use the exposure override or aperture or shutter settings to give twice and/or one-half the metered exposure.

Digital shooters, on the other hand, can use a shoot and review approach, checking the exposure of the picture just taken on the preview screen on the back of the camera, to ensure the correct settings have been used before proceeding.

Film users will need to make sure that contrasty pictures like these are followed up with sympathetic printing by your processing lab. Otherwise, the lab could strain to 'correct' the very effect you wanted to produce. If necessary, ask for a reprint, explaining what you were aiming for.

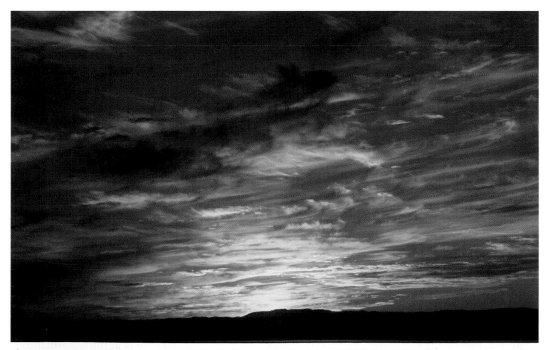

Figure 14.11 To ensure that your sunset shots are not recorded as too light and washed out, tilt the camera towards the sky to take your exposure reading first before recomposing. This way, the dark foreground detail will not affect the overall exposure of the picture. Image courtesy of www.ablestock.com.

15 Changing focal length

The creative controls your camera lens offers include:

- focus control (allowing a sharp image of things at your main subject distance, and so giving them emphasis); and
- aperture control (allowing changes in depth of field as well as helping to control the amount of exposure).

But your camera offers a third possibility, which is to alter its lens focal length. When you change focal length you alter the image size. This makes a difference to how much of your subject the camera now 'gets into the frame'.

Two practical advantages stem from changing the focal length of the lens that you use:

1 You can fill up the frame without having to move closer or further away from your subject.
2 The perspective, or look, of your picture can be altered by changing your subject distance and altering focal length.

'Normal' focal length

A normal (or 'standard') lens for a film-based 35 mm SLR camera has a focal length of 50 mm. On a 35 mm compact, a lens of 35 mm focal length or less is often fitted as standard, mainly for space-saving reasons. These lenses give an angle of view of 46° or 60° respectively. A 50 mm lens is accepted as making the images of objects at different distances in a scene appear in about the same proportions as seen in real life (judged from a typical size final print held at reading distance).

Changing to a lens of longer focal length (also described as a telephoto lens) makes the image bigger. So you have a narrower angle of view and fill up your picture with only part of the scene. A change to a shorter focal length (a wider angle lens) has the opposite effects (see Figures 15.1 and 15.2). But beware, the more extreme these changes are from normal focal length, the more unnatural the sizes and shapes of objects at different distances in your picture begin to appear.

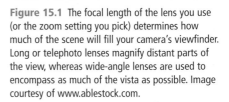

Figure 15.1 The focal length of the lens you use (or the zoom setting you pick) determines how much of the scene will fill your camera's viewfinder. Long or telephoto lenses magnify distant parts of the view, whereas wide-angle lenses are used to encompass as much of the vista as possible. Image courtesy of www.ablestock.com.

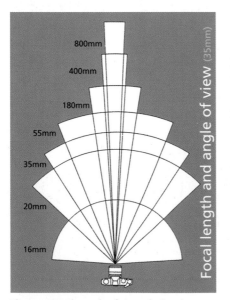

Figure 15.2 The angle of view of a lens is a measure of the amount of the scene that a lens includes in the photograph. Wide-angle lenses have a small focal length but a large angle of view; long lenses are the opposite.

Normal lenses and digital cameras

One of the factors that determines what is a normal lens is the size of the film or sensor in relation to the focal length of the lens. As most digital cameras have a sensor size that is smaller than a 35 mm frame, normal lenses for these cameras tend to have focal lengths shorter than 50 mm. This is even true for the SLR digital cameras that use the same lenses as the film camera version. To accurately compare the perspective of digital camera lenses, look for values that indicate the lens's '35 mm comparative' focal length. This converts the actual lens size to its equivalent on a 35 mm film camera.

How changes are made

Compact cameras have non-removable lenses, so changes of focal length have to take place internally. Most compacts have a zoom lens, meaning it will change focal length in steps or by smooth continuous movement, which is usually powered by a motor. Pressing a 'T' (telephoto) button progressively increases focal length and narrows the angle of view. Pressing 'W' (wide angle) has the opposite effect. The zoom range, as written on the lens rim, might be 35–70 mm. This lens makes image details twice as large at 70 mm than at 35 mm and is described as a 2 × zoom. The compact's viewfinder optics zoom at the same time, to show how much your picture now includes.

Single lens reflex cameras have detachable lenses. You might start off with a normal 50 mm lens, which combines a large maximum aperture (f1.8) and a very reasonable price (because of the large numbers made). This normal lens can be interchanged with any of a very wide range of wide-angle or telephoto fixed focal length lenses. They could include anything from an extreme 8 mm fish-eye through to an extreme 1000 mm super telephoto (see Figure 15.3). Alternatively, the most popular lens that you can attach to your SLR is a variable zoom lens, where the focal length is controlled by a ring on the lens mount. Most SLR camera are supplied with this type of lens as the default (see Figure 15.4).

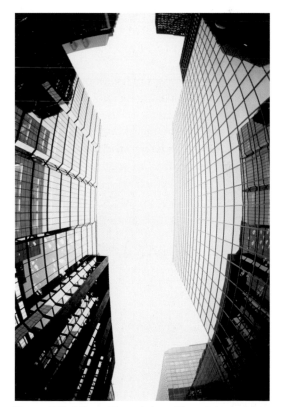

Figure 15.3 A fixed wide- and ultra-wide-angle lens can be added to many cameras and produces dramatic images displaying highly exaggerated perspective. Image courtesy of www.ablestock.com.

Zoom lenses can cover a middle range (35–70 mm) or a tele zoom (70–210 mm, for example) or wide-angle range (18–35 mm). More recently, some manufactures have even started to produce super-zooms that can cover a focal range as broad as 28–200 mm. Bear in mind, though,

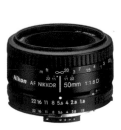

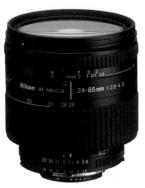

Zoom lens or variable focal
length lens - 24mm - 85mm

Fixed focal length
lens - 50mm

Figure 15.4 Fixed focal length lenses provide a single angle of view and are less popular than zoom lenses, which can be adjusted to provide a variety of focal lengths and therefore angles of view.

that general, non-professional, versions of these lenses – zooms, wide-angles or telephotos – tend to offer a maximum aperture of only f3.5 or f4 at best. Zooms and telephotos are also bigger and heavier than normal fixed focal length types. Professional models offer better maximum apertures but at a price and weight premium.

All this said, one of the real advantages of using a zoom lens with an SLR camera is the fact that any changes in focal length, depth of field and image size are all accurately seen in the viewfinder, thanks to the SLR camera's optical system.

Using a longer focal length

A very useful reason for changing to a longer focal length telephoto lens is so that you can keep your distance from the subject and yet still make it fill your picture. In portraiture photography, changing to 70 or 100 mm allows you to take a head-and-shoulders type photograph without being so overbearingly close that you make the person self-conscious, or creating steepened perspective which distorts the face. Candid shots of children or animals are more easily shot with a 135 or 150 mm focal length lens from a greater distance, where you can keep out of their way. At sports events too, you are seldom permitted to approach close enough to capture action details with a normal lens. Both here and when photographing animals or birds in the wild, a lens of 210 mm or longer is worthwhile (see Figure 15.5).

Long focal length lenses are also useful for picking out high-up, inaccessible details in monuments or architecture, or to shoot landscape from a distance so that mountains on the horizon look relatively large and more dominant.

Remember, however, that longer focal length means less depth of field, so you must be very

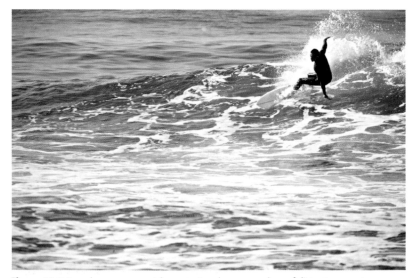

Figure 15.5 Long lenses are great for capturing close-up versions of distant scenes. Image courtesy of www.ablestock.com.

exact with your focusing. The more magnified image also calls for greater care to avoid camera shake than when using the normal focal length. So keep a tripod handy to help steady those zoomed-in photographs.

Using a shorter focal length

Zooming or changing to a shorter, wider angle, focal length (28 mm, for example) is especially useful when you are photographing in a tight space – perhaps showing a building or the interior of a room – without being able to move back far enough to get it all in with a normal lens. It will also allow you to include sweeping foregrounds in shots of architecture or landscape. The differences in scale between things close to you and objects furthest away are more exaggerated with wide lenses (see Figures 15.6 and 15.7). This effect can make people seem grotesque, even menacing. When you use lenses of 24 mm or shorter they begin to distort shapes, particularly near the corners of your picture. Another change you will notice when using a short focal length lens is the extra depth of field it gives, relative to a normal or a telephoto lens used at the same f number setting.

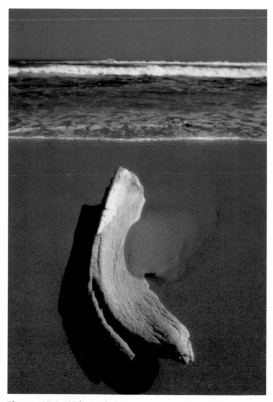

Figure 15.6 Wide-angle lenses provide quite a different perspective, making close subjects appear large in the frame and distant image parts much smaller. Image courtesy of www.ablestock.com.

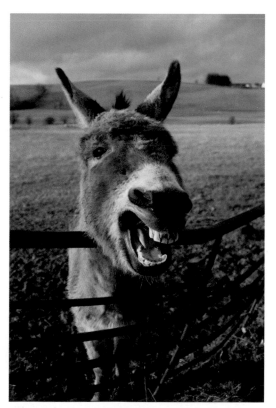

Figure 15.7 The wider the lens, the more dramatic the exaggerated perspective effect becomes. This is the reason why these lenses are not recommended for portrait photography and should be used with care for images where it is important not to show the type of distortion evident here. Image courtesy of www.ablestock.com.

Controlling perspective

It used to be said that the camera cannot lie, but using different focal length lenses you have almost as much freedom to control perspective in a photograph as an artist has when drawing by hand. Perspective is an important way of implying depth, as well as height and width, in a two-dimensional picture. A photograph of a scene such as a landscape shows elements smaller and closer together towards the far distance, and parallel lines seem to taper towards the background. The more steeply such lines appear to converge (the greater the difference in scale), the deeper a picture seems to the eye and the greater visual depth.

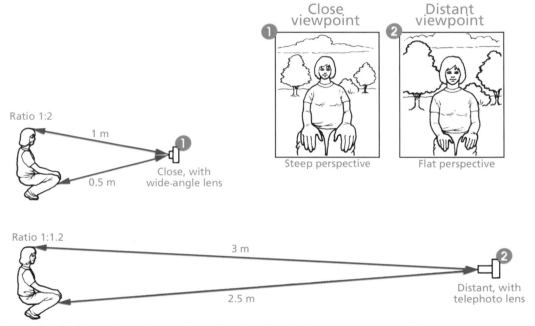

Figure 15.8 Whether drawing or photographing, a close viewpoint gives the steepest perspective (change of apparent size between nearest and furthest elements). Moving back reduces this ratio of nearest and furthest distances, flattening perspective.

As Figure 15.8 shows, it's all a matter of relative distances. Suppose you photograph (or just look) at someone from a close viewpoint so that their hands are only half as far from you as their face. Instead of hands and face being about equal in size, normal human proportions, the hands look twice as big.

Perspective is steep. But if you move much further back, your distance from both hands and face becomes more equal. Hands are only 1.2 times as big as the face. Perspective is flattened. Of course,

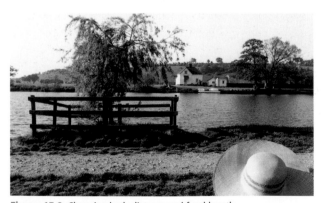

Figure 15.9 Changing both distance and focal length.

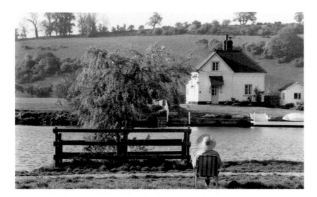

Figure 15.10 Changing both distance and focal length.

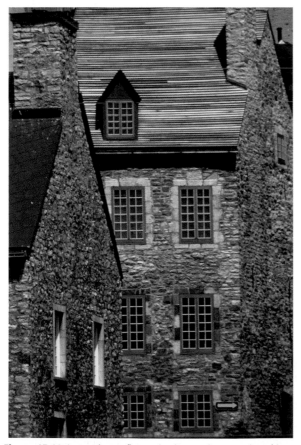

Figure 15.11 Longer lenses flatten the distance between the subjects in a scene. Here the buildings almost look as if they are sitting right next to each other rather than across the street. Image courtesy of www.ablestock.com.

being further away too, everything is imaged smaller – but by changing to a longer focal length lens you can fill up your picture again.

So to steepen perspective the rule is to move closer and then get everything in by either zooming to wide or changing to a wide-angle lens. A shot like Figure 15.9 makes you feel close to the person with the hat and distant from the cottage across the river. It was shot using a 35 mm lens with the camera some 10 m from the fenced tree. In Figure 15.10, the camera was moved to three times this distance and then the lens changed to a 100 mm to restore the tree to about its previous image size. But look what has happened to the cottage and the seated figure! There is now much less scale difference between foreground and background elements. With the camera further away, perspective has been flattened (painters would call this 'foreshortening') and the photograph has a cramped-up feel. Figure 15.11 also makes use of this foreshortening technique to flatten the distance between the two buildings in the picture.

Extremely short or long focal length lenses give results so unlike human vision they are really special effects devices. Figure 15.12, shot with an 8 mm fish-eye lens on an SLR, demonstrates its extreme depth of field as well as plenty of distortion (the building behind was one long straight wall). Lenses of this kind are very expensive, but lower cost 'fish-eye attachments' that fit over the front of a normal lens provide a more affordable option.

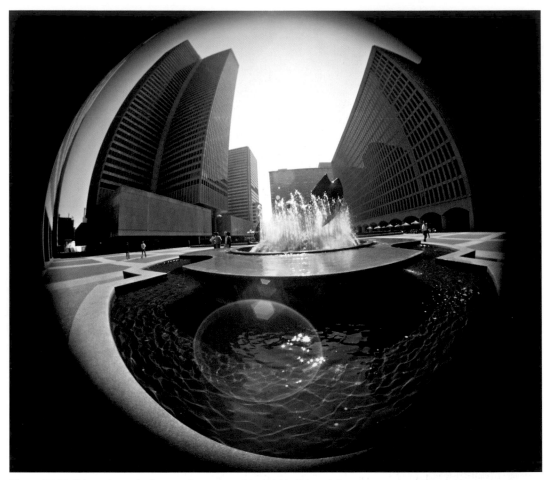

Figure 15.12 Fish-eye lenses (or lens attachments) provide a highly distorted view of scenes that with some lenses equals a 180° view. Notice also the large depth of field produced by virtue of the fact that this is an ultra-wide-angle lens. Image courtesy of www.ablestock.com.

16 Flash and its control

Flash is a very convenient way of providing enough light for photographing in low light situations. After all, most compact and many SLR cameras contain small flash lights built into the camera; its pulse of light is brief enough to prevent camera shake and freeze most subject movement, and it matches the color of daylight.

Unfortunately, this compact, handy light source has its shortcomings too. As explained below, in portraiture it is easy to get an effect called 'red eye' with every shot. Small, built-in flash units give harsh illumination slammed 'flat on' to your subject, resulting in ugly and very unnatural looking lighting effects. Subjects often show a dark, sharp-edged shadow line cast to one side of them onto background detail (see Figure 16.2).

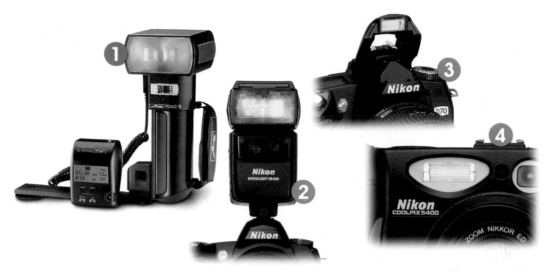

Figure 16.1 The flash lights for modern cameras come in a range of designs. (1) Until recently, the most powerful models, generally used by professional press and wedding photographers, attached to the camera using an angled bracket. Positioning the flash to the side of the camera also had the advantage of minimizing the occurrence of red eye. (2) Many cameras have a 'hot shoe' flash mount located on the top of the camera body. This connection is used to attach a portable flash unit. (3) Less powerful than either of the two previous flash types, the pop-up flash units found on many SLR cameras are suitable for illuminating distances up to about 3 or 4 meters. (4) Built-in 'twinkle' flashes, like those found in most compact cameras, are fine for close portraits and even some fill-flash work, but because of their proximity to the lens often suffer from red eye problems.

Any reflective surface like gloss paint or glass, square-on to the camera, records as a flare spot (see Figure 16.3). Nearest parts of a scene receive more light than furthest parts, often destroying the normal sense of depth and distance. Finally, flash pictures have a uniformity of lighting – which tends to make one shot look much like every other.

Don't, however, let this put you off flash photography. Most of these defects can be avoided or minimized (particularly if you can use a separate, clip-on flash unit). Flash is really useful when natural light is excessively contrasty or from the wrong direction, or impossibly dim for

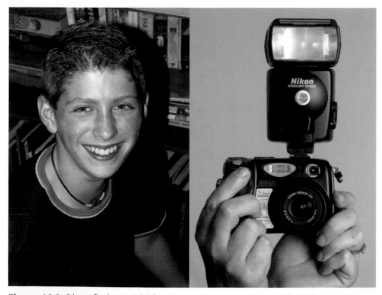

Figure 16.2 Direct flash, straight from your camera, provides very flat lighting with strong, hard-edged dark shadows.

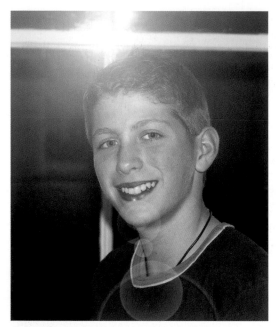

Figure 16.3 Watch the background of the scenes you photograph with flash. Glass or gloss surfaces directly behind your subject will reflect the flashlight back into the camera lens, causing a brilliant 'hot spot' to appear in the photograph.

active subjects indoors. Just don't allow it to become the answer for all your indoor photography – especially if having a camera with a wide aperture lens loaded with fast film (or digital camera set to a high ISO value) allows you to work using existing light.

Cameras with built-in flash

With the exception of some single-use types, virtually all compact 35 mm, APS film and digital cameras today are designed with a small flash unit built in. The vast majority of SLR auto-focusing cameras are similarly equipped. Manual single lens reflexes more often have a flash shoe with electrical contacts ('hot shoe') on top of the camera body. This will accept one of a range of more powerful slip-on flashguns.

In both instances the flash unit takes a few seconds to charge up when switched on, and after each flash. Wiring in the camera synchronizes the flash of light to the camera shutter's open period when you take the picture. Some cameras automatically switch on the flash when the metering system detects dim lighting conditions; it is important, though, to be able to switch it off when you want to shoot by existing light.

'Red eye'

When you look at someone's face the pupil in the center of each eye appears naturally black. In actual fact, the light-sensitive retina at the back of the eye is pink, but is too recessed and shaded to appear colored under normal lighting conditions. However, the flash that is built into a small camera body is only displaced an inch or so to one side of the lens. Like an optician's lamp used to closely examine eyes, the flash easily lights up that part of the retina normally seen as dark. The result is portraits showing 'red eye'.

Camera designers go to great lengths to minimize the defect – the flash source often slides out or hinges up (Figure 16.2) to locate it further from the lens. Another approach is to make the flash give one or more flickering 'pre-flashes' just before flashing at full power with the shutter. This is done to make the eyes of whoever you are photographing react by narrowing their pupil size, which in turn results in reducing the occurrence of red eye.

In addition to these techniques, you can help minimize red eye by angling the camera to avoid straight-on portraits. This may also avoid glare from any reflective surfaces square-on in the background. You may even be able to diffuse and so spread the light with a loop of tracing paper over the flash window. But the best approach of all, if your camera accepts an add-on flashgun, is to 'bounce' the light and avoid red eye altogether.

Using bounce flash

Instead of pointing the flash direct from the camera you will get far more natural, less problematic results by bouncing the light off some nearby white surface (Figures 16.4 and 16.5). This might be a ceiling or wall indoors, or even white card or plastic in a camera-attachable support, which is usable outside too. Most accessory flashguns can be tilted or swiveled so that you can point them upwards or sideways.

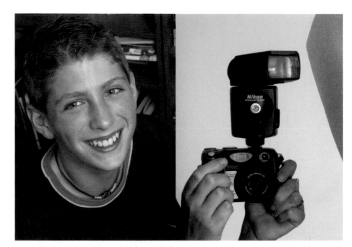

Figure 16.4 Bouncing your flash off a white card reflector to the side of your subject creates a similar effect to soft window light.

The bounced surface then effectively becomes the light source for the image, providing a soft and even light similar to that available on an overcast day. Using this type of flash set-up you avoid the worst aspects of direct flash and red eye. The less flat-on lighting gives you much better subject modeling and sense of form. And instead of light intensity falling away from front to back, most of the room is lit in an even and natural-looking way – from above.

Be careful, though, not to bounce the flash off a tinted ceiling or when surrounded by strongly colored walls. The overall color cast this gives is much less acceptable in a photograph than in real life. Also, ceiling-bounced flash should be directed at an area above the camera rather than above the subject. Otherwise, the subject receives too much top lighting, resulting in overshadowed eyes and a deep shadow below the chin.

Accessory flash units

Provided your camera has some form of electrical contacts for flash such as a hot shoe, you can mount a separate flashgun on top of the body. Here the flash head itself is sufficiently spaced from the lens to avoid red eye and it still fires when triggered by the shutter. There are three main types of small add-on flashguns (see Figure 16.6).

The simplest type does not tilt, has one fixed light output, and a table on the back shows the

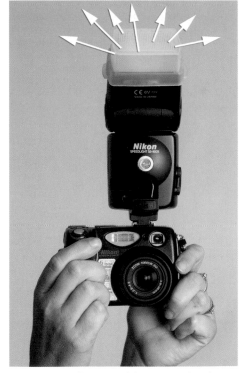

Figure 16.5 With some models you can soften the light using a flash attachment designed to spread the light coming from your flash. Some models are supplied with diffusion attachments designed for just this purpose, or you can purchase a diffuser from a third-party supplier.

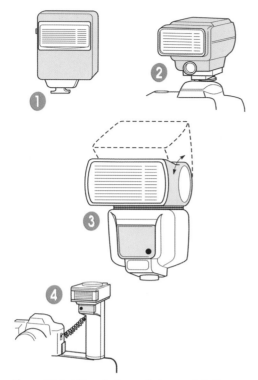

Figure 16.6 Add-on flashguns that connect via the camera's 'hot shoe' or cable. (1) Low-cost basic unit. (2) Semi-automatic with tilting head. (3, 4) More powerful dedicated types.

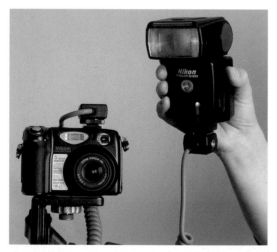

Figure 16.7 You can use your flash as a studio light replacement and can free the unit from its hot shoe base by using an extension cable. The cable maintains a link for all the flow of exposure and triggering information, whilst allowing the photographer to position the flash head away from the camera body.

aperture to set for different flash-to-subject distances and ISO values. Though not used often these days, this type of flash is still available and is often coupled with manual SLR cameras.

The second kind is self-contained and semi-automatic. The ISO value and camera lens aperture you have set are also set on the flashgun. When the picture is taken, a sensor on the front of the unit measures how much light is reflected off your subject and cuts ('quenches') the duration of flash. The head tilts for bouncing light, but you must always have the sensor facing your subject, not the ceiling.

Then there are 'dedicated' flash units, which when connected into an SLR or advanced compact metering circuit, pick up information on the ISO value that is set and uses the camera's own metering system to measure and control flash power and duration.

It may be impossible to connect these styles of flash units with the most basic of compact cameras, namely those that don't contain a connection for external flash. However, it is worth experimenting with a self-contained 'slave' unit, which someone can hold for you, perhaps pointed at the ceiling. The slave has a light-detecting trigger that responds to your camera's built-in flash and instantaneously flashes at the same time. You can then use the external unit to provide bounced or diffused lighting of your main subject. With some units it is even possible to take the flash off the camera and use it to the side, providing very directional lighting (see Figure 16.7).

Exposure and flash

With simple compact cameras that contain no adjustments, the built-in flash gives sufficient light for recording a correct exposure at a fixed aperture (typically f5.6 for an ISO value of 100) and at one set distance (typically 2.1 m or 7 ft). A flash of this power is said to have a 'guide number' of 12 (f5.6 × 2.1 m) – see Appendix K for guide number, aperture and distance chart.

Anything in your picture much closer or further away will be over- or underexposed respectively. The same applies to the simplest add-on flash units with a fixed light output.

Most flash units that are built into entry-level compact cameras are like self-contained automatic flash units, as they contain a small light sensor pointing at your subject. The closer and lighter your main subject, and the faster the ISO value set, the briefer the duration of your flash will be. So for a really microsecond flash, which is able to show spraying water droplets as frozen 'lumps of ice', work close and load fast film or set your digital camera to a high ISO value.

All self-regulating flash units, whether built-in or used as an add-on, only maintain correct exposure over a range of flash-to-subject distances. At the basic level, the distance range is often between 1.5 and 3.5 m. The more advanced the system (e.g. dedicated units), the wider the range of distances over which it will adjust to maintain correct exposure. But don't expect to be able to light a cathedral interior with amateur flash equipment. The same goes for using an auto-flash camera in the audience at a pop concert. The power of these units is often so limited that it will probably just record people a few meters ahead of your position, with all the rest of the scene disappearing into a sea of black.

Switching on the flash on a camera with built-in flash automatically sets the shutter to a speed (typically 1/60 second) short enough to hand-hold the camera, but not too short to 'clip' the flash. When you add a flash unit to a manual SLR you may have to perform this function yourself and set the shutter speed to 'X' (the default flash sync speed) or any slower setting to synchronize properly for flash.

Fill-in flash

An excellent way of using flash on the camera is as auxiliary or 'fill-in' illumination for the existing lighting. When you shoot towards the light, as in Figures 16.8 and 16.9, a low-powered flash on the camera (built-in or clip-on) illuminates what would otherwise be dark shadows. Provided the flash is not overwhelming, the results look entirely natural – you have simply reduced excessive lighting contrast. An auto-focus compact or SLR camera that offers 'fill-flash' mode will make the necessary settings for this style of shooting for you.

Fill-in flash from the camera is also useful for room interiors, which may include a window and where the existing light alone leaves heavy black shadows. If possible, use a powerful flashgun in these circumstances and bounce

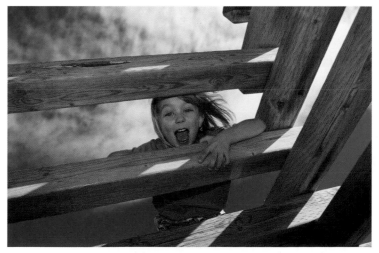

Figure 16.8 Candid portraits taken outside, where there is little or no control over lighting conditions, can generally benefit from a little fill-flash provided by the camera's built-in flash unit. The flash lightens the shadows caused by the sun's strong and contrasty light. Image courtesy of www.ablestock.com.

the light off a suitable wall or surface not included in the picture. This will produce the most even fill-in effect for the scene.

'Open flash'

An interesting way to use a separate flashgun, without needing any extra equipment, is called open flash technique. This technique involves working in a blacked out room, or outdoors at night. You set the camera up on a firm support such as a tripod and lock the shutter open on 'B'. Then, holding the flash unit freely detached from the camera but pointed at your subject, you press its flash test firing button. Having fired the flash once and allowed it to recharge, you can fire it several more times each from different positions around the subject before closing the shutter again. The result looks as though you have used several lights from different directions.

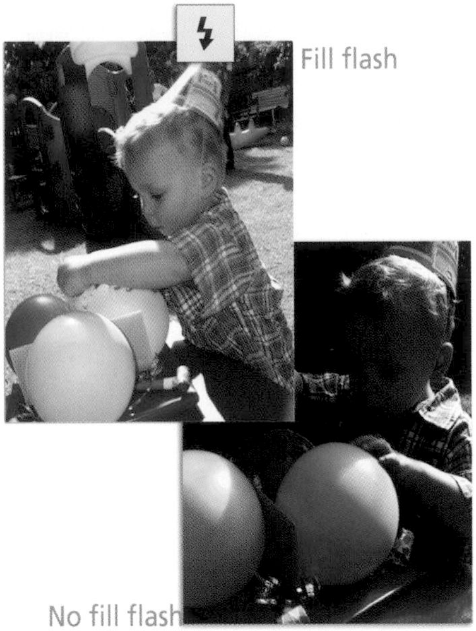

Open flash allows you to photograph the garden or part of your house as if floodlit.

Fill flash

No fill flash

Figure 16.9 Most medium-priced cameras contain exposure systems that can balance the light available in the scene (ambient) with that being emitted from the flash. Some models even have controls that enable the strength of the flash's output to be varied to suit the scene.

Calculate exposure from the guide number given for your flash. This is flash-to-subject distance times the lens f-number needed. If the guide number is 30 (meters) with the film you are using then set the lens to f8 and fire each flash from about 3.75 m (12 ft) away from its part of the subject. Plan out roughly where you should be for every flash, to light a different area. The total time the shutter remains open is not important provided there is little or no other lighting present.

Alternatively, if the flash unit you are using has a built-in sensor, then match ISO and f-stop values from the camera with those on the flash and then proceed to paint your subject with the flash light, allowing the unit to automatically govern its output.

1 Shallow depth of field. Set your camera lens to the smallest f-stop number and longest focal length it contains. Proceed to photograph a series of objects at the closest distance possible. Notice how the long focal length, small f-stop and close distance create images with very small depth of field or areas of focus.

2 All things sharp. Shoot a second series of pictures with the reverse settings to those above – i.e. use wide-angle lenses (or zoom settings), big f-stop numbers and medium 'subject-to-camera' distances. Notice that the images you create with these settings have large zones of focus extending from the foreground into the distance.

3 Dramatic architecture using exaggerated perspective (see Figure 15.3). Many wide- and ultra-wide-angle lenses produce images displaying highly exaggerated perspective.

(continued)

PROJECTS

Subjects close to the lens loom large and those in the distance seem microscopic in comparison. This type of perspective not only gives us a wider angle of view, but also provides us with a great opportunity to create some very dramatic pictures. Graphic architectural photographs with strong hard-edged lines and contrasting shapes and colors work particularly well. Using a modern building in your local area as a starting point, compose and photograph a series of dramatic, wide-angle architectural images. Don't be afraid to try a range of different angles – shoot up, shoot down, move in closer, try a little further back.

4 Panning techniques. As we have seen, using a slow shutter speed blurs the moving subjects in an image. An extension of this technique involves the photographer moving with the motion of the subject. The aim is for the photographer to keep the subject in the frame during the exposure. When this technique is coupled with a slow shutter speed, it's possible to produce shots that have sharp subjects and blurred backgrounds. Try starting with speeds of 1/30 second, gradually reducing them to around 1/4 second. Practice by shooting a subject that contains repeated action, such as a cycling or amateur motor sports event.

5 Flash blur. To achieve this effect you need to set your camera on a slower than normal sync shutter speed. The short flash duration will freeze part of the action and the long shutter will provide a sense of motion. The results combine stillness and movement. Remember to make sure that the light is balanced between the flash exposure and the ambient light exposure. If you are not using a dedicated flash system, this will mean ensuring that the f-stop needed for the flash exposure is the same as that suggested for the shutter speed by the camera's metering system. Again, photograph a subject that contains inherent movement.

6 Experiment with blur. With a camera offering settable shutter speeds, expose a series of images at settings of ISO 100 and 1/8 second. Include people and traffic on the move, preferably close. Use your camera hand-held, on a support, and panning (in various directions). Compare results.

7 Advance a sunset. Take a quick sequence of four color pictures of a landscape at late dusk. Give the first one correct exposure, progressively halved as you continue. Which print gives the most atmospheric result?

8 Angles of view. Using a cardboard frame sliding on a transparent ruler, simulate the use of different focal length lenses. A 24 mm × 36 mm slide mount positioned 50 mm from your eye matches the angle of view of a 35 mm SLR normal lens.

9 Repeating images. With a separate flashgun create a 'stroboscopic' action picture. Have the camera on a tripod with shutter locked open on 'B'. Shoot a light-colored moving figure (dancer) against a dark background in a darkened room, using a separate flashgun set in a position to one side. Make four or five test button flashes, altering the figure after each one. Follow the guide number for one flash when setting the f-number or match the f-stop and ISO values from the camera with those on the flash (if it contains a self-regulating sensor).

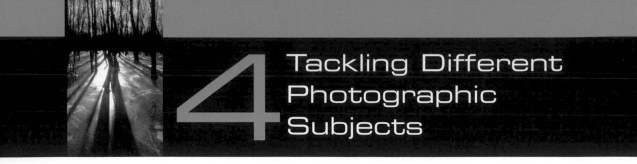
Many aspects of picture composition apply to all photography, as the examples in Part 1 showed. Technical controls too, such as the camera settings you make, choice of lenses and uses of flash, also play an influential role. But then again, the kind of subject you choose to photograph presents its own possibilities and problems. Part 4 looks, therefore, at a range of subject situations with these points in mind. Potentially interesting subjects include people, places, animals, landscapes, small objects in close-up . . . the list is almost endless. Despite the range of these topics, it is probably true to say that all of us at sometime will want to, or need to, photograph people, so this is where we will start.

17 People

Subjects here may be individuals or groups, posed or unposed, ranging from family and friends you know and can control, to candid shots of strangers. In all instances, it pays to pre-plan your shot as far as you can – which means concern for background and setting, direction of the light, and how 'tight' to frame the person (full length, half length, head and shoulders, head shot). At the same time, you must always remain able to respond quickly to any fleeting expression or unexpected moment of action or reaction, as it may occur. For example, the excitement and joyful expression on the face of the swinging child in Figure 17.1 could be lost a moment later; similarly, the baby's quizzical expression in Figure 17.2.

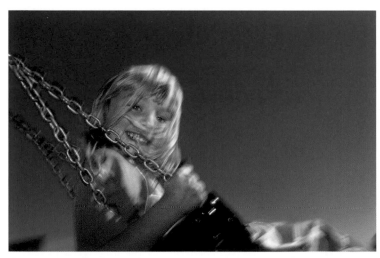

Figure 17.1 Candid photography requires quick work and a sense of anticipation in order to capture the fleeting expressions that can sum up the character of a subject or the feeling of the moment. Image courtesy of www.ablestock.com.

Babies are the least self-conscious people. The main problem with these young subjects is how to maneuver or support a young baby so they are not just shown lying down. Try photographing over the shoulder of the supporting adult, or have the baby looking over the back of an armchair. Avoid direct, harsh sunlight. If your camera offers a zoom lens, set this to its longest focal length (T) or change to a long focal length type. A lens of 85 or 100 mm is ideal for a 35 mm camera; even used at its closest focus setting, such a lens will give you a large but undistorted image.

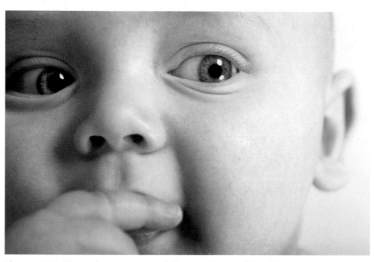

Figure 17.2 Plenty of patience is needed when photographing children and pets, as both subjects are unpredictable and great expressions like this one cannot be delivered on demand, but rather need to be waited for and then quickly captured. Image courtesy of www.ablestock.com.

As children begin to grow up, they quickly become conscious of the camera. It is often better then to give them something to do – set up simple situations that are typical for the child, then wait for something to happen without over-directing the occasion. The girl on the swing in Figure 17.1 was just such a 'can you see me?' activity for the individual concerned, improvised on the spot for the photograph.

Pairs

Portraying people in pairs allows you to relate them to each other in various ways. The relationship may be simply to do with comparative shapes and the individuals themselves remaining anonymous. Or it may be the highly personalized warmth and friendliness of the two brothers (Figure 17.3), both to each other and the person behind the camera. In this semi-posed shot, the boy in black stole into what was planned as a single portrait. The pale background helps to create a strong combined shape, and plain garments avoid distraction from faces. Lighting here was flash bounced off a white ceiling.

In other instances, expressions can have quite different connotations. The candid shot of the two elderly Italians (Figure 17.4) has a rather sinister air. The hats, the shades and the gesticulating hand seem to suggest some plot or business deal. A whole story can be dreamt up around such a picture – when, in fact, it was probably just a couple of old pals on a day out.

Your shot may be a largely constructed situation or taken incognito, but picking exactly the right moment can be quite difficult when two facial expressions have to be considered. Expect to take a number of exposures; you may find out anyway that a short series of two or three prints in an album forms an interesting 'animated'-type sequence that has more depth than a single photograph.

Groups

Organizing people in groups is rather different to photographing them as individuals or in pairs. For one thing, each person is less likely to be self-conscious – there is a sense of safety in numbers, and a touch of collective purpose and fun. This is a good feature to preserve in your

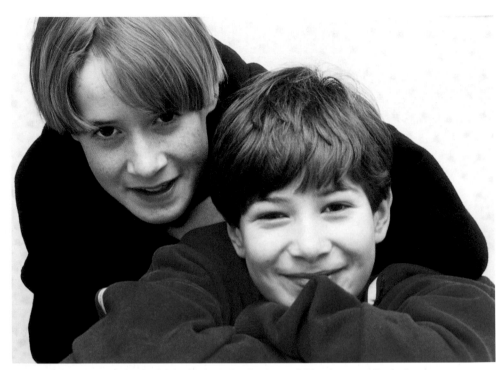

Figure 17.3 Clothes, pose and plain background help to give the picture of this pair an overall cohesive shape.

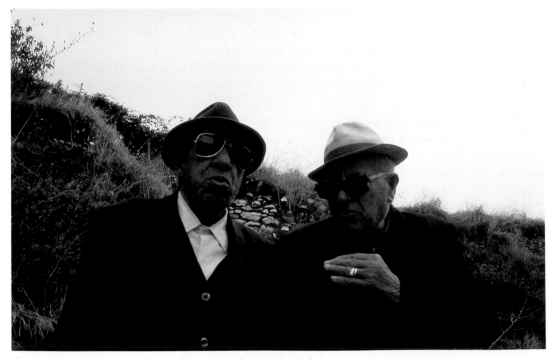

Figure 17.4 Expressions and garb give this passing pair a conspiratorial air.

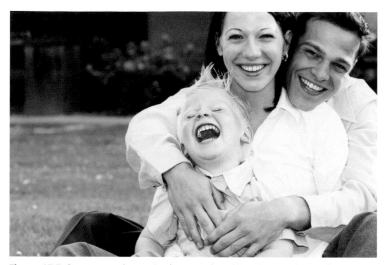

Figure 17.5 Spontaneous interaction between the subjects in your picture often creates a picture that is more full of life than one that is carefully composed or orchestrated. Image courtesy of www.ablestock.com.

picture rather than have everyone wooden-looking and bored. For similar reasons, don't take too long to set up and shoot (see Figure 17.5).

Groups of large numbers of people tend to call for a formal approach, and here it helps to prepare some form of structure, perhaps one or two rows of chairs. This guides people to where to sit or stand, and your camera position can also be prepared in advance. Smaller groups can be much more informally organized, participants jostling together naturally and given freedom to relate to one another, although still under your direction.

Most groups are linked to occasions and it is always helpful to build your group around a center of common interest – which might be the football and cup for a winning team, or a new puppy with its family of proud owners. Begin by picking an appropriate setting. Often, this means avoiding distracting and irrelevant strong shapes or colors in the background. With close, small groups you can help matters by having everyone at about the same distance from you, but keeping background detail much further away and out of focus (see depth of field, page 58).

Sometimes, though, showing the detail of the environment contributes greatly to your shot. Leaving space around the casual group in Figure 17.6 helps to convey the idea of an adventurous gang of youngsters.

If at all possible, avoid harsh direct sunlight that will cast dark shadows from one person onto another or, if the sun is behind your camera, causes everyone to screw up their eyes. Aim to use soft, even light from a hazy or overcast sky. Alternatively, try to find a location where there is some large white surface (the white-painted wall of a house, for example) behind the camera. This will reflect back diffused light into the shadows to dilute and soften them. For small groups, fill-in flash may also be a possibility.

Always try to locate the camera far enough back from the group to allow you to include everyone using a normal focal length lens. Working closer with a wide-angle or zoom lens at shortest focal length setting can make faces at the edges of a group appear distorted.

Every group shot calls for your direction to some degree. Consider its overall structure – gaps may need closing by making people move closer together (see Figures 17.7 and 17.8). With large formal groups you can aim for a strictly regular pattern of faces and clothing. To help with the composition of small groups, some photographers try to form a triangle shape with the main subject parts of their picture (see Figure 17.9). Ask if everyone has unobstructed sight of the camera lens. Always shoot several exposures because of the practical difficulty of getting

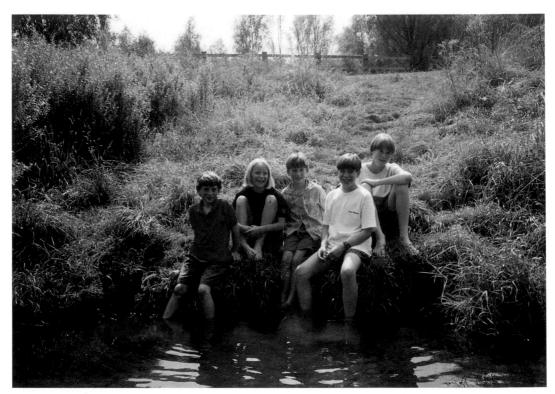

Figure 17.6 Showing surroundings can usefully add a sense of place – it would be wrong to tightly crop this informal group. Image courtesy of Celia Ridley.

everyone with the right expression, eyes open, etc. Having several versions also gives you the opportunity to digitally mix heads into one composite.

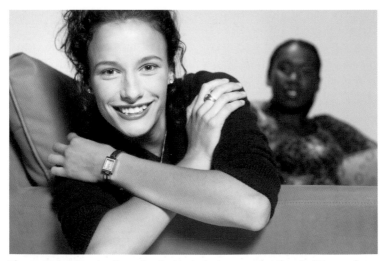

Figure 17.7 When shooting pairs of subjects, try to ensure that there isn't too much visual space between the two sitters. Here the distance was closed by overlapping the foreground sitter with the subjects at the rear. Image courtesy of www.ablestock.com.

Candids

To take portraits of friends and strangers without them being aware calls for delicate handling. But results can be rewarding in warmth and gentle humour. Candid shots of strangers are easier if you begin in crowded places like a market or station, where most people are concentrating on doing other things. Observe situations carefully, especially relationships (real or apparent). These

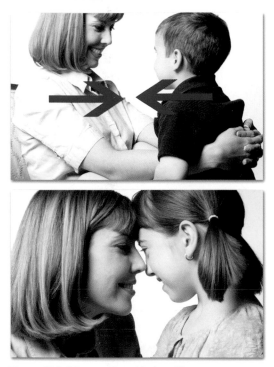

Figure 17.8 When working with the subjects, encourage them to interact closely so that there is little gap between the sitters in the final photograph. Image courtesy of www.ablestock.com.

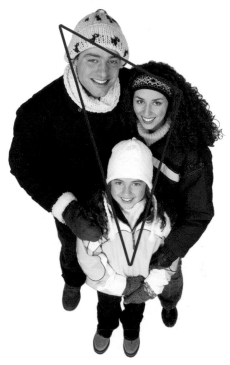

Figure 17.9 Creating a good composition with the members of a small group can be a difficult prospect. Here the photographer has chosen a higher point of view and arranged the subjects in a triangle shape. Image courtesy of www.ablestock.com.

may occur between people and pets, or notices, or other people, or just the way people fit within a patterned environment.

An auto-focus, auto-exposure camera is helpful for candids, but working manually you can often pre-focus on something the same distance away in another direction, and read exposure off the back of your hand. Avoid auto-wind cameras with noisy motors. Remember not to obstruct people when photographing in the street, and always ask permission to shoot on private property.

18 Places

Unlike people, places of habitation – towns, cities, buildings, etc. – are obviously fixed in position relative to their surroundings. This does not mean, however, that picture possibilities are fixed as well, and you cannot produce your own personal portrait of a place. It is just that good, interpretive shots of permanent structures require more careful organization of viewpoint and patience over lighting than most people imagine. The best picture is seldom the first quick snap.

Decide what you feel strongly about a place – this might be easiest to do when you visit the area freshly for the first time, or it may come from a longer stay giving greater insight into what the environment is really like. Compare Figures 18.1 and 18.2, which both show architecture. The

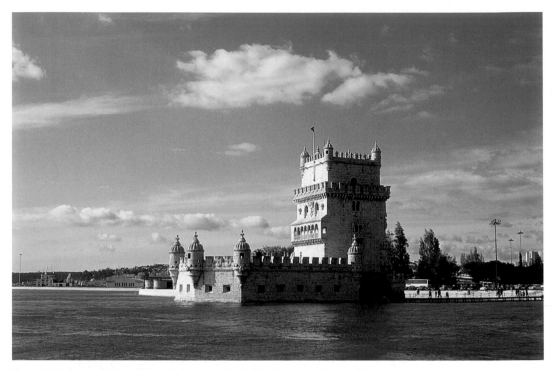

Figure 18.1 Tower of Belem, Lisbon. A shot timed for the lighting to strongly reveal form.

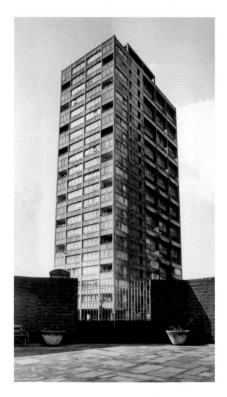

Portuguese Tower of Belem, photographed from a tourist boat, is an attractive pictorial record. (It is also a somewhat conventional postcard-type view.) The concrete tower block, in London, has received a totally different and much more personal treatment. It takes a stance about buildings – interpreting the block as some sort of prison, cut off from the rest of the world. To help achieve this, a distant viewpoint that is flat-on to the wall was carefully selected by eye – aligning wall, tower and shadow, so that they seem connected. The effect is one of shallow space, with wall and railings 'attached' to the tower and caging it in. Then, the lens focal length was changed to 80 mm to fill up the frame from this spot. Printing the shot in black and white helps to merge the different elements as well as increase its somber feel.

Choosing the lighting

Lighting also has a big part to play in the look and feel of your place pictures. Direct sun side-lighting falling

Figure 18.2 A viewpoint chosen to produce false attachment of foreground to background gives a caged-in feeling to this building.

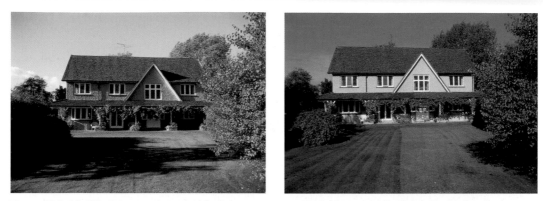

Figure 18.3 A building's texture, pattern and form change appearance as the sun moves direction during the day.

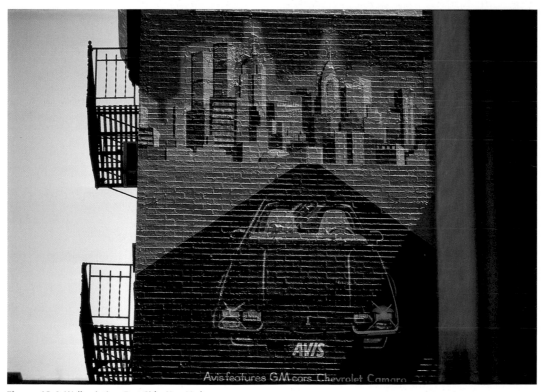

Figure 18.4 Wall painting, East Side, New York.

across your scene can pick out specific landmarks and contrast them against dark backgrounds or shaded backgrounds. This can be a good technique to use to direct the attention of your audience to a specific part of the scene. Softer lighting can create a flattening, downbeat effect, reflecting the gray of the lighting. Overcast conditions do have the advantage of ensuring that details are recorded in the lightest (well-lit) and darkest areas (shadows) of the scene.

Whenever possible, think out the sun's position moving from east to west throughout the day and its relation to the subject or scene you are photographing. If the sun is in the wrong

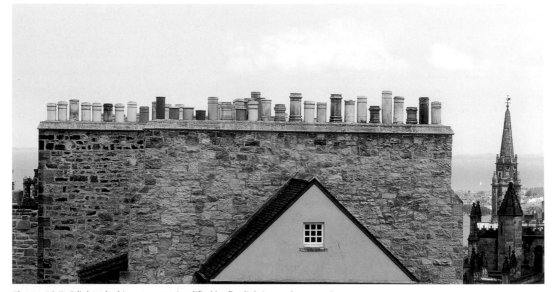

Figure 18.5 Edinburgh chimney-pots, simplified by flat lighting and perspective.

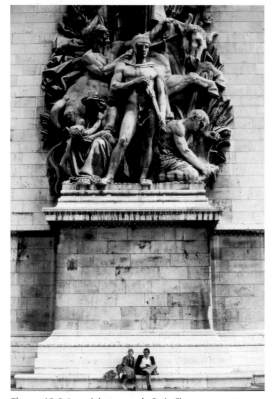

Figure 18.6 Imperial stonework, Paris. Figures contrast warlords and provide scale.

position it may be necessary to come back at a time when its direction will best suit the subject matter (see Figure 18.3). The same applies to choosing a day when weather conditions give direct sunlight or soft diffused light. Harsh, glancing light is essential to show the surface texture of objects such as bricks or cobble streets (see Figure 18.4). On the other hand, the pattern of varied chimney pot designs photographed across the roofs of local houses would be over-complicated by their shadows if recorded in harsh light (see Figure 18.5). Overcast conditions here, together with choice of viewpoint, help to keep the picture on one flat plane. The result is a sense of the eccentric or surreal.

Remember that the best times for interesting, fast-changing lighting effects are either in the early morning or late afternoon. But be prepared to work quickly when sun-cast shadows are an important feature – they change position minute by minute (or may disappear altogether) while you are adjusting the camera. Again, don't overlook the transformation of building exteriors at dusk, when internal lighting brightens the windows but you can still separate building shapes from the sky.

You can often sum up a whole city or village by just showing part of one building. Look for images that suggest the atmosphere and culture of the environment. But try to avoid hackneyed shots; instead, try suggesting the famous or well-recognized landmarks through a reflection or shadow. Signs and logos can form titles. Or you may want to bring together a 'collection' of shots of selected details such as mail-boxes, house names or interesting doors and windows. All these 'sketches' of what strikes you as special and most characteristic about a place will build up a highly personalized set of photographs. Leave the general views of famous sites to the excellent work of professionals shooting under optimum conditions – on sale at tourist centers.

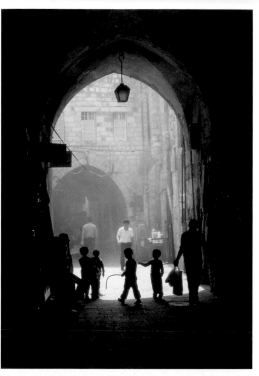

Figure 18.7 Arab quarter, Jerusalem. Exposure was measured for the central area, to preserve the darkness of the foreground.

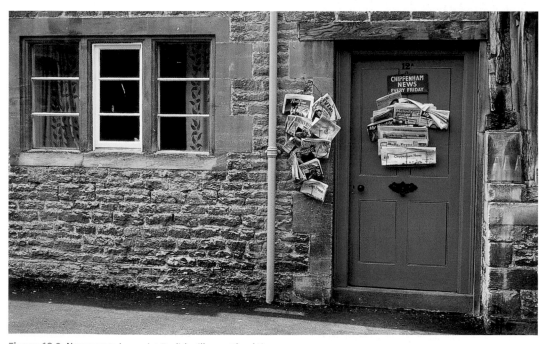

Figure 18.8 Newsagents in a quiet English village, at lunchtime.

People and places

Several other visual devices are worth remembering to help strengthen things you want to say through your pictures. For example, the size and scale of a structure can be usefully shown by the inclusion of figures (see Figure 18.6). Provided the figures you include relate to the environment in the photograph they can be also used as symbols – for example, showing the solitary outline of a person at a window in a vast, impersonal office block communicates more about the place of humans generally in the built environment rather than the life of the individual depicted specifically (see Figure 18.7).

On the other hand, the complete absence of inhabitants may also be important. Often, it is the hints of life that are left behind in a picture that can speak louder about how individuals live, work and dwell within a space than if the images were full of people. The audience is left to use their own imaginations to populate the space (see Figure 18.8).

Even when a destination is unexpectedly cold, bleak and empty, instead of sunny and colorful as anticipated, it can be worth shooting some pictures. Try to make them express this paradox in your glum impression of the day, perhaps by combining the sun and sea as depicted on painted signboards with the awful reality of the bleak day.

Whatever your personal reaction to a new place – perhaps good, maybe bad – aim to communicate it through your photography. New York City is impressive with its soaring architecture, but perhaps you notice too its features of public neglect (holes in the road, garbage) contrasting with corporate splendor (marble-faced commercial buildings). The discordance you recognize may become the basis of the images that you record of your visit.

Pictures of places don't always have to be linked to vacations and travel. You can practice your skills locally – encapsulating a street or an industrial park . . . even your own school or workplace. For a longer-term project, you may choose to take pictures once or twice every year from the same spot to create a series documenting the development of a garden. By always including family members in the shots, the images will also show how children grow and develop.

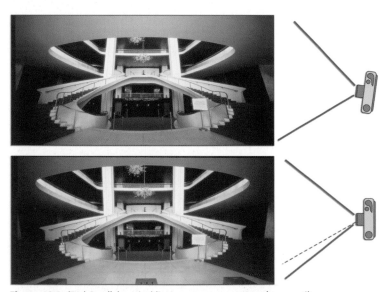

Figure 18.9 (Top) Parallel vertical lines appear to converge when you tilt your camera upwards. (Bottom) Keeping the camera back vertical and later cropping off excessive foreground is one solution.

Interiors of buildings

If you are a beginner, then making pictures of the interiors of buildings may sound difficult, but the abilities of modern camera equipment has made this task easier than ever before. A wide-angle (or at least a shorter-than-normal focal length) lens is usually necessary. This is because there seldom seems to be enough space to get back far enough to include what the eye sees when looking around an interior. Entry-level compact cameras with their 30 or 35 mm standard lenses have an advantage here. A 28 mm lens (or equivalent on digital cameras) is probably ideal, as shorter focal lengths start to create distortion of shapes near the corners of your picture.

Be cautious about tilting the camera when it is fitted with wide-angle lenses. Such an action creates images where the edges of buildings taper as they move away from the camera. This effect is often called 'converging verticals' and is acceptable to the eye when the photograph is obviously looking upwards or even down. But there is nothing more distracting than slightly non-parallel vertical lines in a straight-on view of a building or architectural interior. As Figure 18.9 shows, you can eliminate this effect by keeping the back of the camera vertical and either moving back or cropping off the unwanted extra foreground from your final image.

Even though you will use wide-angle lenses for most of your architectural pictures, you will also find that a long focal length lens, such as 100 or 135 mm, is useful for photographing out-of-the-way details within a large interior. Picking out interesting architectural features can suggest the whole.

Lighting

The main problem here is contrast, and to a lesser extent the dimness and color of the light. The lighting range between, say, the most shadowy corner of an interior and outside detail shown through a window is often beyond the exposure capabilities of your film or sensor. To avoid this

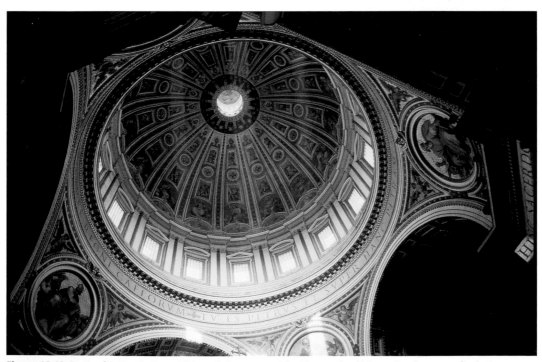

Figure 18.10 Dome of St Peter's, Rome. Wide-angle lens, exposed for 1/8 second at f5.6, pressing the camera firmly to a handrail.

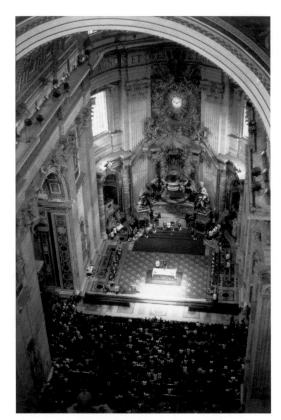

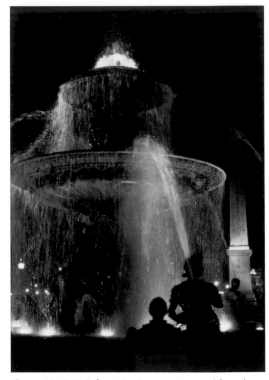

Figure 18.12 Paris fountains. Exposure was read from the central, lit water area.

Figure 18.11 Mass in St Peter's. Mixed artificial light and daylight. The altar area records orange on daylight film.

problem you could exclude windows, keeping them behind you or to one side out of frame, but where windows need including as an important architectural feature:

1 Shoot when the sky is overcast.
2 Pick a viewpoint where windows in other walls help illuminate interior detail.
3 Capture a series of bracketed exposures from which you can select the best image later. After all, some degree of window 'burn out' may prove atmospheric and acceptable provided you have retained important detail in shadow areas.
4 With smaller domestic size interiors, fill-in flash from the camera can reduce contrast, but don't expect success using this technique in a space as vast as a cathedral, especially using a camera with a tiny built-in flash!

Dimness of light need be no problem provided your camera offers long exposure times and you have some kind of firm camera support – improvised or, preferably, a tripod (see Figure 18.10). Some cameras offer timed exposures of up to 30 seconds. By selecting aperture priority mode and setting an f-number chosen for depth of field, the camera's metering system will automatically hold the shutter open for a calculated period. If you time this with a watch you can then change to manual mode and take shots at half and double this exposure time to get a range of results. Or better still, if your camera has an exposure compensation system, simply adjust the feature to add one stop more and one stop less exposure.

Even during daytime, the interiors of large public buildings are often illuminated by artificial light mixed with light through windows and entrances. In most cases, the interior light is a warmer color than daylight – a difference barely noticed by the eyes of someone there at the time but exaggerated in a color photograph (see Figure 18.11). In such a mixture of lighting, it is

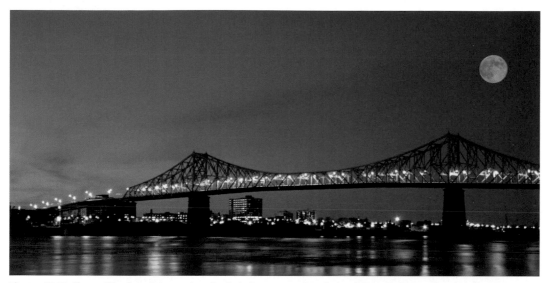

Figure 18.13 The sparkle of city lights against the dusk sky creates a theatrical and dramatic picture. Shooting the same scene on a moonless night, and at a later time, will produce a series of small pin lights against a predominantly black scene, but photographing at dusk means that there is enough light in the sky and on the water to provide texture, detail and color. Image courtesy of www.ablestock.com.

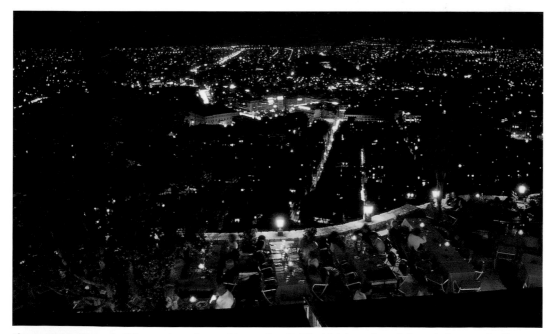

Figure 18.14 Athens. An SLR set to Av mode gave 12 seconds at f8. Mixed lighting – domestic lamps in foreground café.

still best to continue to use normal daylight-type film, with no color correction filtering, as totally removing the orangey artificial light can turn daylit areas unacceptably bluish. Some digital camera users have the advantage of being able to take several versions of the same mixed lighting image with different white balance settings. Later on, with the series of pictures displayed on screen, they can select the picture with the best overall color.

Cities at night

At night, floodlit monuments and city vistas have a special magic (see Figure 18.12). They are transformed from the mundane into a theatre-like spectacle. As with interiors, contrast is your main problem with these photographic subjects. Shooting at dusk is helpful, but sometimes the sparkle and pattern of lights against a solid black sky can really make your picture (see Figures 18.13 and 18.14). Wet streets after rain, reflecting illumination from shop windows and street lamps, will also help reduce contrast. But even so, dark objects still just showing detail to the eye will become silhouettes in photographs when you expose correctly for brightly lit areas. So pick a viewpoint that places interesting and relevant black shapes in the foreground, where they can add depth to the picture.

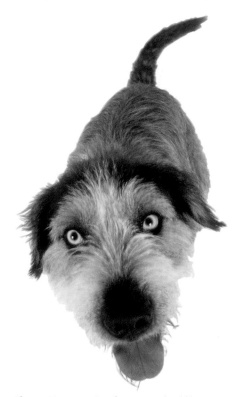

Advanced compacts and all SLRs can expose correctly for floodlit subjects (typically 1 second at f5.6 on ISO 200 film). Just ensure that you measure illumination from close enough to fill up the frame with the brightly lit surfaces. Note also that film behaves as if it is less sensitive when used for long exposures in dim light. For instance, for exposures of 10 seconds or longer, most color films halve their sensitivity. To compensate for this effect, set your lens aperture to one f-number wider (smaller number) or use the camera's exposure compensation system to override the exposure settings.

Figure 19.1 Portraits of your pets should be no less full of life and character than those of your friends or family, but just like these images, such personality-filled pictures require much patience and skill to capture. Image courtesy of www. ablestock.com.

19 Animal portraits

(see Figure 19.1)

Photographing family pets and rural animals is rather like photographing young children. You need a lot of patience because they cannot be told what to do; they are unselfconscious (although capable of showing off) and their relationships with people are a great source of situation pictures.

For best results always take the camera to the animal rather than the reverse. In other words, don't put the animal in a false or unfamiliar environment just because this is more convenient for your photography. Animals do not really belong in studios.

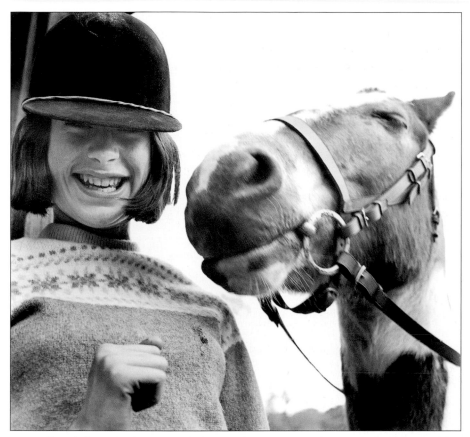

Figure 19.2 A self-satisfied animal with its owner. The low angle here gives strong shapes, and a final line around the print edges holds things together.

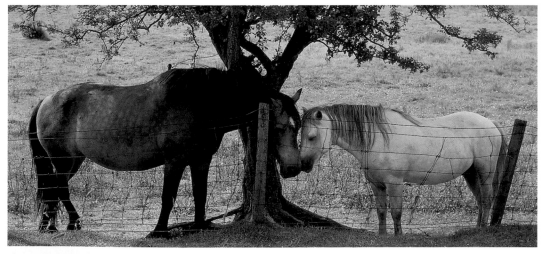

Figure 19.3 On a hot day, horses behave a bit like humans.

Showing character

As much as possible, try to convey the individual character of the animal you are photographing. Often, you can do this by showing the bonds between a pet and its owners, particularly children. It is also possible to show the interaction between animals, although you may have to keep your distance and so avoid disturbing them by your presence (see Figures 19.2 and 19.3).

Decide what is a typical activity and environment for your particular animal. Large pets like ponies and big dogs are often more placid than small dogs and kittens. Even so, it is not helpful to overexcite them by making the photography a 'big event'. You can suggest size by including other things in the picture to give a sense of scale. Also, make good use of camera viewpoint. A looming great horse can be shown close from a low angle, but use a normal or long focal length lens – coming in close with a wider angle gives ugly, steep perspective. A small cat or puppy looks tiny cradled in someone's arms, or photographed from a high viewpoint perhaps in front of a pile of crates and casks. Create candid images of your pet by photographing from the end of the garden, inside the house or across the street with your zoom lens on telephoto setting.

Small active animals are often by nature excitable and difficult to control. If this is a valid part of your pet's character it should be shown. Maybe it is good at leaping for balls, rolling on its back or just lapping up milk? Try setting up simple attractions – a ball on a string or a throwable stick – and then await natural developments patiently . . . But don't over-manage and degrade your pet by, say, dressing it up or putting it into ridiculous situations. The movement of an animal rushing around might be portrayed via a short series of shots, like a sequence of stills from a movie. Try to keep your viewpoint for the series consistent, so that the action appears rather as if on a stage. Another approach is to pan your camera to follow the action (easiest with the lens zoomed or changed to tele) and shooting at 1/30 or 1/15 second. The blurred surroundings and moving limbs then become a feature of your pictures, although you will need to take plenty of shots on a hit-or-miss basis.

Have a helper – preferably the owner – to control the animal and if necessary attract its attention just at the key moment. But make sure you brief the helper to stand near you behind the camera, and not to call the animal until requested. Another approach is to give the animal time to lose interest in you and your camera and return to its normal activities, even if this is just dozing in the sun (see Figure 19.4).

Lighting and exposure

As in human portraiture, soft, even daylight is usually 'kinder' and easier to expose for than contrasty direct light. Try to avoid flash indoors, or if you do use it, bounce the light off the ceiling. 'Red eye' from flash on the camera is just as prevalent with animals as human beings. So be sure to use the red eye reduction techniques

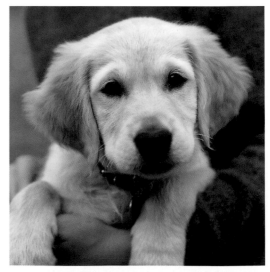

Figure 19.4 Cradling in a helper's arms provides scale and also keeps this lively young animal under control.

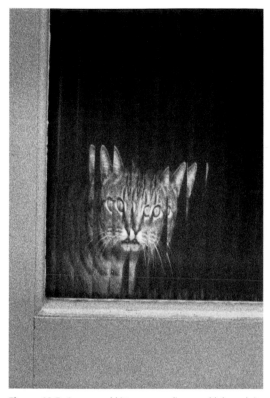

Figure 19.5 One scared kitten sees a dizzy world through its front door.

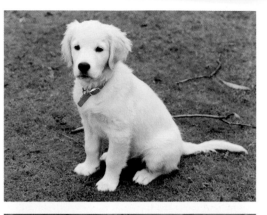

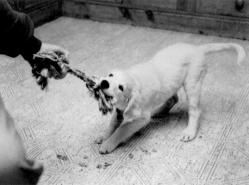

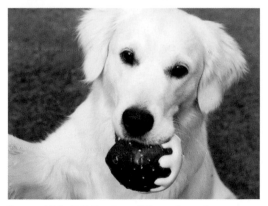

Figures 19.6–19.8 Puppies and kittens change interests from one moment to the next. With a helper you can set up an active game. But include the quieter moment when your pet is intent on studying something new (top). Keep well back and zoom to 'tele'.

outlined in the portrait section. Load medium/fast film, say ISO 400, or set the ISO to a high value for digital cameras, so that you can still use a fast shutter speed with the available light.

If you have a multi-mode exposure system camera, select shutter priority (Tv or S) and set the shutter to 1/250 for outdoors use unless you want subject movement blur. When using a manual camera set this same shutter speed, then change the aperture setting until a reading off the animal's coat signals correct exposure. Having all your camera controls set in advance will avoid loss of pictures due to fiddling with adjustments at the last minute. You need to combine patience with quick reactions, watching your animal through the viewfinder all the time, to be ready to shoot the most fleeting situation. A rapid auto-focus camera is helpful when an animal is liable to move about unexpectedly, especially if it is also close.

Backgrounds

Think carefully about the surroundings and background against which your subject will be shown. Many animal pictures are ruined because assertive and irrelevant details clutter up your photograph. Animals cannot be directed in the same way as people, and what may start out as a good background easily changes to something worse as you follow your subject into a different setting. The safest background to pick is a relatively large area of similar color, tone and texture. A large stretch of grass is a good option, especially when the camera viewpoint is high enough to make this fill the frame. Alternatively, by bending your knees and shooting from a low angle you can use the sky as a background.

Better still, pick surroundings showing something of your particular animal's own habitat, adding character and enriching the portrait. A scared kitten neurotically observing a confusing world through its reeded glass front door is one case in point; a pair of horses gently dozing under the shade of a tree is another.

Not all animal portraits are set up, of course. Always look out for opportunist pictures (for which a compact camera is the quickest to bring into operation). Just like candid shots of people, you will discover a rich source of animal relationship pictures at gatherings – pet shows, livestock markets, pony races, farmyards, even dogs' homes – where plenty of 'animal action' is always going on (see Figures 19.5–19.8).

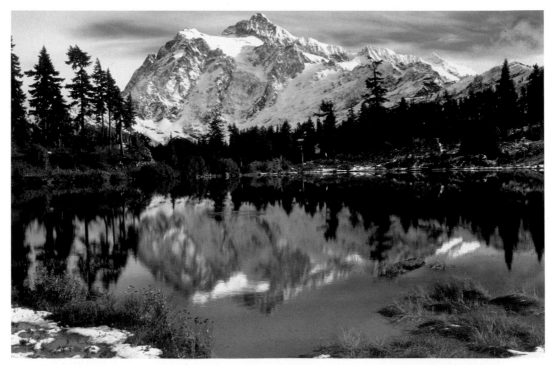

Figure 20.1 Just like a stage set, where the lighting, props, scenery and players all need to work together for a good performance, so too do many different elements need to combine to create a great landscape photograph. Many of these elements are out of the control of the landscape photographer, whose best skill is being in the 'right place at the right time'. Image courtesy of www.ablestock.com.

20 Landscapes

Successful photography of landscapes (meaning here natural scenes, principally in rural locations) goes beyond just accurate physical description. The challenge is to capture the atmosphere and essence of location, perhaps in a romanticized or dramatized way. The colors, pattern of shapes, sense of depth and distance, changes of mood which go along with variations in weather conditions, all contribute here. In fact, a landscape is rather like a stage set (see Figure 20.1).

However, photographs often fail to capture what it felt like to actually be there. Of course, elements such as sounds and smell, the wind in your face, the three-dimensional feeling of open space are all lost in a two-dimensional picture. But there is still plenty you can retain by careful selection of when and from where your shot is taken.

Paramount of all the factors that affect the way that landscape images are recorded is lighting, and since we are dealing here with natural light, the time of day, the weather, even time of year, all have a strong influence on results. You can argue that not much of this is under

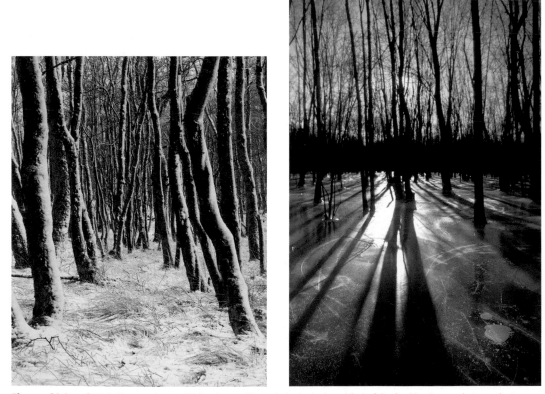

Figures 20.2 and 20.3 The weather and light play a critical role in the look and feel of the final landscape photograph. As seen in these examples, the same type of landscape can take on many dramatically different appearances, depending on the conditions at the time. Images courtesy of www.ablestock.com.

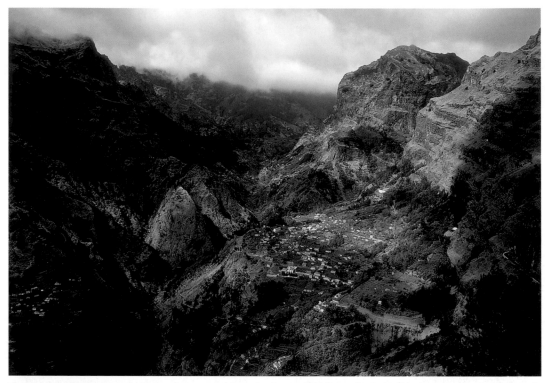

Figure 20.4 Lighting dramatically transforms mountainous landscapes. This deep valley in Madeira kept changing as patches of sunlight drifted through.

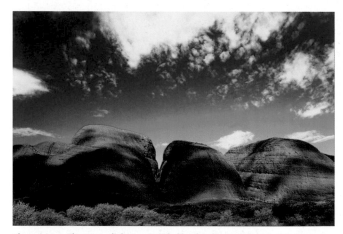

Figure 20.5 The strong lighting provided by the direct sunlight in this image is tempered by the addition of carefully positioned clouds (and their shadows) in the overall image. The landscape photographer needs to be patient when waiting for the lighting conditions and moving elements, like clouds, to be positioned in such a way that it suits the whole picture. Image courtesy of www.ablestock.com.

your control, and certainly there is always an element of seizing an opportunity when by luck you find yourself in the right place at the right time. But you can also help yourself by anticipation. Don't shoot second best – notice when conditions are not quite right and aim to return again earlier or later in the day when the weather is different or perhaps when you can bring a different item of photographic equipment with you (lens, film type, tripod, etc.; see Figures 20.2 and 20.3).

A landscape is basically immobile but it is certainly not unchanging, and there is often a decisive moment in its appearance that will not reappear for another week . . . or another year. Good landscape photographers therefore have to be good planners. They aim to get themselves into the right location before the right time – set up and patiently awaiting a scene to 'unfold'.

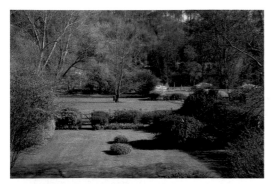

Figure 20.6 Spring, April.

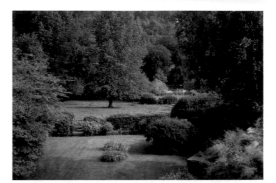

Figure 20.7 Summer, July.

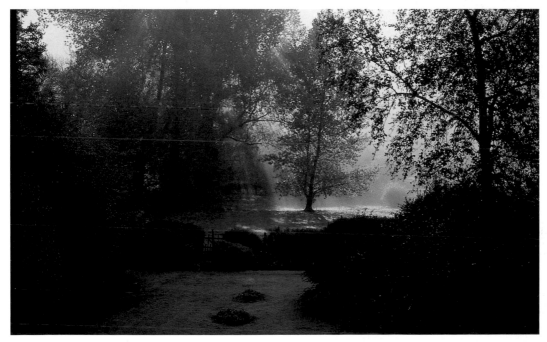

Figure 20.8 Autumn, October.

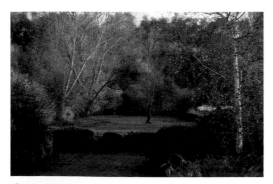

Figure 20.9 Autumn, November.

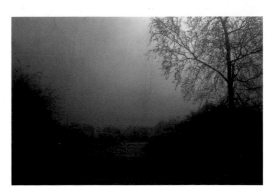

Figure 20.10 Winter, January.

Lighting

If you look through the viewfinder at a landscape as if it were a stage, your framing up and composing is like stage-setting. But then comes the all-important lighting of this theatrical space. Time of day affects mainly the direction of the light; weather conditions affect its quality (hard, semi-diffused, soft) as well as its distribution across the scene. Picture, for example, a mountainous landscape complete with wind-blown cloud cover providing dappled patches of direct sunlight that constantly move across the scene. Every moment the appearance of the landscape changes, which means firing the shutter just when a patch of illumination is in the right place to pick out an important feature or focus point like a few scattered houses (see Figure 20.4).

Cloudless sunny days, so common in the tropics, often provide monotonous lighting. Under these conditions it is more interesting to shoot early or late in the day. Shadows during these periods are long and contribute strongly to the texture of a picture. It is also important to notice that clear direct light displays the colors in the scene at their most vibrant. In contrast, hazier conditions give the same hues a more pastel appearance (see Figure 20.5).

The combination of lighting, weather and season of the year has a powerful influence on a landscape's appearance, particularly noticeable in temperate parts of the world such as Europe. Changes in season bring about great changes in the way that the landscape appears (see Figures 20.6–20.10). Remember that, visually, the most rapidly changing, interesting seasons for landscapes are spring and autumn. Snow-covered scenes in winter need direct sunlight in order to 'sparkle', unless you want a moody, somber

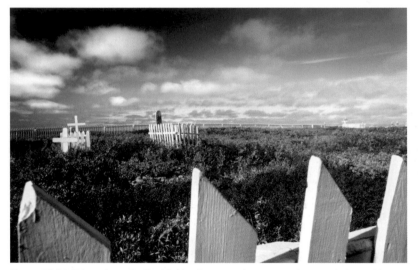

Figure 20.11 Using a large depth of field to keep most image parts sharp can help combine foreground, middle ground and background elements. Image courtesy of www.ablestock.com.

effect. Very hazy conditions are good for atmosphere but can easily become dull. It may be best then to shoot against the light and base your picture on silhouetted foreground shapes linked to grayer shapes further away.

Camera technique

The basic elements when framing up a landscape are its foreground, middle ground and background. Each of these areas should relate in some way, and be relevant to the others (see Figure 20.11). Consider how high to place the horizon – a decision that often determines the ratio of the three parts. Beginners often position the horizon dead center. Don't overdo this though, for unless you consciously plan a symmetrical composition, splitting the picture into equal halves can make it weaker and indecisive. Always avoid tilting the horizon, which seems to happen most easily when you use the camera on its side to shoot a vertical format picture. Keep the foreground interesting or at least filled, preferably in some way that provides a lead-in to the main elements in your picture. Even a plain foreground looks good if in shadow, contributing depth to the picture when contrasted against a lighter background.

A zoom lens that offers a short focal length or a wide-angle lens of about 28 mm are very useful for landscape work – particularly when the foreground is important or when you just want to 'open up' the whole of a scenic view. Secondly, a lens of moderately long focal length such as 135 mm is occasionally handy when you want a distant element in your picture – mountains on the horizon, for example – to loom large relative to mid-distance and foreground.

When your lighting is uneven, decide the key part of your landscape and measure exposure for this part – perhaps turning and reading off nearby ground that is receiving the same light. Some photographers use a number 2 graduated gray filter attached to the front of their camera lens to prevent overexposure bleaching important sky detail when setting the correct exposure for darker ground area. Other filters that are useful for landscape work include a deep orange color and a polarizing filter. The former is used for black and white photography, to darken the monochrome reproduction of blue sky and so make white clouds appear more bold. The polarizing filter, which appears overall gray, is also useful for color photography. It can reduce the glare or sheen of light reflected from surfaces such as glossy foliage, water or glass, as well as darkening blue sky at right angles to the direction of clear sunlight. The polarizing filter can therefore help to intensify subject colors, although colorless itself.

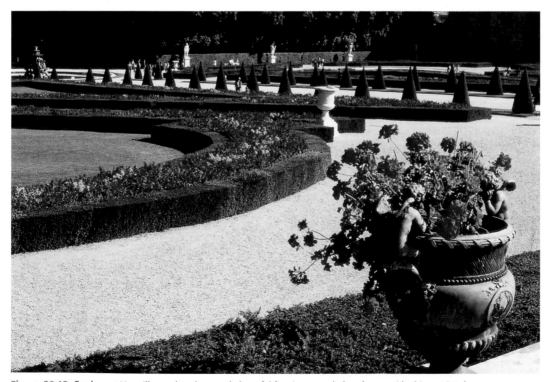

Figure 20.12 Gardens at Versailles, a shot that needed careful framing to exclude colors outside this restricted range.

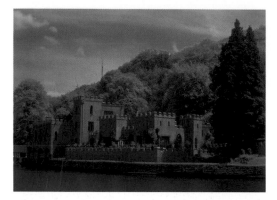

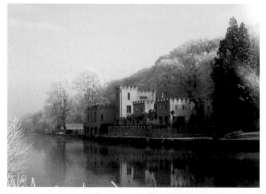

Figures 20.13 and 20.14 (Top) Landscape shot on false color, infrared 35 mm. Results are most dramatic when the picture includes young foliage in direct sunlight. (Bottom) The same scene taken on regular color film in winter.

Finally a small, easily carried tripod greatly extends the possibilities of landscape work. It frees you from concern over slow shutter speeds when time of day, weather conditions and dark tones of the scene itself combine to form a dim (but often dramatic) image.

Color in landscape

The intensity of colors in landscape photography is enormously influenced by atmospheric conditions, plus the color, type and intensity of the light and technical matters such as choice of film or saturation setting for digital shooters and the use of filtration. For instance, direct, warm evening light shortly after a downpour can give intense and saturated colors. Water provides a very interesting foreground for landscapes. Changes in its surface – from still to rippled by breeze – mix colors, reflections and shapes.

A much more formal man-made landscape, like the gardens at Versailles, already has a scheme of tightly restricted colors built in. In hard, clear sunlight, the brilliance of red and green and a touch of yellow appears most strongly to the eye (see Figure 20.12).

For film users, the choice of color film (and the color paper that negatives are printed on) can fine-tune results, emphasizing the richness of certain hues in a landscape or give more muted, subtle results. Experiment with different maker's brands. And if you produce your own color prints through a computer printer, various software programs will allow you to 'tweak' the final color balance in different directions. Don't overdo this manipulation, though (see Figures 20.13 and 20.14).

Skies

Clouds, sunsets, vapour trails and rainbows all form an important and ever-changing element in land and seascapes. The contents of skies can also form abstract images of their own. American photographer Alfred Stieglitz called his photographs of clouds 'equivalents' – their shapes and tones evoking emotions such as love, foreboding, exuberance, even ageing and death.

The best times of year for interesting skies are during spring and autumn. Cloud shapes appear most dramatic when back- or side-lit, in ways which strongly separate them from the general tone of the sky. For example, the sun may have just set, leaving a brilliant sky background and silhouetted shapes. Conversely, during unsettled weather, clouds can appear intensely bright against a dark background bank of storm clouds. Often, a 'skyscape' needs a weight of tone to form a base to your picture. You might achieve this by composing darker parts of a cloud mass low in the frame or by including a strip of land across the bottom of the shot.

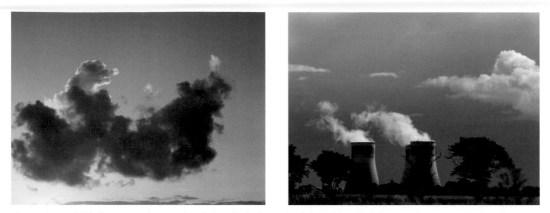

Figure 20.15 With the setting sun on or just below the horizon, cloud shape becomes strong.

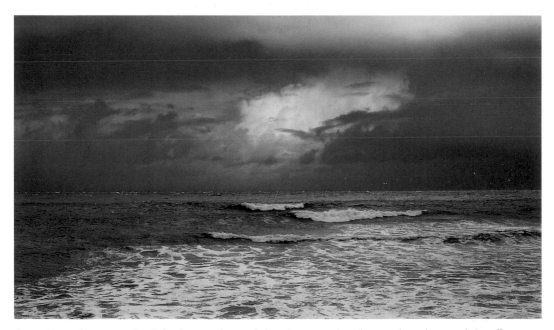

Figure 20.16 This seascape in rain has become almost colorless. Gray tone values plus a gentle sea have a calming effect.

Where possible, make elements in this lower part of your picture complement sky contents in some way. Trees may be useful in helping to frame the sun when this figures in your image (see Figures 20.15 and 20.16).

Warning: the sun's bright globe loses its energy and can be harmlessly imaged late in the evening, when the light passes through miles of haze. But never point your camera direct at the sun in clear sky at other times of day. Like using binoculars under such conditions, the intensity of light can damage your eyes. The camera's exposure meter too is temporarily blinded and can give rogue readings for several minutes afterwards. Also, digital sensors may be permanently damaged if used to capture a photograph of the sun directly.

Even though the sun is not shown in many sky images, you must decide carefully how you will measure exposure for these pictures. It's easy to overexpose when your camera metering system becomes too influenced by a darker land mass also in the picture. The consequence is that cloud texture and sky colors appear burned out. Choose which part of the picture should finally appear a midtone – midway between darkest and lightest details – then fill the entire frame with this or a visually matching area while you measure and set exposure (then set the AF lock on automatic exposure cameras). If possible, make one or two bracketed exposures, giving less rather than more exposure. Make sure your final picture is printed dark enough to give exactly the feeling for shadow and light that you wanted.

21 Close-up subjects

Working close-up (within 30 cm or so of your subject) opens up a whole new spectrum of picture possibilities. You can not only record small objects so that they fill the frame, but interesting, even dramatic pictures can be made from details of relatively ordinary things that you might not otherwise consider for photography. A cabbage, or a few clothes pegs, or just the page edges of a thick book are examples of hundreds of simple subjects that can be explored for hours in close-up. Along with plants and flowers, and weathered or

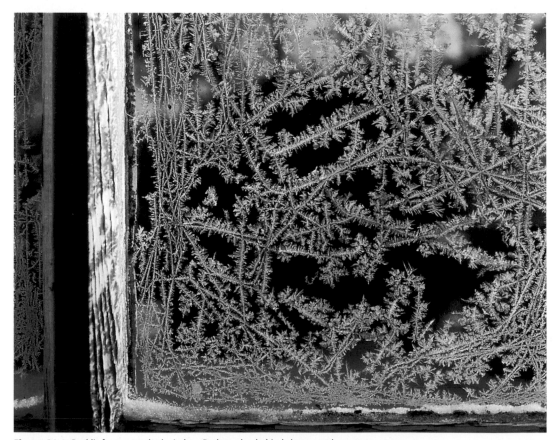

Figure 21.1 Backlit frost on a shed window. Dark garden behind shows up the pattern.

corroded materials, they provide a rich source of pictures based on color, shape, pattern and texture (see Figure 21.1).

Close-up photography is also useful to record possessions for identification purposes. Items of special value to you can be logged in detail, against possible damage or theft, leading to an insurance claim. If you are an enthusiast then your collection of stamps, coins or model cars can be visually catalogued this way and then scanned into a computer file. Photographing inanimate objects in close-up is also an excellent self-teaching process for control of lighting and picture composition generally, working in your own time.

Technically, the main challenges in close-up work are to:

1 Sharply focus and accurately frame your subject.
2 Achieve sufficient depth of field, which shrinks alarmingly with close subjects.
3 Arrange suitable lighting.

Focus and framing

The closer your subject, the more the camera lens must be located further forward of the film or sensor to give you a sharp image. Basic, fixed focus cameras do not sharply image subjects nearer than about 1.5 m, unless you can add a supplementary close up lens. A typical 35 mm compact camera allows focus adjustment down to 0.6 m (20 in) and the more expensive models to 0.45 m (12 in). The latter means that you can fill the picture with a subject about 6.5 cm wide. Some cameras have a so-called macro setting for their closest focusing distance. It may mean there is a gap between the lens's continuous focusing adjustment and its positioning for the closer distance. This is more limiting than to be able to focus 'all the way down' but will still enable you to capture good close-up pictures (see Figures 21.2–21.4).

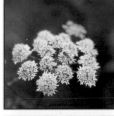
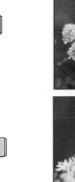
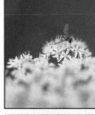

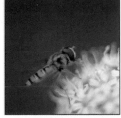

The macro setting on many digital compact cameras allows you to focus extremely closely. In some newer models, this can be as close as 2 cm from the front lens element. This, plus the ability to review the image immediately, makes these cameras prime candidates for close-up work.

Figures 21.2–21.4 Close focusing with an SLR. (Top) Fifty-millimeter lens used at its closest setting, no ring. (Center) With a 1 cm ring added. (Bottom) Using a 5 cm ring instead.

One way to adapt any camera for close subjects is to fit a close-up lens element over the main lens, which shortens its focal length. These supplementary lenses, like reading glasses, are rated in different dioptre power according to strength. Fitting a +1 close-up lens to a fixed-focus 50 mm lens camera, for example, makes it focus subjects 87 cm distant. Used on a focusing compact with a camera lens set for 0.6 m, it sharply focuses subjects 30 cm away.

The main difficulty using a close-up lens on a compact camera is that the separate viewfinder system becomes even more inaccurate the nearer the subject. A close-up lens is more practical on

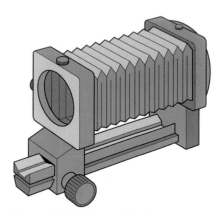

Figure 21.5 A bellows unit for close work.

a digital camera, where you can observe focus and composition accurately on the electronic display screen. Similarly, any single lens reflex film camera has a viewfinding system that allows you to see exactly what is being imaged.

However, close-up lenses – particularly the most powerful types – do reduce the overall imaging quality of your main lens. This is where an SLR camera scores heavily over a compact. For, instead of adding a lens, you can detach its regular high-quality lens from the camera body and fit an extension ring between the two. The extra spacing this gives reduces the minimum focusing distance. This might mean that your normal lens, which focuses from infinity down to 0.45 m, now offers a range from 0.45 to 0.27 m (so the subject is imaged on film about one-quarter life size).

By using extension rings of different lengths – singly or several at once – you can move in closer still. The degree of extension, and therefore how close a subject can still be focused, is even greater if you fit a bellows unit rather than extension rings. Generally, when using bellows or extension rings, auto-focus lenses have to be manually focused (see Figure 21.5).

Most SLR zoom lenses offer a macro setting on the focusing scale. This adjusts components inside the lens so you can sharply focus subjects an inch or so from its front surface. Often, the range of subject distances is very restricted. For best quality and greatest flexibility in close-up work, change your SLR camera lens to a more expensive macro lens, specially designed for close subjects. Its focusing scale allows continuous focusing down to about 0.2 m and thereafter closer still if you add rings or bellows.

If you have no macro lens, you can achieve maximum magnification with your SLR camera equipment by combining your shortest focal length lens with your longest extension tube or bellows. In other words, if you own a simple extension ring, fitting it behind a 28 mm lens instead of a normal 50 mm type will sharply focus your subject about 30 per cent larger. However, you will be working much closer, which may result in the camera casting a shadow. This close proximity also makes three-dimensional subjects record with steepened perspective.

Depth of field

Depth of field decreases as you move closer to your subject, even though you use the same lens aperture (e.g. a lens focused on something 1.5 m away might give nearly 20 cm depth of field, but this shrinks to only 3 cm depth when the same lens is focused for 0.45 m). This means that your focusing must be very precise – there is little latitude for error. Where possible, arrange your camera viewpoint so that all the parts of the subject you need to show pin sharp are about the same distance from the lens. Provided that every part of the subject where you must show detail is sharp, rendering things at other distances out of focus helps to isolate them, erasing clutter. A manual camera with depth of field preview button is very useful here – observing image appearance as you alter the lens aperture setting will give you a good idea of the extent of sharp detail (although you must get used to the screen getting

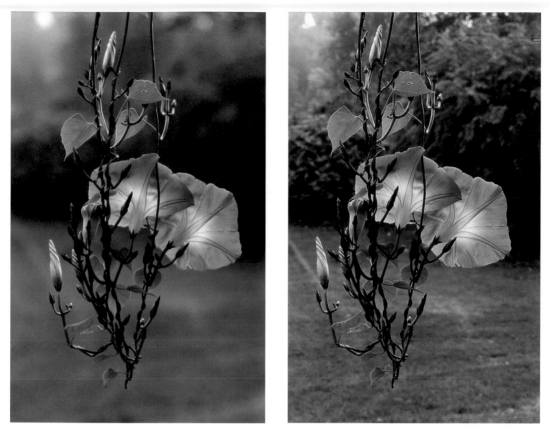

Figures 21.6 and 21.7 Morning glory. (Left) Using f4 and 1/250 second. (Right) Using f16 and 1/15 second. The former version has a less distracting background and looks more three-dimensional. Hazy daylight from above and behind helps to reveal form.

darker as the aperture is reduced in size). Alternatively, digital camera users can use the 'shoot and review' process to ensure that the zone of focus is where you want it (see Figures 21.6 and 21.7).

Garden flower close-ups

Flowers are a rich source of color, pattern, texture and form. Lighting is therefore very important. Shooting against diffused sunlight out in the garden is a good way to show the transparency of petals and leaves, emphasized by shadowed background. Back- or side-lighting also reveals the stalks and other structural detail in a three-dimensional way. Direct sunlight from the side is good for emphasizing texture (see Figure 21.8). Even when sunlight is diffused, fit a lens hood or shade to your lens to minimize light scatter and flare caused by light falling on the front element of the lens. Measure the majority of your exposure from the delicate petal detail – if this approach results in dark stalks it is still more acceptable than burnt-out flower colors. Use soft, even lighting for strongly patterned flowers, as it will cause less confusion than direct light, which will add shadow and texture to the picture as well.

One advantage of working so close to a small subject is that it is not difficult to modify natural light to suit your needs. Something as simple as a piece of tracing paper hung between a

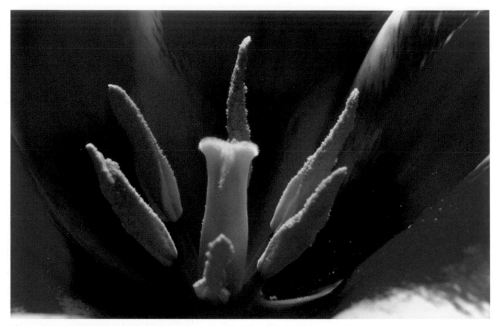

Figure 21.8 Good lighting is essential for close-up work, as low light levels can contribute to aperture and shutter speed settings that produce shallow depth of field and perhaps even some camera shake. Image courtesy of www.ablestock.com.

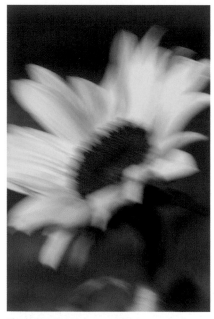

Figure 21.9 In breezy conditions, ensure that you are using a fast shutter speed and then be prepared to shoot several images of the one flower set to ensure that one of the series is captured with no subject movement. Image courtesy of www.ablestock.com.

plant and direct sunlight will bathe everything in soft, even illumination. A hand mirror can direct sunlight into the shadow areas and a white card held close behind the camera reduces the excessive contrast of backlit shots.

Movement blur

A feature of working outdoors you will discover is that small movements of the flower caused by the slightest breeze are magnified by image size and recorded as blur. As a result, if the subject keeps swaying out of focus there will be an increased risk of movement blur (see Figure 21.9).

A shield made of card on the windward side and positioned just outside the picture area will help reduce the movement. In addition, selecting a high ISO value or a fast film will allow you to set a combination of brief shutter speed (perhaps 1/125 second to reduce blur and allow camera hand-holding) plus a really small aperture to produce sufficient depth of field.

Be careful, though, as the faster the film or higher the ISO value, the more grain is apparent in the final picture. Too much grain and you will destroy the finer qualities of your image, especially if you plan a big print.

The best approach is to work using a tripod, or at least partly support the camera on top of a stick or 'monopod' reaching to the ground. A monopod with the camera attached can minimize movement blur yet still allow quick adjustments to distance.

When using a manual or semi-automatic camera on aperture priority mode, first set an aperture to achieve the depth of field you need and then shoot at the shutter speed indicated to give correct exposure. Clamping the flower in some way – perhaps holding its stem with your hand just outside the picture area – will also help.

Flash is a handy source of movement-freezing illumination in a close-up situation. If possible, have a flashgun on an extended lead – so that you can position it from the best angle for the subject features you want to show, using the light either direct or diffused with tracing paper. Flash on or near the camera can be useful when working with daylight to dilute or lighten shadows, leaving sunlight from above to pick out the form. Flash will also suppress unwanted background or surroundings by under-lighting them, but take care that this does not give you unnatural looking results.

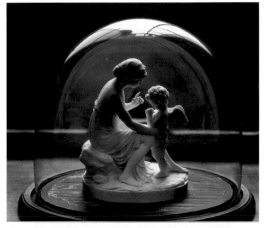

Figure 21.10 This piece was lit by a wide rear window. Shooting from a distance avoided steep perspective and hid camera reflection.

Close-ups indoors

Being able to work close up means that you can find all kinds of subjects indoors. You may use these subjects for factual record purposes, or to create artistic pictures. You might, for example, create a 'portrait' of someone through a still life group of related possessions and personal memorabilia. For a child, this might be the contents of their schoolbag; for an aged relative, it may be pictures and objects displayed on a bureau. Much of this work can be done by using the existing daylight as your source of light. Hazy sunlight through cloud (not blue sky) will give most accurate color, and if you can work in a room with a large window, this will help to avoid uneven illumination. Figure 21.10 was photographed this way. For this type of indoors work a tripod is practically essential – it not only gives you the freedom to give longer exposures without camera shake, but anchors viewpoint and distance in one spot while you build up your picture, bit by bit.

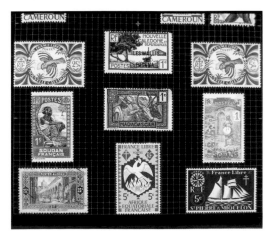

Figure 21.11 Copied on a window sill, lit by soft overcast daylight from above, and white card below the lens to fill in.

Copying flat surface subjects

The most important factors in photographing or making copies of physically flat subjects such as drawings, sheets of stamps, etc. are:

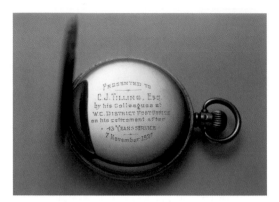

Figure 21.12 Shot with a 50 mm lens and extension ring. Tracing paper diffused daylight.

1 To be square-on to your subject.
2 To have it evenly lit.

Unless the back of your camera is truly parallel to the surface you are copying, horizontal and/or vertical lines will converge. Look very carefully around the edges of the frame to ensure that the borders of your subject line up – don't be tempted to tilt the camera a bit if the picture is not quite central (shift it sideways instead).

When using daylight through a window, come close to the glass so you have the widest possible width of illumination, e.g. lay your subject flat on a bay window sill. Evenness is further improved if you place a white card vertically facing the window on the room side of your subject just outside the picture area. Be careful about measuring exposure when your subject is on a background sheet of a very different tone, as in Figure 21.11. Stamps displayed on a black, or white, page will be over- or underexposed respectively by a general light reading. It is best to cover the whole page with a mid-gray card

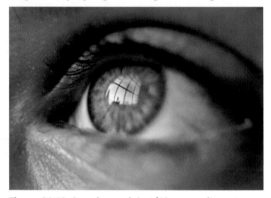

Figure 21.13 Same lens and ring; f16 was used to get eye and distant window sharp.

and measure off this surface, set the aperture and shutter speed, and then remove the card before exposing.

Reflective subjects

Reflective surfaces such as glass or shiny metal need special lighting care; otherwise, shadowy reflections of the camera will confuse detail. Sometimes you can help matters by shooting from further away, using a longer focal length lens on an extension tube. This way, the camera can be far enough back to be a small, unsharp, almost invisible reflection (see Figure 21.12).

A large sheet of tracing paper used close to your subject is the best way of controlling reflection. Angle the camera so that the tracing paper surface (through which all the lighting passed) is shown as an even white reflection off the reflective surface.

Some close-up shots stretch depth of field to its limits. For instance, with extreme close-ups of a face it can be almost impossible to get nose, eyes and ears all sharp. For the biggest depth of field possible, set the lens to the smallest aperture (f22 or f32) and, with the depth of field preview button pushed, examine the dim image as you move the camera fractionally backwards and forwards; all the important elements in your picture are just within the depth-of-field boundaries (see Figure 21.13).

Tackling self-set themes

A good way to extend your photography is to work to a particular topic or theme – something chosen yourself, or set perhaps in a competition. This will challenge you to organize ideas and plan your approach, and actually having to carry out an assignment encourages you to solve technical problems, gaining experience and confidence.

Themes might place greatest emphasis on the subject itself (a person or thing) or on shapes or structures. Or again they may be concerned with underlying concepts, such as humour and emotions of various kinds.

Singles or series?

Your result might be a single picture, or a pair or sequence of photographs. One picture can sum up a simple concept, such as joy or sorrow, whereas taking two separate photographs offers opportunities for comparisons and contrasts when presented together. Sometimes it's helpful or even necessary to make features such as background, positioning in the frame and angle of view similar in both pictures to show up differences in your main subjects. A longer series of pictures gives scope to tell a story or explain a process, show changes of time and place, and thus develop a theme.

Subject-based themes

Several subject themes have been touched on in this part of the book, but there are many more, such as sports activities, natural history and still life, for you to choose from. Perhaps you decide to work to a portrait theme. Think of all the ways you can show an individual – at work, at home with their possessions, with family and friends, traveling, relaxing or practicing a hobby. You need patience and time to get to know your subject well, observing mannerisms and seeking out representative aspects of their life.

Another way of working is to shoot a collective portrait, say one picture of every family in a street or apartment block. Here you might show each at their own front door, keeping your viewpoint and lighting similar to provide continuity. Allow the groups to pose themselves. Even show their reactions to being photographed – some showing off, others shy.

Structural themes

Here the project might center on movement or color, or shapes. You might build a set of pictures from 'found' subjects that all share a common color scheme but have many variations in content, scale and/or texture. One might be blue sky with clouds, another a group of blue-painted signs, a house with blue curtains or a close-up of blue flowers. Make sure each shot is a satisfying image within itself, as well as working as a part of the whole series.

To begin a project on the theme 'light', you could consider qualities such as brilliance, reflection, color, cast shadow and so on. Observe the effects of light on various surfaces under different atmospheric conditions. Next, work through your list, eliminating similarities and identifying six or so characteristics you want to show. Then find suitable subjects (don't overlook the macro world) and techniques to communicate strongly each aspect of the theme.

Emotive and narrative themes

Projects based on the dominant feelings a viewer reads out of your picture are arguably more difficult to plan and tackle. A sense of jubilation, or stress, implied menace, despair, loneliness or close friendship are all feelings that can form the basis of an interesting series. Your chosen approach might be factual and objective, or implied through the shape of a shadow or plant structure, or something colorful but quite abstract.

Alternatively, you may want to work in a more storytelling or narrative way. You could use your sequence of images to illustrate a

(continued)

poem, or cover a passage of time, or a journey from one place to another. A picture series like this needs visual variety as well as continuity if all the photographs are to work as individual pictures and also as part of a series. Start off with a strong general view as an establishing shot, then move in to concentrate on particular areas, including close-ups and lively (but not puzzling) viewpoints. The final photograph might bring the viewer full circle, e.g. the opening picture reshot at dusk.

1 Pick a letter of the alphabet and photograph five different found objects that look like the letter shape. Don't forget to use close-up as well as distant shots to add variety to your series.

2 Sum up your impressions of one of the following places in three or four pictures: (a) a graveyard; (b) the seashore; (c) a modern industrial park.

3 Try to illustrate the color red in three pictures without actually photographing any objects colored with the hue.

4 Make a short series of pictures of owners and pets to prove or disprove the theory that they grow to resemble one another.

5 Create a descriptive portrait of the character of a family member by photographing three images containing places and things that are important to the subject. Don't include the subject in any of the pictures.

6 Produce two or three animal 'head and shoulders' portraits of either: (a) a dog; (b) a tame rabbit or hamster; or (c) a cat. Try to convey character through showing what they do. Include the owner if relevant.

7 Photograph a series of valuable items to record them for insurance purposes. Include a ruler alongside for scale.

8 Using hands as an expression of emotion, produce three pictures, each conveying one of the following: anger; tenderness; tension; prayer.

9 Illustrate three of the following themes using a pair of pictures in each case: simple/complex; young/old; tall/short; hard/soft.

10 Make a documentary series of four pictures on either 'children at play', 'shopping' or 'a day off'.

Troubleshooting

Everyone makes mistakes some time, but it is how you see these mistakes that will determine whether you will make the same mistakes later on. See each unexpected result as a chance to learn more about photography and its techniques. In fact, I would go so far as to say that if you are not making mistakes then you are probably not learning as much as you could about how to use your equipment and make better pictures.

The best approach when you receive unexpected results from processing or when viewing your day's shooting on your computer is to identify what went wrong. Was it the film, or the camera, or (most likely) the way you used your equipment? Or maybe it's all due to the lab that processed and printed your results? Identifying the source of the error will help you fix the problem, as well as ensure that the mistake doesn't happen again.

22 Film users: assessing the results from the lab

a. Loading film

A fault most often experienced by beginners using film cameras happens during the loading of the film. If the leading edge of the film is not properly attached to the take-up spool in the camera or positioned in the area indicated for automatic cameras, then after closing the camera back the film remains stationary even though you wind on after each exposure. Then when you send the film for processing you will receive a blank (clear because it is unexposed) film in return (see Figure 22.5).

Fault prevention: check that the film is winding on correctly by watching the film rewind leaver turn when the film is advancing. Open and reattach the film if it is not turning with each newly advanced frame. Auto-winding cameras should warn of this fault via a beep or an indicator on the LCD panel.

b. Unloading film

Another very common error is to open the camera before you have rewound your exposed film back into its light-proof cassette. Single-use cameras avoid these problems by having the film ready loaded and sealed in. Cameras (including APS) with automatic loading and rewind are also unlikely to allow wind-on errors to occur, as the camera has built-in safeguards that ensure the film is correctly wound (see Figure 22.1).

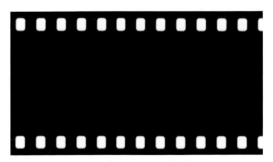

Figure 22.1 Negative film completely black.

Fault prevention: always double check that you have wound back your film before opening the camera back.

c. Marks on prints but not the negatives

When you notice a fault on a print, the first thing to do is to compare it very closely against the returned negative (the film that was initially exposed in the camera). If this negative looks normal and shows a lot more detail in the shadows or highlights than its associated print, or the print shows a blemish that cannot be seen on the negative, ask for a reprint. (If you have shot slides it is often easier to pin down faults, as the chain of processing does not then include possible printing errors.)

Fault correction: take the offending image back to the processing lab along with the negative, point out the area of concern, such as a dust mark or blemish, and ask for a corrected reprint.

d. Film completely black

If your film is completely black and without data numbers or lettering visible along the edges, it is most likely to have been heavily fogged (exposed) to light in some way. Perhaps the camera back was open as the film was rewound. Or a child, playing, pulled the film from its cassette (and then wound it back in). Alternatively, your camera back may not be sealing correctly and therefore letting light leak onto the film whilst you are photographing. Exceptionally, this can be the result of chemical fogging during processing (see Figures 22.1–22.7).

Fault prevention: inspect the seals on the edge of the camera back to ensure a light-tight fit. If in doubt, have a technician examine and repair any light leaks. Also, be careful not to

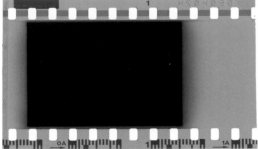

Figure 22.2 One black frame, but the rest of the film with no pictures.

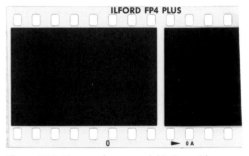

Figure 22.3 Separate frames, each black or with a vastly dense picture. Black and white film.

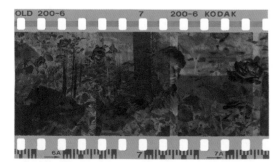

Figure 22.4 A continuous jumble of overlapping images and frame lines.

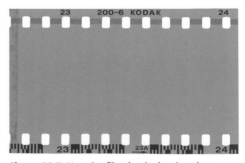

Figure 22.5 Negative film that is clear but shows edge numbers and data.

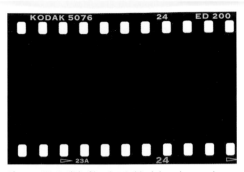

Figure 22.6 Slide film that is black but shows edge numbers and data.

inadvertently expose the film when rewinding it back into its canister.

e. Film mainly clear

The film has one frame black, near the beginning. The rest is clear film, although data can be read along its edges. This film was correctly positioned for the first picture but then failed to move on because it became detached from the camera's take-up spool. All your shots were therefore exposed on the one frame.

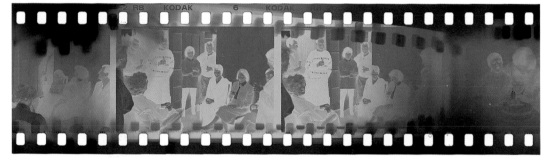

Figure 22.7 Color negative film with dark patches and patterns over pictures.

Fault prevention: check that the rewind is turning when advancing the film. Open and reattach the film if it is not turning with each newly advanced frame. Auto-winding cameras should warn of this fault via a beep or an indicator on the LCD panel.

f. Each frame completely black

Each frame can be seen, but is just solid black. This usually results from every picture having been grossly overexposed. Maybe the shutter sticks, remaining open for several seconds. Or the lens aperture remains fully open despite the bright conditions. Your exposure metering system may have a major fault, or you set the film speed wildly wrong (e.g. ISO 32 for ISO 3200 film). For more advanced cameras, check that the exposure compensation system wasn't inadvertently set to add extra light to each exposure (see Figure 22.3).

Fault prevention: initially check that the ISO value on the camera matched the film that was used and that the exposure compensation system was set to zero. If there was no problem with these two areas, take your camera to a technician to ensure that the shutter, aperture and exposure system are functioning correctly.

g. Overlapping images

If the film is an end-to-end mix of overlapping images and frame lines, then you have probably put the same film through the camera twice (see Figure 22.4).

Fault prevention: winding an exposed film completely back into its cassette, or folding over its protruding end, will signal to you that the film is used and will help to avoid this happening.

h. Clear film with edge numbers

If your film is clear, having no images, but edge data and numbers can still be clearly seen, then you have probably sent an unexposed negative film for processing. If a processed slide film is returned and it is completely black but the edge numbers are still clear, then an unexposed film was sent for processing (see Figure 22.5).

Fault prevention: clearly label exposed films, or make sure that the tongue of the film is wound completely back into the canister when used.

i. Fogged areas with a perforated pattern

Indeterminate shaped patches of fog and perforation shape patterns along the whole length of the film, as well as images, usually means that your film has been partially fogged to light, probably during processing. With some processing systems, films are spliced end to end before going into the machine. Other systems place the film in a light-tight container before adding the chemistry. If light briefly enters the machine or the tank during processing, then the loosely coiled film may print its perforations onto the film surface beneath it (see Figure 22.7).

Fault prevention: for self-processed film, make sure that the tank lid is secured carefully before proceeding with processing. For machine-processed images, talk to your lab about the problem.

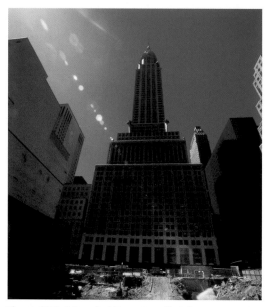

Figure 22.8 A line of white spots and beads.

j. A line of white spots and beads

This 'necklace' of flare spots is caused by internal reflection within the lens when shooting towards the sun. This happens most easily when using a wide-angle or zoom lens. (On an SLR camera you may not actually see this defect if you are viewing the image at widest aperture.) The size and shape of spots alter as you change f-number (see Figure 22.8).

Fault prevention: shade the lens with your hand or a lens hood, or shift the camera into the shadow of a building.

k. Black hair shape

This is the result of a small hair being on the actual film surface when this shot was taken (or on a slide scanned into the computer; see Figure 22.9).

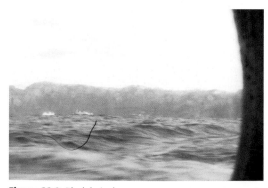

Figure 22.9 Black hair shape.

Fault prevention: check the cleanliness of the space between lens and film plane in the (empty) camera. With an SLR, lock the shutter open on 'B' to access this area. Clean slides before scanning.

l. White hair shape

Unlike the previous fault, this is the result of a hair being temporarily on the negative surface during printing or scanning (see Figure 22.10).

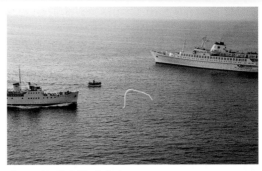

Figure 22.10 White hair shape.

Fault prevention and correction: ensure that negatives are clean before they go into the enlarger. You may be able to disguise the mark by print spotting (see page 237) or via digital manipulation (see page 159). If this picture was printed by a lab, then request a reprint.

m. Pale print from overexposed negative

This can be caused by a faulty light measuring system or even batteries with a low charge. Similar results can be obtained if the ISO setting is too low for the film being used, if the lens aperture was stuck fully open or the shutter was sluggish (see Figure 22.11).

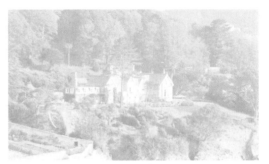

Figure 22.11 Pale print from overexposed negative.

Fault prevention: check over your camera functions, looking through the back of the (empty) camera body to ensure that all are working correctly. If in doubt, take the camera to a technician for a service.

n. Print from underexposed negative

When a simple camera is loaded with slow film and used in dim lighting, the negative will be underexposed. The same effect will result if slow film is loaded in the camera but an ultra-fast ISO value is set on the camera (see Figure 22.12).

Fault prevention: keep to sunny conditions when you are photographing with very basic equipment. If possible, check what ISO value

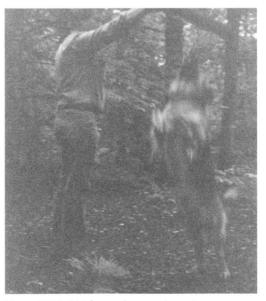

Figure 22.12 Print from underexposed negative.

the camera is set for. (As this is typical of the best print possible off a nearly transparent negative, you are unlikely to improve on the result.)

23 General shooting faults

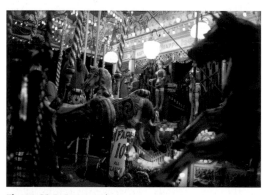

Figure 23.1 Orange color.

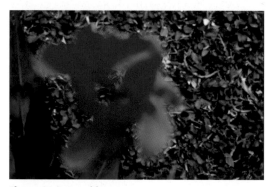

Figure 23.2 Out of focus.

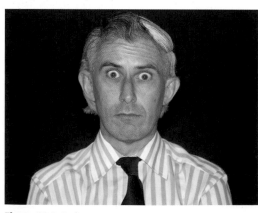

Figure 23.3 Red eye.

a. Orange color

If your slides end up with an all-over orange color, it is generally because the film was exposed to a subject lit by domestic-type (tungsten) light bulbs (see Figure 23.1).

Fault prevention: shoot with a blue (80A) filter over the lens. Daylight color negative film gives a print with a similar cast, but this can be given considerable correction during either darkroom or digital printing. Digital shooters can avoid these problems by selecting a tungsten or auto setting for the camera's white balance feature.

b. Out of focus

Out of focus pictures can be caused by using a fixed focus lens camera too close to the subject (see Figure 23.2).

Fault prevention: don't exceed your camera's closest focus limit – often only about 1 m.

c. Red eye

Red eye is caused by the flash on the camera lighting up the pink retina at the back of the eyes when it is normally shadowed and therefore seen as black (see Figure 23.3).

Fault prevention: use a camera with a flash unit higher or further to one side of the lens. Better still, bounce or diffuse the flash light.

d. Yellow color cast all over

An overall color cast can be caused by photographing under a colored (yellow) awning, or using bounced flash light that is

reflecting off a colored (yellow) surface
(see Figure 23.4).

Fault prevention and correction: to
prevent this situation, recognize such
lighting conditions and use an alternative way
to light the scene. To correct the problem
after shooting on color negative film, request
that the lab reprint the photograph, giving
the maximum correction of cast. Digital
camera users should turn their white
balance setting to automatic to minimize
the cast.

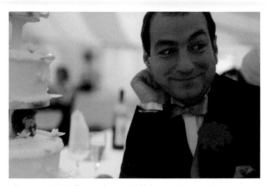

Figure 23.4 Yellow color cast all over.

e. Only the background is sharply focused

This can occur when an auto-focus camera has
been focused for the central zone of the
picture, which happens to be the background,
rather than the main subject, which is
positioned off-center. A similar situation results
when the AF mechanism is jammed or when
the manual focus lens was set for the wrong
distance (see Figure 23.5).

Fault prevention: use AF lock for
off center subjects. With a manual lens, always
set the distance for your main subject – and
don't move after focusing.

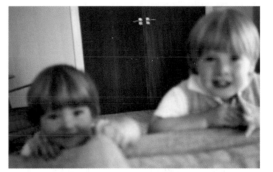

Figure 23.5 Only the background is sharply focused.

f. Wrong moment to shoot

Releasing the shutter just as someone or
something unexpectedly barges into the
picture (see Figure 23.6).

Fault prevention: try to anticipate what is
about to happen between camera and subject.
A compact camera has the advantage that,
through its viewfinder, you still see some of the
scene just outside your picture limits. This lets
you anticipate the action more easily. Also,
make sure you have enough film left to allow
several shots when people are swarming
around you. But keep one or two of these
'mistakes' for a special place in the family
album.

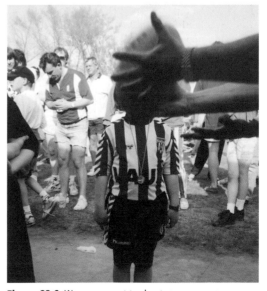

Figure 23.6 Wrong moment to shoot.

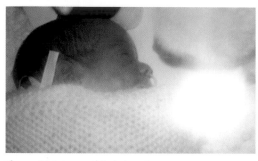

Figure 23.7 Large white hot spot.

g. Large white hot spot

Inbuilt flash from the camera reflected straight off the plastic window of this baby's incubator (see Figure 23.7).

Fault prevention: do not shoot 'flat on' to windows, glass or plastic – angle your viewpoint. Where possible, shoot by natural daylight, loading fast film if necessary (or using a higher ISO value for digital users), to avoid using flash.

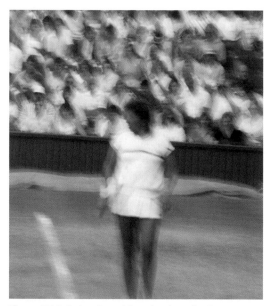

Figure 23.8 Entire picture blurred and smudged.

h. Entire picture, even static elements, blurred and smudged

This situation is caused by camera shake. In poor light, with slow film, an auto-exposure camera may have selected a slow (1/8 second or longer) shutter speed, at which setting the camera could not be held sufficiently still by hand to record a sharp picture. An alternative explanation is that the firing button was jabbed hard instead of squeezing gently when exposing (see Figure 23.8).

Fault prevention: use a higher ISO value (digital users) or load faster film when poor light is expected. Watch for 'shake' warning light with auto cameras – then improvise some firm support or use a tripod for shooting. With manual set cameras, select the widest lens aperture possible, to allow the use of the fastest possible shutter speed for the situation (without underexposing).

i. Ring of light

The picture was taken with the camera pointed directly towards the sun. The simple compact camera, having a shiny rim to its lens, reflected the sunlight into the picture (see Figure 23.9).

Fault prevention: anticipate light flare from these conditions and adjust camera direction to account for them. In this example, tilting the camera downwards or shifting slightly to the

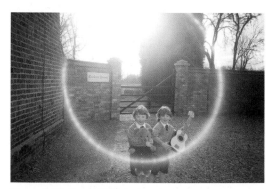

Figure 23.9 Ring of light.

right would allow the tree to shade the lens from the sunlight. Alternatively, you can fit a lens hood or shade the front of the lens with your hand.

j. Bands of orange or red, showing up most clearly in dark areas

Light has entered the camera or cassette and has fogged the film. Perhaps the back was opened, or there is a missing screw in the camera body itself (see Figure 23.10).

Fault prevention: always fully rewind the film immediately after your final exposure, before anyone can open the camera. Never load your camera in strong sunlight.

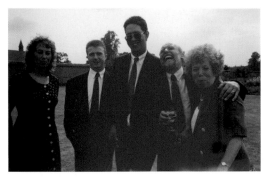

Figure 23.10 Bands of orange or red, showing up most clearly in dark areas.

k. Mis-framed picture

This is caused by an inaccurate framing through the viewfinder and generally occurs when using a compact camera quite close to the subject whilst ignoring its parallax correction guide lines (see Figure 23.11).

Fault prevention: follow your camera's instructions for viewfinder compensation when photographing near subjects. Always ensure your eye clearly sees all four corners of the rectangular frame line at one time, especially if you wear glasses. Digital users can more accurately frame using the LCD screen on the back of the camera rather than the viewfinder.

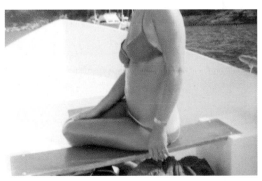

Figure 23.11 Mis-framed picture.

l. Main subject too dark

The camera's overall light reading was influenced too much by a large, bright area in the scene. In this case, it is the window behind the main subject (see Figure 23.12).

Fault prevention: read exposure from close to the figure, then apply the camera's AE lock. Alternatively, use fill-in flash, or pick another background.

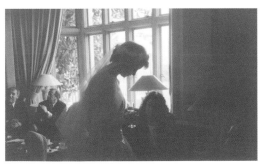

Figure 23.12 Main subject too dark.

m. White dog appears yellow

Fault in printing. The large area of strong blue background in this picture has confused the lab's automatic printing equipment. It has intensified yellow to counteract what it measures as excess blue in the picture, turning the white coat cream (see Figure 23.13).

Fault correction: return to the photo lab and have a corrected reprint made.

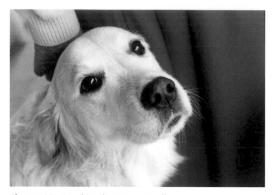

Figure 23.13 White dog appears yellow.

n. Subject appears distorted in shape

The subject was photographed with a short focal length (wide-angle). The nose of the horse was too close to the camera (see Figure 23.14).

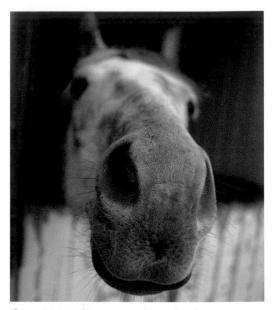

Figure 23.14 Subject appears distorted in shape.

Fault prevention: move further back from the subject and then change to a longer focal length (or have the smaller image enlarged out of the center of your picture).

24 Digital users: checking images on the desktop

a. Marks on the scanned picture

The photograph contains marks on the surface after scanning. This usually occurs because of dust or scratches on the glass plate on the top of the scanner or on the photograph or negative (see Figure 24.1).

Fault correction: clean the glass plate and photograph carefully before placing and scanning your picture. If you still have marks, use a retouching tool to remove them (see the 'Removing unwanted details in the software' section for more details).

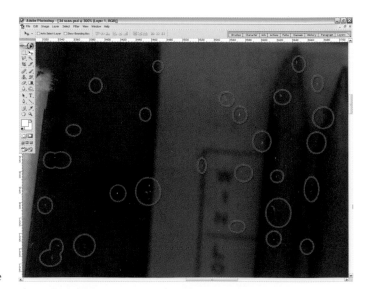

Figure 24.1 Marks on the scanned picture.

b. The scanned color picture appears black and white

After scanning a color picture it appears black and white on screen. This is the result of the 'original' or 'media' option in the scanner software being set to black and white and not color.

Fault correction: rescan the picture, making sure that the software is set to color original or color photograph.

c. The scanned picture is too bright

The picture looks too bright overall. Light areas of the photograph appear to be completely white with no details. The picture has been scanned with the wrong 'exposure' or 'brightness' setting (see Figure 24.2).

Fault correction: rescan the picture, but this time move the brightness or exposure slider towards the dark end of the scale before scanning.

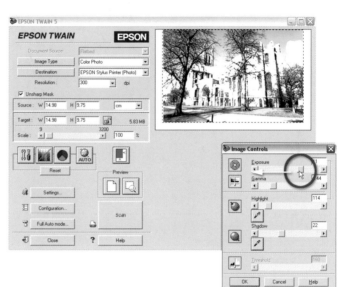

Figure 24.2 The scanned picture is too bright.

d. The scanned picture is too dark

The picture looks too dark overall. There is no detail in the shadow parts of the photograph. This results from the picture having been scanned with the wrong 'exposure' or 'brightness' setting (see Figure 24.3).

Fault correction: rescan the picture, but this time slide the brightness or exposure slider towards the light end of the scale before scanning.

e. The scanned picture looks washed out

The picture has no vibrant colors and looks washed out. This occurs when the contrast control in the scanner software is set too low.

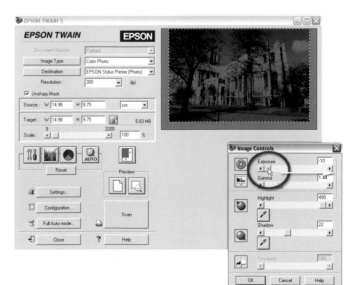

Figure 24.3 The scanned picture is too dark.

Fault correction: rescan the photograph, altering the scanner's contrast setting to a higher value.

f. Writing in the scanned picture is back to front

The message on a billboard in the picture is back to front. The cause of this problem is the negative or slide was placed into the scanner back to front.

Fault correction: turn the film or slide over and scan again.

g. The scanned picture has too much contrast

The delicate light areas and shadow details of the picture can't be seen and have been converted to completely white and completely black. This results from the contrast control in the scanner software being set too high (see Figure 24.4).

Fault correction: rescan the photograph, altering the scanner's contrast setting to a lower value.

h. When I print my scanned picture it is fuzzy

The print of a scanned image is fuzzy, not very clear or is made up of rectangular blocks of color. To get the best quality prints from your scanned pictures you must make sure that you match the scan quality (resolution) with the output requirements. A fuzzy or unclear print is usually the result of using a scan quality setting that is too low.

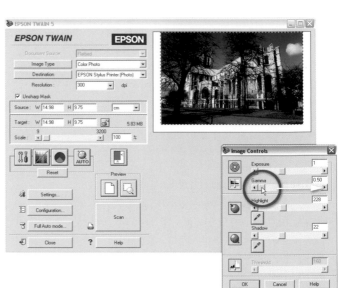

Figure 24.4 The scanned picture has too much contrast.

Fault correction: rescan the picture using a higher scan quality setting (resolution).

i. Surface puddling when printing

Prints with this problem show puddles of wet ink on the surface of the paper. This situation results from too much ink being applied to the surface (see Figure 24.5).

Figure 24.5 Surface puddling when printing.

Fault correction: select another paper or media type in the printer dialog that better suits the printing paper you are using.

j. Edge bleeding

The edges of the print appear fuzzy and shadow areas are clogged and too dark. This usually occurs when using a watercolor or uncoated paper (see Figure 24.6).

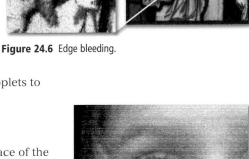

Figure 24.6 Edge bleeding.

Fault correction: try choosing a media or paper type such as 'Plain Paper' or 'Backlit Film'. These measures will change the amount of ink being applied and the spacing of the ink droplets to account for the absorbency of the paper.

k. Banding

Thin horizontal white lines appear across the surface of the photograph. This problem usually results from one or more of the print heads being clogged (see Figure 24.7).

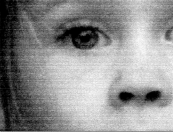

Fault correction: consult your printer's manual to find out how to activate the cleaning sequence. Once completed, print a 'nozzle test' page to check that all are working correctly. If banding still occurs after several cleaning attempts, it may be necessary to install a new cartridge.

Figure 24.7 Banding.

l. Weird colors

The picture looks great on screen but prints with strange colors. Using inks not made by your printer manufacturer can cause the colors in your print to be radically different to those displayed on screen.

Fault correction and prevention: replace non-genuine inks with those made by your printer manufacturer.

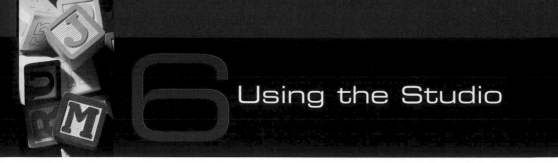

6 Using the Studio

A photographic studio is the rather grand term for any room where you can clear enough space to take pictures. Working in a studio should offer you full control over subject, camera position, lights and background, and is without doubt the best place to learn the basics of lighting and composition. A studio allows you time to experiment, especially with portraits or still life shots. You can keep essential bits and pieces on hand and leave things set up. This is a great help in allowing you to shoot, check results and, if necessary, retake the picture with improvements (see Figures 25.1 and 25.2).

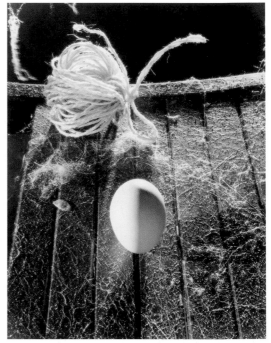

Figure 25.2 Working with light in the studio, you can make pictures from simple oddments.

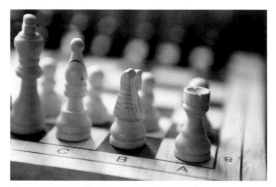

Figure 25.1 Working in a studio gives you the opportunity to fine-tune lighting, zone of focus and compositional skills. Image courtesy of www.ablestock.com.

25 Layout and lighting

Your 'studio' may simply be an empty spare bedroom, or better still a garage, outhouse or barn. It should be blacked out so that all lighting is under your control. In the studio shown in Figure 25.3, a large room has been cleared. Walls and ceiling are matt white and the floor gray, to avoid reflecting color onto every subject. White surfaces are also important for 'bouncing' light when required. The window has a removable blind and the glass behind is covered with tracing paper. If daylight is needed, the light coming through the window is therefore soft and diffused.

To start, you don't need a lot of lighting units. A couple of basic photographic lamps are perfectly suitable. These come in two main kinds – spotlights and floodlights. They need to be mounted on height-adjustable floor stands and have tilting heads. The 'boom' stand is an ideal

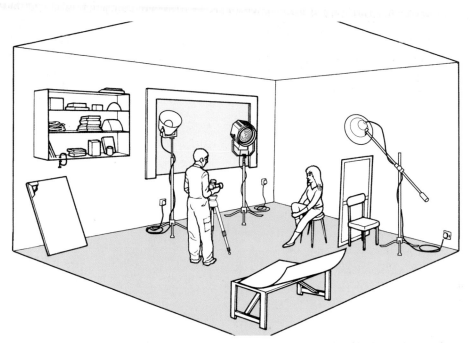

Figure 25.3 A room cleared to form a temporary studio. The table with curved card background is used for still lifes.

way to position a lamp high up to backlight a figure or illuminate the background (see Figure 25.4).

As an alternative, many top-of-camera flash units can now also be used off the camera. Two such flash guns, using either sync cords or wireless links, can be employed instead of the photographic lamps for most studio work. They have the advantage of being balanced for daylight film (or white balance setting) and the exposure of many models can be automatically calculated via special flash readings in the camera. The downside is that most of these portable, on-camera models do not contain any modeling lamps and so it is very difficult to predict the positioning and quality of the

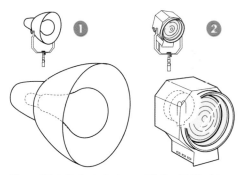

Figure 25.4 Basic studio lamps. (1) Floodlight, giving soft, even lighting. (2) Spotlight, giving hard lighting like direct sunlight. Its lamp focuses for narrow or wide beam.

light that they are emitting. Digital shooters have an advantage in this respect, being able to shoot and assess the resultant lighting via the LCD screen on the back of the camera. Changes can then be made to the lighting set-up before reshooting again.

As well as lighting, you will also need a stool for portraits and one or two reflector boards and diffusers. These can be made from white card and tracing paper stretched over a simple frame. Have a table to support small still life subjects at a convenient height. You will also need lots of useful small items – sticky tape, string, blocks of wood to prop things up with, modeling clay, wire and drawing pins.

Lighting equipment

Floodlights are the general name for lighting units that give even illumination and cause solid objects to cast shadows with soft edges. The effect is similar to hazy cloud conditions outdoors. Typically, a floodlight has a 500-watt diffused glass bulb surrounded by a large open reflector. A traditional desk lamp produces similar effects, although being much dimmer, and is really only usable for still life subjects because of the longer shutter speed necessary for the exposure.

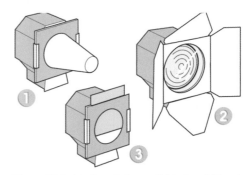

In contrast, a spotlight uses a small clear glass 500-watt lamp in a lamp house with a moulded lens at the front. A lever shifts the lamp, making the unit give out light in either a narrow or broad beam. Different attachments help you to shade off parts of the light. Spotlighting is harsh, causing sharp-edged shadows like direct sunlight, especially when set to broad beam. The nearest domestic substitute for a photographic spotlight is a bulb

Figure 25.5 Attachments for spotlights. Snoot (1) and barndoors (2) limit the light beam and shade the camera from split illumination. (3) Holder for colored acetate filters.

having an integral reflector, or you could use a slide projector (see Figure 25.5).

Unless you only work in black and white, however, you must ensure that the light from all your lighting units matches in color. One-hundred-watt lamps, for example, give yellower (as well as dimmer) light than 500-watt lamps, and so are best avoided for color photography. Then, having matched up your illumination, you can fit a color correction filter (see Table 25.1) to suit the daylight film you are using. Digital shooters can switch the white balance setting to tungsten or, better still, use the custom option to match the color of the light precisely to the sensor.

Table 25.1 Camera filters and white balance settings for color-balancing studio lighting

Light source	Filter needed for daylight film	Filter needed for tungsten film	White balance setting on a digital camera
Flash	No filter	85B	Daylight
Warm white fluorescent tubes	Fluor. correction or 40 magenta	81EF	Fluorescent
500 W lamps (3200 K)	80A	No filter	Tungsten
100 W domestic lamps	Not recommended	82B	Custom

As mentioned previously, another approach is to use flash in your studio, linking several flash units together either with cords or with newer models via wireless connections. You can then shoot on unfiltered daylight-type color film or the daylight white balance setting, since flash is the same color as sunlight. Flash heads for studio work often have built-in modeling lamps so that you can forecast how and where subject shadows and highlights will appear.

Controlling lighting

Exploring lighting, given the freedom offered by a studio, is interesting and creative – but be prepared to learn one step at a time. Firstly, if you are shooting in color, match up the color balance of your film with the color of your lighting as closely as possible. Table 25.1 shows the code number of the blue conversion filter needed over the camera lens with daylight color film (print or slide) using 500-watt lamps. A few color films, mostly slide, are balanced for artificial light and so need different filtering, or none at all. These films are often referred to as tungsten balanced films.

Start off with a still life subject because it is easier to take your time experimenting with this than when shooting a portrait. Set up your camera on a tripod and compose the subject. You can then keep returning to check appearance through the camera viewfinder for every change of lighting, knowing that nothing else has altered.

Direction

Keep to one light source at first. The aim of most studio lighting is to give a fairly natural appearance as if lit by the sun. This means having one predominant source of light and shadows, positioned high rather than low down. Set up your light source (a spotlight, for example) somewhere above camera height and to one side of the subject. Adjust it to give the best lighting direction for showing up form, texture and shape – whatever you consider the most important features of your subject to stress. Figures 25.6 and 25.7 illustrate how simply changing direction picks out or flattens different parts of a three-dimensional subject.

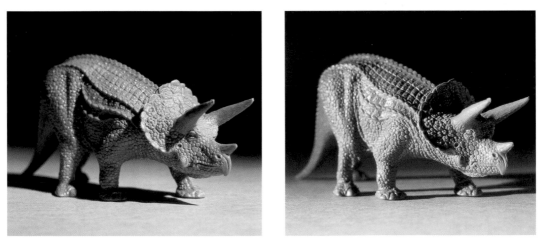

Figures 25.6 and 25.7 Lighting direction. Surface appearances change dramatically when you alter the position of the lamp.

Contrast

Be careful about contrast (the difference in brightness between lit and shadowed parts) at this point. Outdoors, in daylight, the sky always gives some illumination to shadows, but in an otherwise darkened studio direct light from a single lamp can leave very black shadows indeed. You may want to 'fill in' shadows with just enough illumination to record a little detail, using a large white card reflector as shown in Figure 25.8. This throws back very diffused light towards

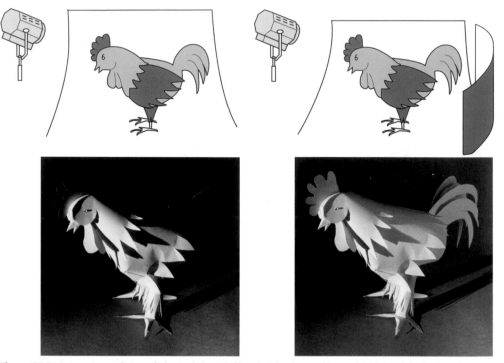

Figure 25.8 Contrast control. A spotlight used alone (left) and with a large white card added (right). Shadows become paler, without additional shadows forming.

the subject and, since it does not produce a second set of clearly defined shadows, you still preserve that 'one light source', natural look.

26 Photographing people in the studio

Like viewpoint and framing, there are no absolute 'rights' or 'wrongs' of organizing lighting. There are basic guidelines (introduced below), but you must decide which subject features you want to emphasize or suppress and the general mood you need to set, and manipulate your lights accordingly. You can dramatize and dominate the subject matter with your lighting, or keep the light simple and subsidiary so that subject features alone make your shot.

Experiment until you can forecast and control how the final picture will look. Remember what you learnt by observing natural lighting outdoors. Think of a spotlight as direct sunlight and diffused or reflected light like slightly hazy sun. The difference is that you can set their position instantly instead of waiting for different times of day for the sun to move. As you get more experienced, it becomes helpful to use more than one lighting unit at a time. Don't allow this to interfere with your main lighting, though, destroying its 'natural light' basis of causing only one set of shadows. The second lamp might, for example, separately illuminate the background behind a portrait or still life. This allows you to separate the subject from the

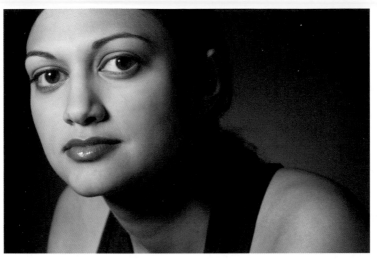

Figure 26.1 Adding another light to the set-up to illuminate the background provides separation between the dark hair of the model and what would be an equally dark background if left unlit. Image courtesy of www.ablestock.com.

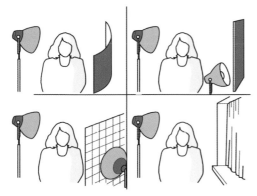

Figure 26.2 A range of methods to reduce light contrast in the studio, without creating a second shadow.

background by making it lighter, or graduated in tone, or even colored (by filtering the light source) – see Figures 26.1 and 26.2.

Basic portrait lighting

One of the key factors to capturing good portraits is making sure that your lighting is up to the task. This involves more than just ensuring that there is enough light to make a good exposure. The quality of the light that you use will help to characterize the style of portraits you make. Good photographers understand and can control the quality of light within their pictures. It is up to you to start to train your eyes to see the differences in light quality and to predict the effect they will have on the way that your subjects are lit. The two main light qualities are:

1 *Direct, strong lighting*, which produces hard-edged, dark shadows and is often used to emphasize texture. In portraiture, this style suits subjects with big and bold personalities and strong facial features.
2 *Soft, diffused light* is more delicate, creates light shadows and is often used to minimize texture. This lighting is by far the most popular style of portrait lighting, as it softly caresses sitters rather than starkly defining them.

Typical portrait lighting set-ups

Most photographers control the quality and the direction of the light used for their portraits. By manipulating these two factors they can produce radically different images of the same sitter. Don't think that these styles are only used in the studio with expensive flash kits; the same

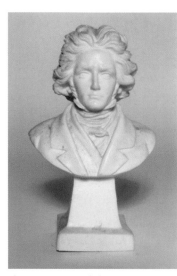

Figure 26.3 Front lighting.

techniques can be used with affordable floodlights or when you are taking pictures with your portable flash gun (or even when shooting outside with the sun as the main light).

Photographers have their own favorite lighting set-ups that they use on a regular basis. Let's look at the most common approaches.

Front lighting

One of the most common styles of lighting is 'direct front'. This is especially true for those photographers whose cameras contain a built-in flash system and for those people who still remember the famous Kodak saying: 'always shoot with the sun behind you'. Pictures illuminated in this way show sharp-edged shadows trailing behind the subject. The fact that the light is coming from the front also means that there will not be much texture in the subject's face.

For most portrait photographs, this style of lighting is neither flattering nor descriptive. You should only use it when you have no other options (see Figure 26.3).

Side-top lighting

Sometimes referred to as Rembrandt lighting, as it copies the way that the famous artist used to light the main figures in his paintings, with this set-up the light is positioned above and to one side of the subject. This provides both texture and form to the face, and is by far the most popular set-up used by portrait photographers (see Figure 26.4).

To get the position of the light just right, make sure that:

• there is a twinkle of light in the subjects eyes (called a 'catch light'); and
• there is a triangle of light on the side of the face that is opposite to the light source.

'Okay,' I hear you say, 'this is all well and good in the studio with movable lights, but I don't have that luxury.' The trick is to use the principles of these lighting set-ups with any source that you have available.

If you are photographing outside, it will not be possible to move the sun to just the right position, so instead move the subject. If the sun is too high, then tilt the subject's head up a little, or wait until the sun moves lower in the sky before photographing.

It is important to teach yourself to see how the lighting in your environment is falling on your subject and then either

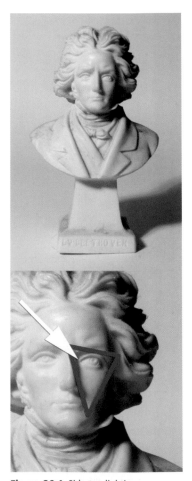

Figure 26.4 Side-top lighting.

modify the lighting to suit (e.g. move the study lamp on the side desk this way or that), or change the position of your subject to take advantage of the lighting that is available.

Lighting from above

Many a photographer, wanting to avoid the flat lighting that accompanies using their camera's flash straight on, simply flips the unit so that it faces skywards. The flash light then bounces off the ceiling and then onto the subject. The results do provide more texture in the face, but often the eyes are hidden in the dark shadows of the brows. Similar results regularly occur when photographing portraits outside when the sun is high. Top lighting is generally not used for portraiture for this reason (see Figure 26.5).

Instead of bouncing your light off the ceiling, try twisting it sidewards and reflecting it off a white wall. This will give you much better results that look and feel like soft window light. If you must shoot in the middle of the day with the sun above, try adding a little fill-flash to lighten the shadows around the eyes. Most modern cameras contain the option for this flash mode and, unlike the bad old days of manual flash calculations, the camera will generally balance the daylight and flash exposures as well.

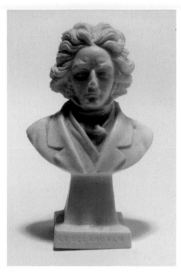

Figure 26.5 Lighting from above.

Lighting from behind

Positioning your main light behind the subject can create particularly dramatic portraits and silhouettes, but in most cases the lack of detail in the subject's face can prove disappointing. By all means play with this lighting approach as it offers very real creative opportunities, but make sure that the positioning of the subject is such that the face doesn't become a big dark chasm (see Figure 26.6).

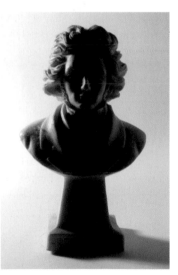

Figure 26.6 Lighting from behind.

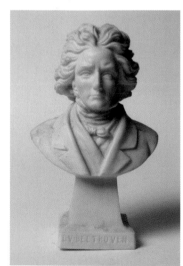

Figure 26.7 Soft diffused light.

Soft diffused light – Rembrandt style

In the previous lighting set-ups, I used a strong direct light source to make the shadow areas and direction of the light completely obvious. But this style of light is rarely used for contemporary portraiture. These days, soft or diffused light is much more popular (see Figure 26.7).

In this example, I positioned the soft light source to the left and above the subject – Rembrandt style. Notice that the triangle of light is still visible but the edges of the shadow areas are much softer.

Professionals use special attachments for their studio flashes, called 'soft boxes', to create this type of soft diffused lighting. Some even use semi-transparent white umbrellas in front of their flash heads. You can replicate the same effect by passing your main light through some diffusion material before it falls onto your subject. You can use drafting or tracing film, or even an offcut of white sail cloth (the sort used by sail makers to construct the sails for sailboards). This also works well when you are photographing outside with the sun as your light source. Just place the diffuser between the sun and your subject.

Alternatively, you can bounce your light off an angled white board, or piece of polystyrene foam, that is positioned top left of the subject. All of these techniques work particularly well at softening the light falling on your subject.

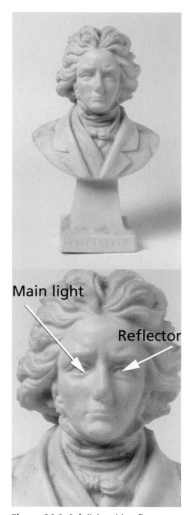

Soft light with reflector

Sometimes a single light, even if it is softened, casts shadows on the subject that are too dark for our camera's sensors to penetrate. So most professionals add a reflector to the opposite side of the subject to lighten the shadows and reveal the details hidden by the lack of light. Reflectors can be made from many different materials, including polystyrene foam and white card, but remember to keep the surface white as any color present here will be added to your shadows (see Figure 26.8).

Reflectors are often used when making portraits in the environment to help ensure that dark shadows don't ruin a good picture.

In practice, with your main light positioned to ensure good texture and form for the face, slowly bring a reflector in from the opposite side. Watch as the shadows lighten. Be sure that, when framing the portrait, the reflector remains out of view. To make a more directional reflector, try adhering aluminum foil to a piece of card.

Figure 26.8 Soft light with reflector.

Lighting and movement

The lighting control you have in the studio can help with many of the experimental approaches to depicting movement, as discussed in Part 9. Figure movements during a long exposure, for example, can be turned into abstract patterns in accurately directed ways. For Figures 26.9 and 26.10, two dancers, in pale reflective clothing, posed some distance in front of a black background. The lighting was two spotlights – positioned left and right at right angles to the camera viewpoint, and screened

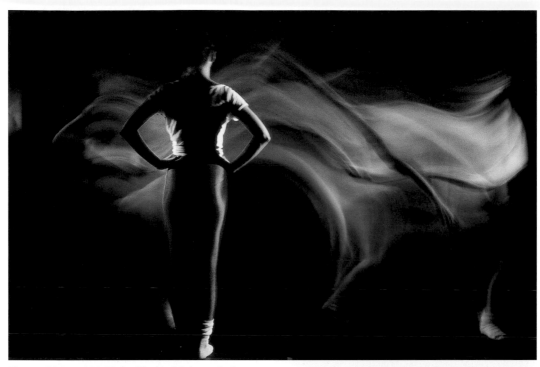

Figures 26.9 and 26.10 Double side-lighting and a long exposure produced each of these expressionist dance images.

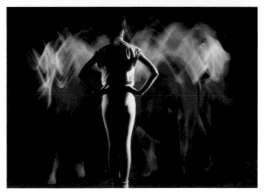

off from both the background and lens. Within the 'slot' of light so formed, one dancer stood completely still while the other moved to the music throughout a five-second exposure. Including a static element, like the still dancer, in your picture gives a counterpoint to all the action going on elsewhere.

27 Photographing objects in the studio

The five studio shots and lighting set-ups in Figures 27.1–27.5 show how mixed changes of lighting can alter subject appearance, especially texture. Figure 27.6 shows where the (single) light source was positioned for each version. In Figure 27.1 the spotlight was positioned at the rear of the stone slab, a little above lens height. Its direct light exaggerates texture but gives such contrast that the film both overexposes highlights and underexposes shadows. Figure 27.2 uses a reflector board close to the camera to return diffused light into the

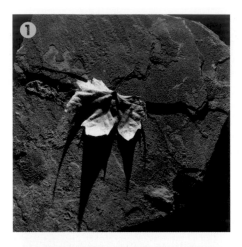

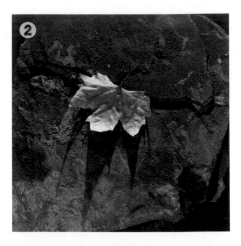

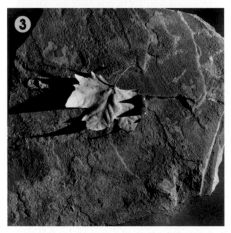

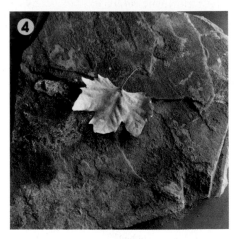

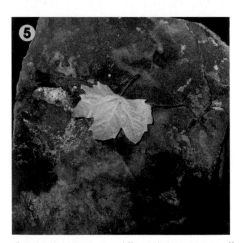

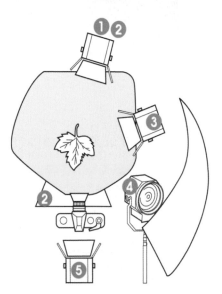

Figures 27.1–27.6 How different lighting set-ups affect texture, detail and form.

shadows. In Figure 27.3 the spotlight is now to one side, changing the direction of the (harsh) shadows. For Figure 27.4 the spotlight was turned away from the leaf altogether, and illuminates a large white card. The result is diffused ('soft') light, still directed from the side but now free of sharp-edged shadows and even less contrast than Figure 27.2. In Figure 27.5 the spotlight is now positioned close to and directly above the camera, and used direct. Like flash on the camera, everything receives light but it is like a drawing without shading, suppressing texture and form.

Arguably, Figure 27.2 gives the best compromise between drama and detail, although as a beginner you will often be tempted by Figure 27.1 because it looks good in the studio. Always remember that your eye can cope with greater contrast than film will successfully record.

Lighting for different surfaces

Over the years, photographers have developed specific lighting set-ups that work well with different subject surfaces. These set-ups, sometimes called lighting 'schema', provide a good starting point when lighting a difficult subject in the studio.

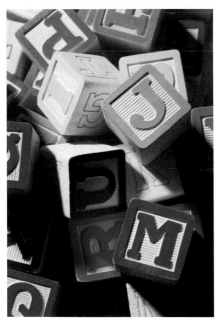

Figure 27.7 The textural qualities of both the blocks themselves and the greater assemblage are emphasized by skimming strong directional light across the surface of the subject. In this way, the shadow provides the sense of texture, but be careful, if the shadow is too dark and not lightened with a reflector or a second weaker light, little or no detail will be seen here. Image courtesy of www.ablestock.com.

Texture

Lighting for texture is all about using strong directional light that skims across the surface of the object, producing shadows as it goes. To show texture you must create shadows, so move your light or your subject around until you see the texture become pronounced. Don't use soft or diffused light sources, even if this results in some dark featureless shadow areas. Instead, set up your main light and then use a reflector to help fill in the shadow regions. Remember the golden rule for texture is light from the side of the object (see Figure 27.7).

Silverware or glossware

Highly reflective surfaces, such as chrome or highly polished, glossy paint, need to be treated quite differently to the textured surfaces above. Aiming a strong light directly at the surface will only result in a bright hot spot, with the rest of the object looking dull and dark. Professionals light these subjects by surrounding the object with a 'tent' of diffusion material that they then light through. The silver or gloss surface then reflects the white surface of the inside of the tent.

Though this sounds a little tricky, in practice, a successful silver jewelry photograph can be taken by suspending a piece of white sailcloth over the top of the

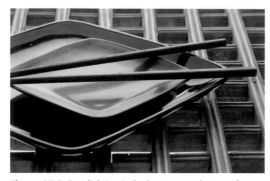

Figure 27.8 Tent lighting is the best approach to use for glossy or silver objects. The surface quality of these objects is only apparent when they are reflecting the white of the lit tent fabric. Image courtesy of www.ablestock.com.

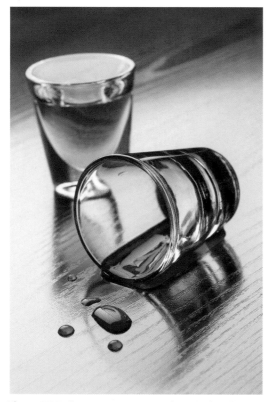

Figure 27.9 The transparency or translucency of a subject is shown in a photograph by lighting it from behind, but don't think that this is only achieved by directing the light onto the subject. Here the surface in and around the subject is lit, and then this illuminated area is photographed through the glasses. Image courtesy of www.ablestock.com.

object and then passing the light through the diffuser. The camera is then positioned so that it is to the side of the diffuser and is not reflected in the jewelry surface (see Figure 27.8).

Glassware

Glass objects pose a similar problem to the previous surface types in that directing a light onto the surface produces a hot spot and doesn't show the translucency of the subject at all. To solve this problem, glassware should be lit from behind. Often, this involves a set-up where light is directed onto a lightly colored background and then photographing through the glass object to the lit surface behind.

Once you build up your confidence with lighting subjects with each of these techniques, stretch your skills by trying to light a subject that contains more than one surface type. For instance, a glass bottle with a silvered label would require you to light the bottle from behind and the label using a broad diffused light (tent) – see Figure 27.9.

Lighting for copying

Photographic copying means accurately recording two-dimensional subjects such as artwork, photoprints, montages and paste-ups. You can turn prints into slides, slides into prints, or color into black and white. The essential technique is to light as evenly as possible, and have the camera set up square-on. Drawings, pictures and clips from papers are best taped against black cardboard, attached to the wall and lit by two floodlights positioned about 30° to the surface. Keep each flood well back from the original to help ensure even illumination. Check lighting with a pencil (Figure 27.10) held at right angles to the original. The two shadows should be equally dark, the same length and together form one straight line.

To copy a slide, you can improvise by laying it horizontally on opal plastic, masked along all four edges with wide strips of black card. Illuminate the plastic from underneath using a floodlight (bounced off white card to avoid heat damage). Support the camera square-on and directly above, fitted with close-up extension tubes or bellows to allow a same-size image. Alternatively, use a slide copying attachment (Figure 27.11) added to an SLR fitted with tubes or bellows. The slide slips into the far end of the attachment, in front of a light diffuser.

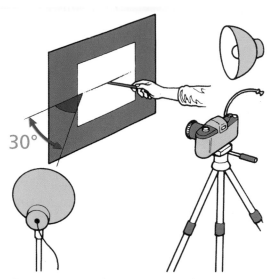

Figure 27.10 Set-up for copying paste-up photoprints, drawings and other flat work.

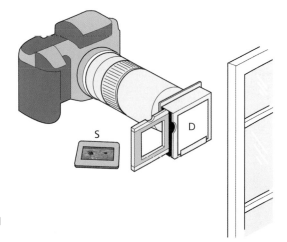

Figure 27.11 Slide copying. S, slide; D, light diffuser. Adjustable length tube fits on the front of the camera lens and extension ring.

1 A great way to help educate your eye as to the way that both portraits and products are lit is to examine how the professionals do it. Select a few example images from product catalogues or the advertising section of the weekend newspapers and analyze how each of the photographs is taken. For clues of lighting set-ups, look for the direction and style of shadows falling from the main subjects, as well as the reflection of light sources in the eyes of the portrait sitters or off the surface of reflective subjects. Once you diagnose the schema used, try to recreate the look of the photograph using your own set-up.

2 Photograph two portraits of a willing friend or relative using two completely different lighting set-ups. Create one with harsh direct lighting that has strong, hard-edged shadows and then use soft,

(*continued*)

PROJECTS

well-diffused light with shadows that are almost totally filled in (with a broad white reflector) for the other.

3 Find a collector of dolls, toy soldiers, unusual teapots, stamps or something similar in your local area. Offer to make a record of some of the pieces in their collection and then go on to use the opportunity to practice your lighting and still life photography skills.

4 Make a photographic copy of a set of montaged prints created with one of the techniques in Part 9 of the book. Ensure that the montage is evenly lit and that the camera is positioned so that it is 'straight on' to the original. Use the resultant image to make a single flat print of the picture.

5 Shoot separately pieces of glassware, silverware and a highly textured object, changing the lighting set-ups to suit each subject as you go. Once you have mastered each of these typical schemas, try photographing a subject that contains two, or more, of these surface types in combination.

7 Digital Processing and Printing

In the previous sections we looked at how to successfully create your own digital pictures (with camera or scanner), so let's now take a deeper look at how to process and print these images.

28 Introducing the digital photography tools

The image editing program

An image editing application is a computer program that can be loaded onto your machine and then used to change and enhance your digital pictures. There are many different programs available for installation on your computer. Some are used for word processing, chart creation or working out the family budget, but it is those that are specifically designed for manipulating pixels and fixing up digital photographs that we will look at here.

Many image retouching programs combine a range of features that can be used for everything from web design, manipulating photographs, creating posters and flyers for your business to making titles for your home movies. Such programs can cost anything from US $40 to over US $500. So which program is a good choice for you (see Figure 28.1)?

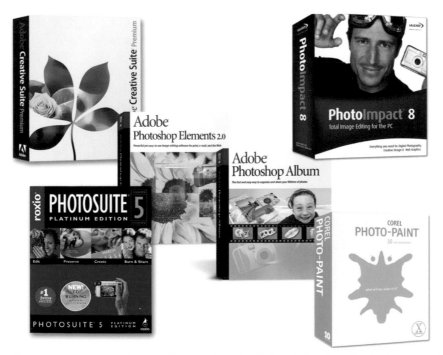

Figure 28.1 There are many different software packages on the market that are designed to edit and enhance your pictures.

What retouching software can do for photos

- Improve/change the color, contrast, brightness, hue and saturation (intensity).

- Change color images to black and white.

- Change black and white to duotone (two colors), tri-tone (three colors) or quad tone (four colors).

- Change mono (black and white) to color using hand coloring tools.

- Remove dust specks, scratches and other damage.

- Invisibly remove parts of an image.

- Repair damaged sections and reduce the effects of ageing in old photos.

- Apply effects to the whole picture or just parts of it.

- Alter images to create stunning artworks.

- Add 2D or 2D text effects.

- Include your images in calendars, cards, report covers, school projects, business cards, letterheads, invitations and more.

- Save to different file formats suitable for web, print and desktop publishing.

- Convert photos into a web page complete with links and animated effects.

- Create special web page buttons and animations.

- Create index or contact sheets.

- Convert your pictures to different color spaces, e.g. CMYK, LAB color, RGB and Grayscale.

- Add artistic effects.

Simply considered, image retouching/manipulation software can be placed in three application levels: enthusiast, semi-pro and professional. Enthusiast programs are generally for fun and games, whilst professional packages are designed for sophisticated image retouching and manipulation in a professional working environment. For most of us, however, it's the 'semi-professional' packages in the mid price range that give the best value, performance and room for growth.

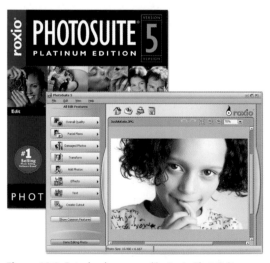

Figure 28.2 Entry-level programs like Roxio PhotoSuite use a simple, easy to follow interface designed to get users editing their pictures quickly. Image courtesy of www.ablestock.com.

Entry-level applications

(see Figure 28.2)

At the base level, you can get your hands on simple image editing software for free. Both the Windows and Macintosh platforms come with basic, though very limited, photo tweaking capabilities. The Mac version really only lets you view images, but it's a start.

As you may already know, desktop scanners and cameras often come bundled with several different application programs, one of which is always a simple image editing package. Most of these 'free' inclusions are very good and though they may not fulfil all your imaging needs, they are a good place to start. For instance, Adobe's Photoshop Elements is a program that is often included.

Besides purely edit-based programs, you will also see a range of products targeting the younger digital imager: programs for morphing one photo into another and liquid paint programs used for creating cool effects. These are tremendous fun but limited in their scope. No detailed restoration or retouching is possible with these!

Semi-professional programs (see Figure 28.3)

In the mid-range category, Adobe Photoshop Elements is definitely a favorite, being essentially a cut-down version of Photoshop, the world-class standard in image retouching programs.

Designed to compete directly with the likes of Jasc's Paintshop Pro, Ulead's PhotoImpact and Roxio's PhotoSuite, Adobe's mid-range package gives desktop photographers top quality image editing tools that can be used for preparing pictures for printing, or web work.

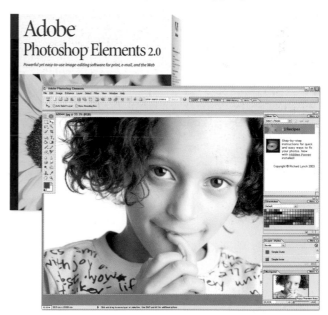

Tools like the panoramic stitching option, called Photomerge, and the File Browser are favorite features. The color management and text and shape tools are the same robust technology that drives Photoshop itself, but Adobe has cleverly simplified the learning process by providing step-by-step interactive recipes for common image manipulation tasks. These, coupled with other helpful features

Figure 28.3 Semi-professional packages give high-quality results with slightly reduced feature sets and an easier to use interface than the professional programs.

like Fill Flash, Adjust Backlighting and the Red Eye Brush tool, make this package a digital photographer's delight.

The mid-range price category (US $60–200) has seen the greatest improvements, often producing results as professional as something created with software costing US $500 or more.

Professional programs (see Figure 28.4)

The top end of town gives you everything that a mid-range program can provide *plus* sophisticated productivity enhancing features with complete editablilty. Programs like Photoshop are designed for total integration with other Adobe products (InDesign, Illustrator,

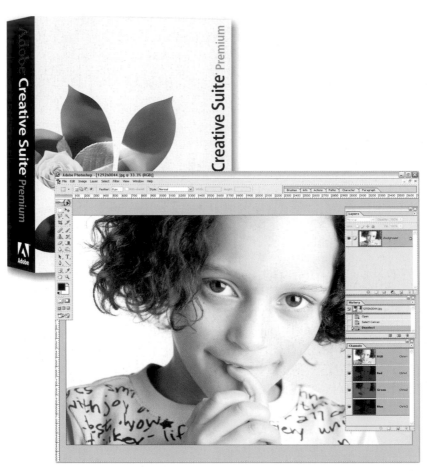

Figure 28.4 For the absolute best quality and greatest control over your pixels, you can't better the industry leader Adobe Photoshop.

Pagemaker) and like-minded programs (Macromedia Dreamweaver, Fireworks). An enthusiast will find it hard to justify spending much more on a program that's unlikely to produce any better inkjet print results than programs like Jasc PaintShop Pro, Adobe Photoshop Elements or Ulead PhotoImpact. The differences between high-end programs and entry-level products are really noticeable in a high turnover production business, especially in the prepress or publishing environment. The array of functions and the level of editability of the files are something that cheaper programs just don't provide in any depth.

What you get for your money
Entry level

■ Support for a limited number of file formats.

■ Basic tool and feature set.

■ Limited file saving options.

■ Some preset special effects or filters.

■ Plenty of template-based activities, such as magazine covers, calendars and cards.

Semi-professional

■ Wide range of file formats supported.

■ The use of separate image layers.

(continued)

- Reasonably unlimited file saving options.

- Wide range of special effects filters.

- Support for third-party plug-in programs to add extra features to the software.

- Inclusion of web-based design features, including image slicing, image optimization and animation.

- Drag and drop web page creation.

Professional

- Multiple file format support.

- Integration with other programs.

- Fully editable layers.

- Fully editable paths.

- Combination of scalable vector and bitmap graphics.

- Sophisticated special effects filters.

- Complex web design features.

- Wide range of editable pro paint and drawing tools.

- Wide range of darkroom manipulation tools.

- Wide range of specialist image adjustment features.

- Support for third-party plug-in programs to add extra features to the software.

Parts of image editing programs

Most editing programs contain a look and feel that is very familiar and pretty much the same from one program to the next. This remains true even if the packages are created by different manufacturers.

The interface is the way that the software package communicates with the user. Each program has its own style, but the majority contain a work space, a set of tools laid out in a toolbar and some menus. You might also encounter some other smaller windows around the edge of the screen. Commonly called dialog boxes and palettes, these windows give you extra details and controls for tools that you are using (see Figure 28.5).

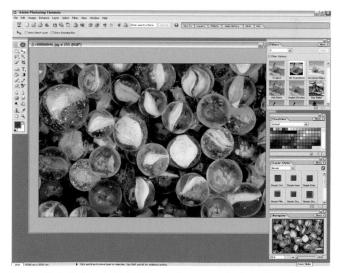

Figure 28.5 The program's interface is the gateway to the editing of your photographs.

Programs have become so complex that sometimes there are so many different boxes, menus and tools on screen that it is difficult to see your picture. Photographers solve this problem by treating themselves to bigger screens or by using two linked screens – one for tools and dialogs, and one for images. Most of us don't have this luxury, so it's important that, right from the start, you arrange the parts of the screen in a way that provides you with the best view of what is important – your image. Get into the habit of being tidy.

Know your tools

Over the years, the tools in most image editing packages have been distilled to a common set of similar icons that perform in very similar ways. The tools themselves can be divided up into several groups, depending on their general function.

Drawing tools (see Figure 28.6)

Designed to allow the user to draw lines or areas of color onto the screen, these tools are mostly used by the digital photographer to add to existing images. Those readers who are more artistically gifted will be able to use this group to generate masterpieces in their own right from blank screens.

Most software packages include basic brush, eraser, pen, line, spray paint and paint bucket tools. The tool draws with colors selected and categorized as either foreground or background.

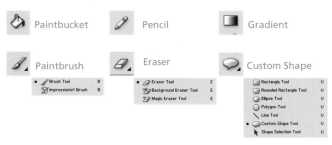

Figure 28.6 Drawing tools.

Selecting tools (see Figure 28.7)

When starting out, most new users apply functions like filters and contrast control to the whole of the image area. By using one, or more, of the selection tools, it is also possible to isolate part of the image and restrict the effect of such changes to this area only.

Used in this way, the three major selection tools – lasso, magic wand and marquee – are some of the most important tools in any program. Good control of the various selection methods in a program is the basis for many digital photography production techniques.

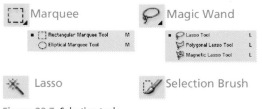

Figure 28.7 Selecting tools.

Text tools (see Figure 28.8)

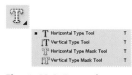

Figure 28.8 Text tools.

Adding and controlling the look of text within an image is becoming more important than ever. The text handling within all the major software packages has become increasingly sophisticated with each new release of the product. Effects that were only possible in text layout programs are now integral parts of the best packages.

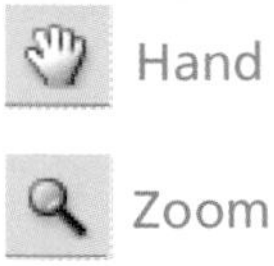

Viewing tools (see Figure 28.9)

This group includes the now infamous magnifying glass for zooming in and out of an image and the move tool used for shifting the view of an enlarged picture.

Figure 28.9 Viewing tools.

Others (see Figure 28.10)

There remains a small group of specialist tools that don't fit into the categories above. Most of them are specifically related to digital photography. In packages like Hotshots they include a 'Red Eye Remover' tool specially designed to eliminate those evil-eyed images that plague compact camera users. Photoshop, on the other hand, supplies both 'dodging' and 'burning-in' tools.

Figure 28.10 Other tools.

Making a menu selection

(see Figure 28.11)

Features not activated via a tool can be found grouped under headings in the menu bar. Headings such as File, Edit, View and Help are common to most programs, but picture editing packages also display choices such as Image, Layer, Select and Filter. Navigating your way around the many choices and remembering where certain

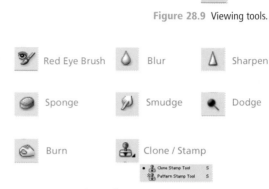

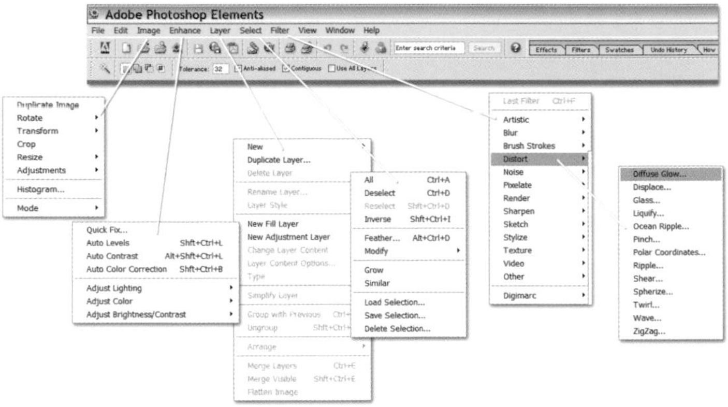

Figure 28.11 Making a menu selection.

options are found takes practice, but after a little while finding your favorite features will become almost automatic.

When writing about how to select a particular option in a menu, authors often use a style of menu shorthand. For instance, 'Image > Image Size' means select the 'Image Size' option, which can be found under the 'Image' menu.

29 First steps in image processing

To start your introduction to image processing, we will concentrate on the following basic steps that most photographers perform after each shooting session:

1 Downloading your pictures from the camera.
2 Viewing your results.
3 Rotating and cropping the photograph.

4 Making a couple of automatic color and tone adjustments.

5 Applying a little sharpening.

6 Saving the picture.

These basic alterations take a standard picture captured by a camera, or scanner, and tweak the pixels so that the resultant photograph is cast free, sharp and displays a good spread of tones.

No matter what image editing program you are using, the tools and features designed to perform these steps are often those first learned. Here the steps are demonstrated using Photoshop Elements, but these basic steps can be performed with any of the main image editing programs currently available on the market. A summary of the tools and menu options needed to perform these steps in Photoshop is also included at the end of each section. A trial version of Photoshop Elements can be obtained by downloading the 30-day demo from the www.adobe.com site.

Step 1. Importing pictures from a camera (see Figure 29.1)

When opening Photoshop Elements for the first time, the user is confronted with the Quick Start or Welcome screen, containing several options. Images can be created from scratch, opened (if previously saved) or acquired from scanner, or digital camera, sources. Clicking the Acquire option will provide the user with a list of image sources. The same list can be found in the Import section of the File menu.

As long as your camera is correctly installed, there should be an item on the list for your make and model. In the example, I

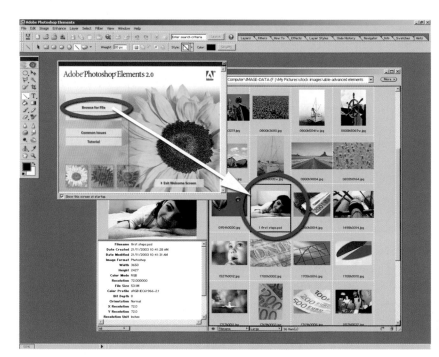

Figure 29.1 Importing pictures from a camera.

selected the camera driver as the images I wanted to import were sitting on the memory card in my digital camera, but you could also obtain your pictures directly from the card using a card reader. A new dialog appears showing thumbnail versions of the pictures. Though some twain plug-ins contain simple enhancement controls, most of these programs are only used for selecting images to be downloaded.

Alternatively, if you have already downloaded the pictures using the camera's transfer software (such as NikonView for Nikon cameras), you can use the Browse for File option to search these photographs on your hard drive. This feature opens up the Elements File Browser, which provides a thumbnail view of all the pictures stored on your computer. Search for the folder, or directory, where you initially downloaded the pictures and locate the photograph you wish to use.

With an image selected, click OK to import the picture into Elements.

This step in Photoshop:
To browse for a picture: File > Browse
To open a picture from a folder: File > Open
To import an image from a connected camera: File > Import

Step 2. Changing a picture's orientation (see Figure 29.2)

Turning your camera to shoot images in portrait mode will generally produce pictures that need to be rotated to vertical after importing. Elements provides a series of dedicated Rotate options under the Image menu designed for this purpose. Here the picture can be turned to the right or left in 90° increments or to custom angles, using the Canvas Custom feature.

There is even an option to rotate the whole picture 180° for those readers, who like me, regularly place prints into their scanners upside down.

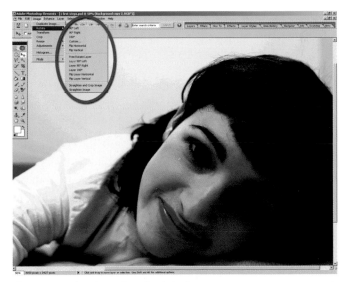

Figure 29.2 Changing a picture's orientation.

This step in Photoshop:
To rotate a picture: Image > Rotate Canvas > Select an option

Step 3. Cropping and straightening (see Figure 29.3)

Most editing programs provide tools that enable the user to crop the size and shape of their images. Elements provides two such methods. The first is to select the Rectangular Marquee tool and draw a selection on the image the size and shape of the required crop. Next choose Image > Crop from the menu bar. The area outside of the marquee is removed and the area inside becomes the new image.

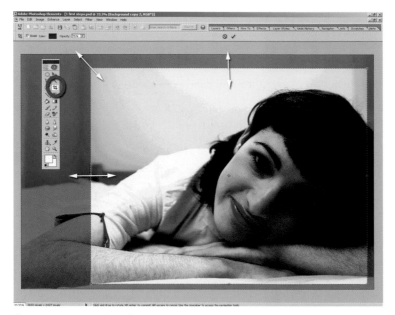

Figure 29.3 Cropping and straightening.

The second method uses the dedicated Crop tool that is located just below the Lasso in the toolbox. Just as with the Marquee tool, a rectangle is drawn around the section of the image that you want to retain. The selection area can be resized at any time by clicking and dragging any of the handles positioned in the corners of the box. To crop the image, click the OK button in the options bar or double-click inside the selected area.

An added benefit of using the Crop tool is the ability to rotate the selection by clicking and dragging the mouse when it is positioned outside the box. To complete the crop, click the OK button in the options bar, but this time the image is also straightened based on the amount that the selection area was rotated.

As well as this manual method, Elements provides an automatic technique for cropping and straightening crooked scans. The bottom two options in the Rotate menu, Straighten Image and Straighten and Crop Image, are specifically designed for this purpose.

> This step in Photoshop:
> *To crop a picture*: use the Crop tool or Rectangular Marquee tool as detailed above

Step 4. Spreading your image tones (see Figure 29.4)

When photographers produce their own monochrome prints, they aim to spread the image tones between maximum black and white; so too should the digital image maker ensure that their pixels are spread across the whole of the possible tonal range. In a full color 24-bit image, this means that the tonal values should extend from 0 (black) to 255 (white).

Elements provides both manual and automatic techniques for adjusting tones. The Auto Contrast and Auto Levels options are both positioned under the Enhance menu. Both features will spread the tones of your image automatically, the difference being that the Auto Levels function adjusts the tones of each of the color channels individually, whereas the Auto Contrast command ignores differences between the spread of the Red, Green and Blue components and just concentrates on adjusting the overall contrast.

If your image has a dominant cast, then using Auto Levels can sometimes neutralize this problem. The results can be unpredictable, though, so if after using the feature the colors in your image are still a little wayward, undo the changes using the Edit > Undo command and use the Auto Contrast feature instead.

If you want a little more control over the placement of your pixel tones, then Adobe has also included the same slider-based Contrast/Brightness and Levels features used in Photoshop in their entry-level software. Both these features, Levels in particular, take back the control for the adjustment from the program and place it squarely in the hands of the user.

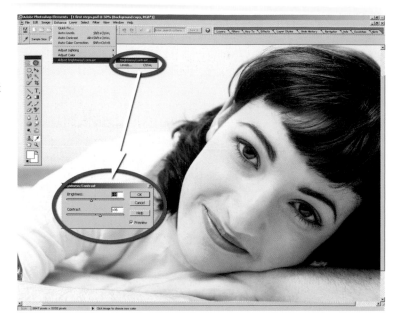

Figure 29.4 Spreading your image tones.

This step in Photoshop:
To automatically adjust the contrast only in a picture: Image > Adjustments > Auto Contrast
To automatically adjust the contrast and color in a picture: Image > Adjustment > Auto Levels
Manual adjustment of contrast and brightness: Image > Adjustments > Brightness/Contrast

---

Step 5. Ridding your pictures of unwanted color casts (see Figure 29.5)

Despite the quality of modern digital cameras' white balance systems, images shot under mixed lighting conditions often contain strange color casts. The regularity of this problem led Adobe to include the specialized Color Cast tool (Enhance > Color > Color Cast) in Elements. Simply click the eyedropper on a section of your image that is meant to be gray (an area that contains equal amounts of red, green and blue values) and the program will adjust all the colors accordingly.

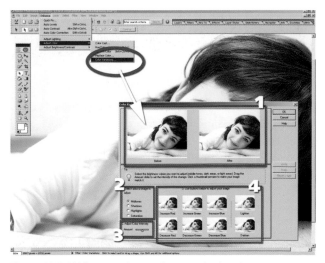

Figure 29.5 Ridding your pictures of unwanted color casts.

This process is very easy and accurate – if you have a gray section in your picture, that is. For those pictures without the convenience of this reference, the Variations feature (Enhance > Variations) provides a visual 'ring-around' guide to cast removal. The feature is divided into four parts. The top of the dialog (1) contains two thumbnails that represent how your image looked before changes and its appearance after. The radio buttons in the middle-left section (2) allow the user to select the parts of the image they wish to alter. In this way, highlights, midtones and shadows can all be adjusted independently. The 'amount' slider (3) in the bottom left controls the strength of the color changes.

The final part, bottom left (4), is taken up with six color and two brightness preview images. These represent how your picture will look with specific colors added or when the picture is brightened or darkened. Clicking on any of these thumbnails will change the 'after' picture by adding the color chosen. To add a color to your image, click on a suitably colored thumbnail. To remove a color, click on its opposite.

> This step in Photoshop:
> *To automatically adjust the color in a picture*: Image > Adjustments > Auto Color
> *To adjust the color in a picture using preview thumbnails*: Image > Adjustment > Variations

Step 6. Applying some sharpening (see Figure 29.6)

The nature of the capture or scan process means that most digital images can profit from a little careful sharpening. I say careful, because the overuse of this tool can cause image errors, or artifacts, that are very difficult to remove. Elements provides several sharpening choices, most automatic, and one with a degree of manual control.

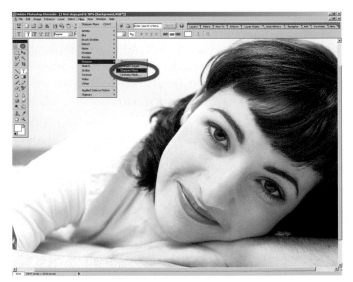

Figure 29.6 Applying some sharpening.

The Sharpen, Sharpen More and Sharpen Edges features found in the Sharpen selection of the Filter menu provide automatic techniques for improving the clarity of your images. The effect is achieved by altering the contrast of adjacent pixels and pixel groups. The Sharpen and Sharpen More options apply the effect to all pixels in the image, whereas the Sharpen Edges only uses the filter on areas where the program detects edges.

The fourth option, the Unsharp Mask filter, provides the user with manual control over which pixels will be changed and how strong the effect will be. The key to using this feature is to make sure that the changes made by the filter are previewed in both the thumbnail and full image at 100 per cent magnification. This will help to ensure that your pictures will not be noticeably over-sharpened.

> This step in Photoshop:
> *To adjust the sharpness in a picture*: the same range of sharpening filters are available in Photoshop as are detailed above – look for them under the Filter > Sharpen menu

Step 7. Saving your images (see Figure 29.7)

The final step in the process is to save all your hard work. The format you choose to save in determines a lot of the functionality of the file. If you are unsure of your needs, always use the native PSD or Photoshop format. These files maintain layers and features like editable text and saved selections and do not use any compression (keeping all the quality that was originally contained in your picture) If you are not using Photoshop or Elements and still want to maintain the best quality in your pictures, then you can use the TIF or Tagged Image File Format, but this option has less

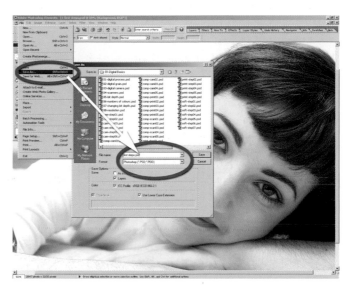

Figure 29.7 Saving your images.

features than the Photoshop format. JPEG and GIF files should only be used for web work or when you need to squeeze you files down to the smallest size possible. Both these formats lose image quality in the reduction process, so keep a PSD or TIF version as a quality backup.

To save your work, select File > Save As, entering the file name and selecting the file format you desire before pressing OK.

> This step in Photoshop:
> *To save pictures in a given format*: you can use the same File > Save As option in Photoshop that was available in Photoshop Elements

30 Editing techniques

Now let's throw a few more techniques into the editing arena for good measure. More than enhancing existing detail, these techniques are designed to change the information in your pictures and so are usually considered editing techniques.

Dust and Scratches (Filter > Noise > Dust and Scratches)

It seems that no matter how careful I am, my scanned images always contain a few dust marks. The Dust and Scratches filter in Photoshop and Elements helps to eliminate these annoying spots

Over-application

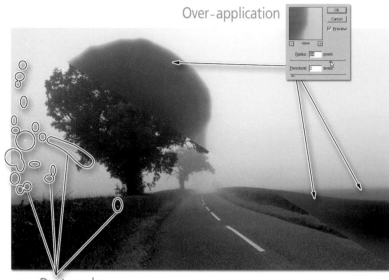

Dust marks

Figure 30.1 Too much Dust and Scratches filtering can destroy image detail and make the picture fuzzy.

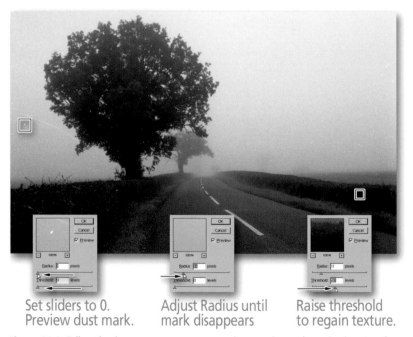

Set sliders to 0. Preview dust mark.

Adjust Radius until mark disappears

Raise threshold to regain texture.

Figure 30.2 Follow the three-step process to ensure that you choose the optimal settings for the Dust and Scratches filter.

by blending or blurring the surrounding pixels to cover the defect. The settings you choose for this filter are critical if you are to maintain image sharpness whilst removing small marks. Too much filtering and your image will appear blurred, too little and the marks will remain (see Figure 30.1).

To find settings that provide a good balance, try adjusting the threshold setting to zero first. Next use the preview box in the filter dialog to highlight a mark that you want to remove. Use the zoom controls to enlarge the view of the defect. Now drag the Radius slider to the right. Find, and set, the lowest radius value where the mark is removed. Next increase the threshold value gradually until the texture of the image is restored and the defect is still removed (see Figure 30.2).

Generally, I only use this filter for removing problem marks in parts of the picture where there is little detail that can be obscured by the filter. This means that, where possible, only use this filter on picture parts such as smoothly graded skies or clear backgrounds.

Clone Stamp

In some instances, the values needed for the Dust and Scratches filter to erase or disguise picture faults are so high that it makes the whole image too blurry for use. In these cases, it is better to use a tool that works with the problem area specifically rather than the whole picture surface.

The Clone Stamp tool (sometimes called the Rubber Stamp tool) samples an area of the image and then paints with the texture, color and tone of this copy onto another part of the picture. This process makes it a great tool to use for removing scratches or repairing tears or creases in a photograph. Backgrounds can be sampled and then painted over dust or scratch marks, and whole areas of a picture can be rebuilt or reconstructed using the information contained in other parts of the image (see Figure 30.3).

Using the Clone Stamp tool is a two-part process. The first step is to select the area that you are going to use as a sample by Alt-clicking (Windows) or Option-clicking (Macintosh) the area (see Figure 30.4). Now move the cursor to where you want to paint and click and drag to start the process (see Figure 30.5).

The size and style of the sampled area are based on the current brush and the opacity setting controls the transparency of the painted section.

Using the Healing Brush – Photoshop only (see Figure 30.6)

Designed to work in a similar way to the Clone tool, the user selects the area to be sampled before painting. The tool achieves great

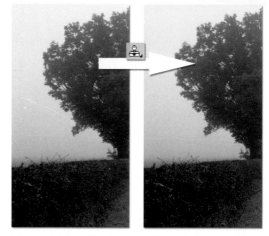

Figure 30.3 The Clone Stamp tool is perfect for retouching the marks that the Dust and Scratches filter cannot erase.

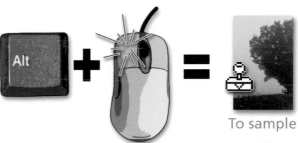

To sample

Figure 30.4 Alt + click (Windows) or Option + click (Mac) to mark the area to be sampled.

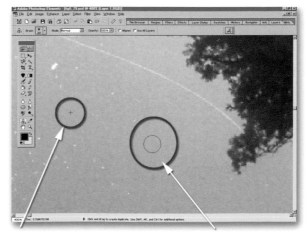

Sample point   Retouching area

Figure 30.5 Move the cursor over the mark and click to paint over with the sampled texture.

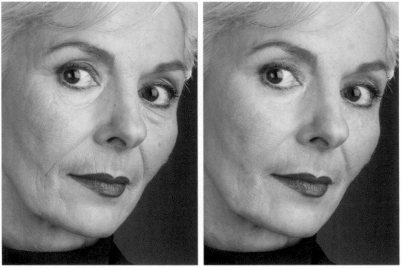

Before   After

Figure 30.6 The Healing Brush, which can be found in more recent versions of Photoshop, is an advanced retouching tool that works in the same basic 'sample and paint' way as the Clone Stamp tool. The difference is that the Healing Brush merges the newly painted area into the pixels that surround the mark, creating a more seamless repair. Image courtesy of www.ablestock.com.

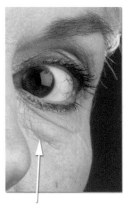

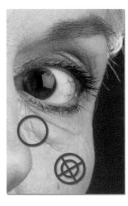

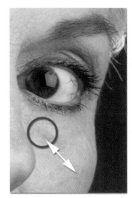

Locate the area to be healed   ALT + Click to set sample point   Click and Drag to heal

Figure 30.7 Use this three-step approach to retouch using the Healing Brush.

results by merging background and source area details as you paint. Just as with the Clone Stamp tool, the size and edged hardness of the current brush determines the characteristics of the Healing tool tip.

To use the Healing Brush, the first step is to locate the areas of the image that need to be retouched. Next, hold down the Alt key and click on the area that will be used as a sample for the brush. Notice that the cursor changes to cross-hairs to indicate the sample area (see Figure 30.7).

Now move the cursor to the area that needs retouching and click and drag the mouse to 'paint' over the problem picture part. After you release the mouse button,

Photoshop merges the newly painted section with the image beneath.

Red eye removal

The dreaded red eye appears all too frequently with images shot using the built-in flash on compact digital cameras. The flash is too close to the lens and the light reflects back from the inside of the subject's pupil, giving the tell-tale red glow. Red eye removal features can be found in most digital photography software and usually consist of a brush tool that replaces the red color with a hue that is more natural.

Photoshop Elements contains a specialist tool to help retouch these problems in our pictures. Called the Red Eye Brush, it changes crimson color in the center of the eye for a more natural-looking black. To use on your own images, pick the tool from the toolbox, select the brush size and type, push the default colors button on the options bar and then click on the red section of the eyes (see Figure 30.8).

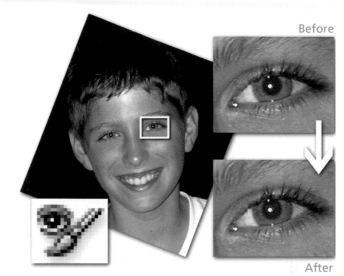

Figure 30.8 You can use a tool like the Red Eye Brush found in Photoshop Elements to remove the worst effects of your flash pictures.

Photoshop CS also contains a version of this feature called the Color Replacement tool. You can find it nestled in the fly-out menu (to display, click and hold the mouse pointer over the small triangle in the bottom-right corner of the tool icon in the toolbox) of the Healing Brush and Patch tool.

Though designed specifically for this purpose, the tool can also be used for changing other colors. To achieve this, click on the 'current' color swatch and use the eyedropper to sample the color you wish to change. Next click on the 'Replacement' swatch to pick the hue that will be used as a substitute. Now, when the brush is dragged over a 'current' color, it will be changed to the 'replacement' hue.

The Tolerance slider controls how similar to the current color a pixel must be, before it is replaced. Low values restrict the effect to precisely the current color; higher values replace a broader range of dissimilar hues.

Red eye removal in practice

Select Red Eye Brush from the toolbox and then choose brush size and type from the options bar. Select Current Color from the sampling menu and then click the Default Colors button to remove red eye or select your own Current and Replacement colors and then adjust the Tolerance slider to suit the image. Drag the brush over the area to be changed to replace the red with a more natural hue (see Figure 30.9).

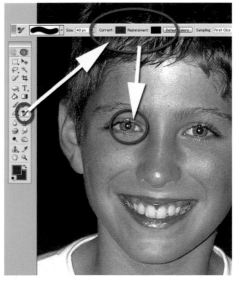

Figure 30.9 Red eye removal in practice.

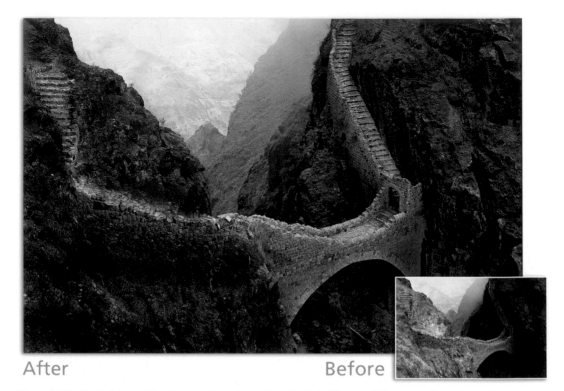

After   Before

Figure 30.10 The dodging and burning-in tools can be used to selectively lighten or darken areas of your pictures. Image courtesy of www.ablestock.com.

The Dodge and Burn-in tools (see Figure 30.10)

Over the years, the people at Adobe have borrowed many traditional darkroom terms and ideas for use in their Photoshop and Photoshop Elements image editing packages. I guess part of the reasoning is that it will be easier for us to understand just how a feature works (and what we should use it for) if we have a historical example to go by.

As we will see in the next part of this book, the Photoshop Elements' dodging and burning-in tools have roots in traditional darkroom techniques that enabled photographers to selectively darken and lighten sections of their pictures. These techniques involve shielding the print from light ('dodging') during exposure or adding extra light ('burning in') after the initial overall exposure. In this way, and unlike brightness changes, which alter the tones across the whole picture, burning-in and dodging techniques are used to darken or lighten just a portion of the picture.

The digital versions of the technique use brush-shaped tools that are dragged over the picture area to be changed. The pixels beneath the dragged brush are either lightened or darkened according to the Exposure value selected and how many times the area is brushed. By selecting different Range options in the tool's options bar, the tonal changes can be limited to either highlights, shadows or midtones.

The same tools are available in both Photoshop and Photoshop Elements.

Dodging and burning in practice

1 With an image open and dodging tool selected, adjust the Brush, size, target tonal Range and Exposure values in the options bar. To start with, use a small, soft-edged brush, select midtones and ensure that the exposure is around 20 per cent (see Figure 30.11).

2 For dark areas of the image, select the dodging tool and, using a series of overlapping brush strokes, click and drag over the area to lighten it. If the lightening effect is too great, Edit > Undo the changes and select a lower exposure value (see Figure 30.12).

3 For lighter parts, switch to the burning-in tool and brush the whole area except the steps (see Figure 30.13).

Applying a filter to your image (see Figure 30.14)

Using a filter to change the way that your picture looks should not be a completely new technique to readers, as we have already looked at a sharpening technique that used the Unsharp Mask filter to crispen our pictures. Here we will look at filters more generally and also find out how we can filter only a part of the picture, leaving the rest unchanged.

The filters in Adobe Photoshop Elements and Photoshop can be found grouped under a series of sub-headings based on their main effect or feature in the Filter menu. Selecting a filter will apply the effect to the current layer or selection. Some filters display a dialog that allows the user to

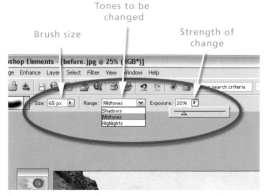

Tones to be changed

Brush size

Strength of change

Figure 30.11 The dodging tool in practice – 1.

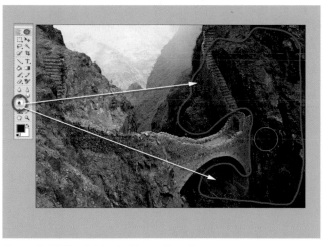

Figure 30.12 The dodging tool in practice – 2.

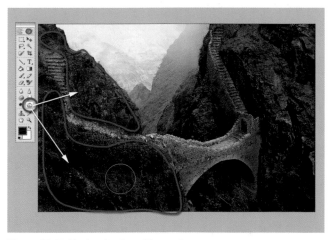

Figure 30.13 The burning-in tool in practice.

Before

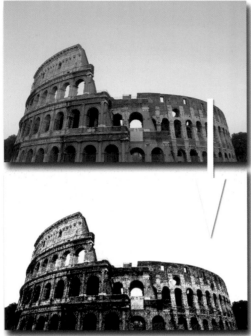

After

Figure 30.14 Digital filters can be used to dramatically alter the way that your pictures appear. In this example, a filter is used to change a color photograph into a 'look-alike' pen and ink drawing. Image courtesy of www.ablestock.com.

change specific settings and preview the filtered image before applying the effect to the whole of the picture (see Figure 30.15). This can be a great time saver, as filtering a large file can take several minutes. If the preview option is not available then, as an alternative, make a partial selection of the image using the Marquee tool first and use this to test the filter. Remember, filter changes can be reversed by using the Undo feature, but not once the changes have been saved to the file.

The number and type of filters available can make selecting which to use a difficult process. To help with this decision, Elements contains a Filter Browser and Photoshop CS a Filter Gallery feature that display thumbnail versions of different filter effects. Clicking the filter preview thumbnail and then the Apply button will alter your image using the filter settings (see Figure 30.16). The selection of filters previewed at any one time can be changed by altering the selection in the pop-up menu at the top of the palette.

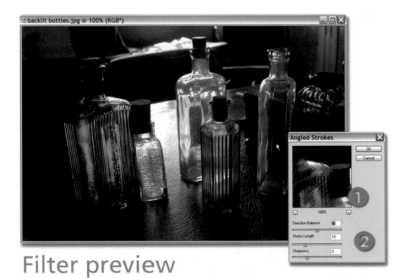

Filter preview

Figure 30.15 Most filters are supplied with a preview and settings dialog that allows the user to view changes before committing them to the full image. (1) Filter preview thumbnail. (2) Filter controls.

Filters in action

1 Check to see that you have selected the layer that you wish to filter (see Figure 30.17).
2 Select Window > Filters or click on the Filters tab in the palette well to display the Filters palette and select or click on the filter to display the preview dialog or to apply. Adjust settings in the preview dialog (if available for the particular filter chosen). Click Apply to finish (see Figure 30.18).

Restricting your filtering (see Figure 30.19)

You can restrict your filtering to just a single part of the picture by isolating this area with a selection tool first before applying a filter. Choose a selection tool, such as the Rectangular Marquee tool, draw a selection of part of the picture, and then choose and apply the filter of your choice. Notice that only the area that was defined by the selection has been changed.

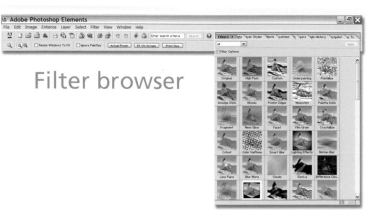

Figure 30.16 Features like the Filter Browser in Photoshop Elements give users a good idea of the types of changes that a filter will make to an image.

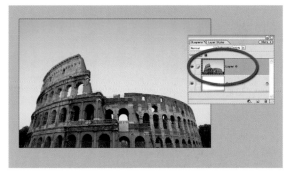

Figure 30.17 Filters in action – 1.

Introduction to layers (see Figure 30.20)

It doesn't take new digital photographers much time before they want to do more with their pictures than simply download and print them. Before you know it, they are adding text to their photographs, combining several images together and even adding fancy borders to their pictures. In some image editing packages, these sorts of activities are performed directly on the picture, which means making corrections, or slight modifications of these changes at a later date, difficult, if not almost impossible.

The leading programs, such as Photoshop, Photoshop Elements, PaintShop Pro and PhotoImpact, use a better approach to image editing by

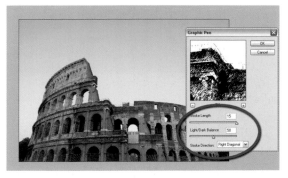

Figure 30.18 Filters in action – 2.

providing a layer system to their files. The system enables users to separate individual components of a picture onto different layers. Each layer can be moved and edited independently. This is a big advantage compared to programs that treat the picture as a flat file, where any changes become a permanent part of the picture.

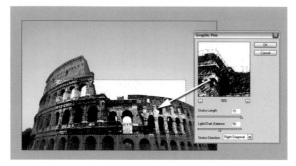

Figure 30.19 By selecting a portion of your picture first before filtering, you can restrict the area where the effect is applied.

Though each program handles this system differently, all provide a palette that you can use to view each of the layers and their content. The layers are positioned one above each other in a stack and the picture you see in the work area is a preview of the image with all layers combined (see Figures 30.21 and 30.22).

Layered pictures are only possible with file formats that support the feature. The Photoshop or PSD format supports layers and so should be used as your primary method of storing your digital pictures. Formats like JPEG and GIF don't support layers.

Getting to know how layers work in your favorite program will help you create more exciting and dynamic images in less time.

Adding text to your pictures (see Figure 30.23)

Combining text and pictures used to be the job of a graphic designer or printer, but the simple text functions that are now included in image retouching programs mean that more and more people are

Figure 30.21 Most layer functions and features can be accessed via buttons and menus in the Layers palette. These features can also be activated from the Layers option in the menu bar.

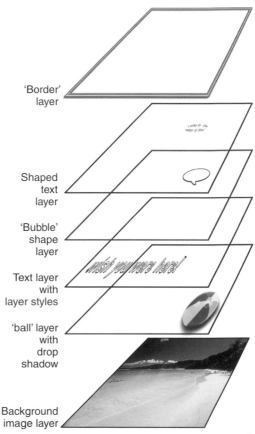

'Border' layer

Shaped text layer

'Bubble' shape layer

Text layer with layer styles

'ball' layer with drop shadow

Background image layer

Figure 30.20 Image parts, text and editing functions can all be separated and saved as individual layers that can be moved and edited independently. Image courtesy of www.ablestock.com.

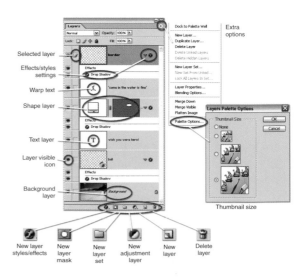

Selected layer

Effects/styles settings

Warp text

Shape layer

Text layer

Layer visible icon

Background layer

Dock to Palette Well
New Layer...
Duplicate Layer...
Delete Layer
Delete Linked Layers
Delete Hidden Layers

New Layer Set...
New Set From Linked...
Lock All Layers in Set...

Layer Properties...
Blending Options...

Merge Down
Merge Visible
Flatten Image

Palette Options...

Extra options

Layers Palette Options

Thumbnail Size
None

OK
Cancel

Thumbnail size

New layer styles/effects

New layer mask

New layer set

New adjustment layer

New layer

Delete layer

trying their hand at adding type to pictures.

Photoshop as well as Photoshop Elements provide the ability to input type directly onto the canvas rather than via a type dialog. This means that you can see and adjust your text to fit and suit the image beneath. As the text is stored on a separate layer to the rest of the picture, it can be moved and altered independent of the other image parts. Just like when you are using a word processing program, changes of size, shape and style can be made at

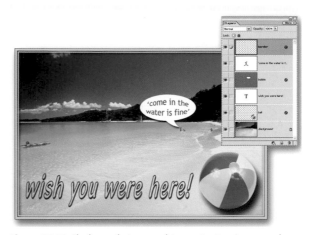

Figure 30.22 The layers that are used to construct an image can be viewed in two ways with Photoshop or Photoshop Elements. The main image window provides a preview of what the picture looks like with all the layers combined and the Layers palette shows each of the layers separated in a layer stack.

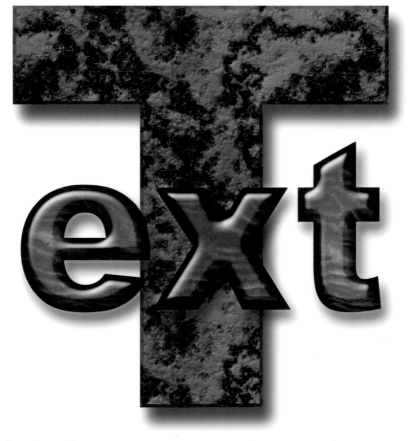

Figure 30.23 Current image editing programs like Elements have a range of sophisticated text features that not only allow you to add text to your pictures, but also control the way that the text looks.

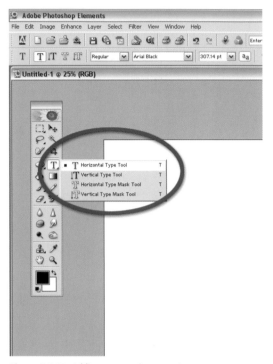

Figure 30.24 Adding text to pictures – 1.

any stage by selecting the text and applying the alterations.

1 Select the Type tool from the toolbox. There are two different versions to choose from – one produces horizontal type and the other vertical. Click on the picture surface at the point where you want the type to start. At this point, you can also choose the type style, font, color and size in the options bar (see Figure 30.24).

2 Enter the text using the keyboard. To begin a new line, press the Enter key. Click the OK button (shaped like a tick) in the options bar to complete the process (see Figure 30.25).

3 To add to the text later, select the Type tool, click next to the existing characters and continue typing (see Figure 30.26).

4 To change the font, style, color or size of the type, select the text and input the altered values in the

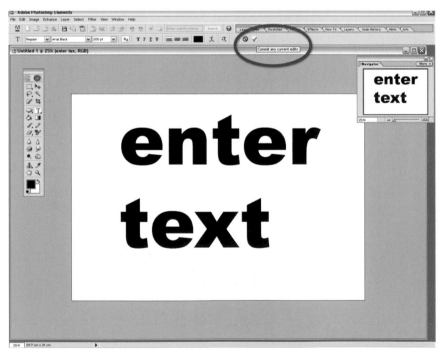

Figure 30.25 Adding text to pictures – 2.

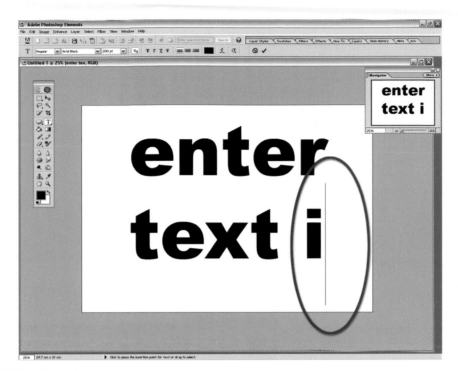

Figure 30.26 Adding text to pictures – 3.

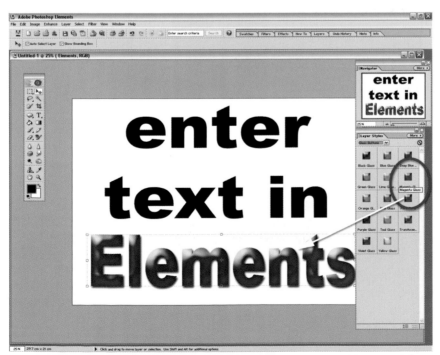

Figure 30.27 Adding text to pictures – 4.

options bar. To add fancy 3D styles and textures to the type, make sure the type layer is selected and then choose one of the Layer Styles options (see Figure 30.27).

31 Printing your digital files

It is one thing to be able to take great pictures with your digital camera and quite another to then produce fantastic photographic prints. With film-based photography, many photographers passed on the responsibility of making a print to their local photo store. In contrast, with the advance of the digital age the center of much digital print production sits squarely on the desk in the form of a tabletop printer.

The quality of the output from these devices continues to improve, as does the archival life of the prints they produce, but the first choice for many shooters for printing is still the local photo-

Table 31.1 Summary of the features of different methods of printing

	DIY desktop printing	Photo-lab printing
Set-up cost	Initial purchase of printer US $100–400	Nil
Cost per print	Moderate	Small
Ease	You will need a little instruction to get started	Very easy to use
Quality	Good	Good
Archival life	Good for some models, average for others	Good
Ability to change results to suit your own taste or ideas	Almost unlimited options to make user changes to how the print looks	Limited options or none
Convenience	Print whenever you want	Limited to shop hours, unless lab has online options

lab. Here, too, times are changing. Not only can they make prints from negatives, but also from digital camera cards and CD-roms.

The decision about whether you print your own, or have your pictures printed for you, is generally a personal one, based on ease and comfort as much as anything. A summary of the current state of play is given in Table 31.1.

If you opt to make your own prints, there are several different printer technologies that can turn your digital pictures into photographs. The most popular, at the moment, is the *inkjet* (or bubble jet) printer, followed by *dye sublimation* and *laser* machines.

The inkjet printer

Starting at a price of around US $50, the ink jet printer provides the cheapest way to enter the world of desktop printing. The ability of an inkjet printer to produce great photographs is based on the production of a combination of fineness of detail and seamless graduation of the color and tone. The machines contain a series of cartridges filled with liquid ink. The ink is forced through a set of tiny print nozzles using either heat or pressure. Different manufactures have slightly different systems, but all are capable of producing very small droplets of ink (some are four times smaller than the diameter of a human hair!). The printer head moves back and forth across the paper laying down color, whilst the roller mechanism gradually feeds the print through the machine. Newer models have multiple sets of nozzles that operate in both directions (bidirectional) to give faster print speeds (see Figure 31.1).

The most sophisticated printers from manufacturers like Canon, Epson and Hewlett Packard also have the ability to produce ink droplets that vary in size. This feature helps create the fine detail in photographic prints.

Most photographic quality printers have very high resolution, approaching 6000 dots per inch, which equates to pictures being created with very small ink droplets, and six or seven different ink colors, enabling these machines to produce the highest quality prints. These printers are often more expensive than standard models, but serious photographers will value the extra quality they are capable of (see Figure 31.2).

Printers optimized for business applications are often capable of producing prints faster than the photographic models. They usually only have three colors and black, and so do not produce photographic images with as much subtlety in tonal change as the special photo models.

One of the real advantages of inkjet printing technologies for digital photography is the

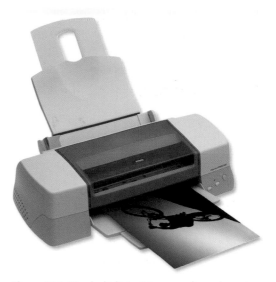

Figure 31.1 Standard inkjet printers use a four-color system containing cyan, magenta, yellow and black to produce color pictures.

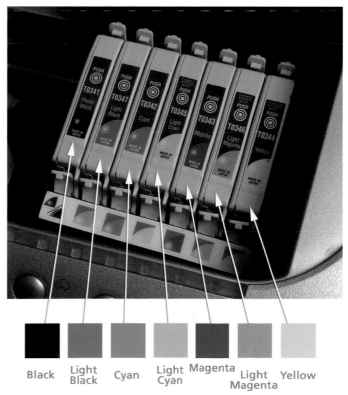

Black | Light Black | Cyan | Light Cyan | Magenta | Light Magenta | Yellow

Figure 31.2 Inkjet printers designed especially for photographic printing often contain five colors plus black, and some models can even print up to A3+ (bigger than A3).

7

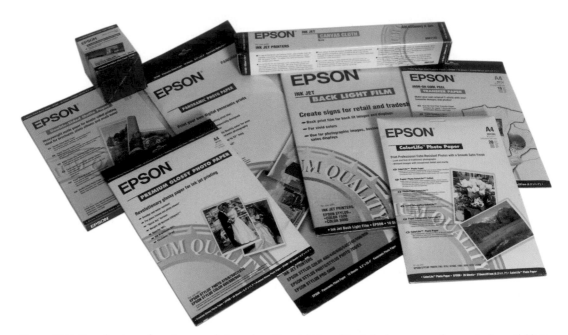

Figure 31.3 One advantage of creating your photographs with an inkjet machine is the large range of paper stocks available to print on.

choice of papers available for printing. Different surfaces (gloss, semi-gloss, matte, iron-on transfer, metallic, magnetic and even plastic), textures (smooth, watercolor and canvas), thickness (from 80 to 300 gsm) and sizes (A4, A3, 10 in × 8 in, 6 in × 4 in, panorama and even roll) can all be feed through the printer. This is not the case with laser, where the choice is limited in surface and thickness, or dye sublimation, where only the specialized paper supplied with the colored ribbons can be used (see Figure 31.3).

Before you start to print

Make sure that your printer is turned on and then with an image editing program open your photograph ready for printing. Select the Print option from the File menu (generally File > Print). This will open up the printer's control panel, often called the printer driver dialog. Check to see that the name of the printer is correctly listed in the Name box. If not, select the correct printer from the drop-down menu. Click on the properties button and choose the 'Main Tab'. Select the media type that matches your paper, the 'Color' option for photographic images and 'Automatic and Quality' settings in the mode section. These options automatically select the highest quality print settings for the paper type you are using. Click OK.

Now with your printer set for the paper, quality and type of print you require, let's output the first image.

Making your first digital print

With an image open in Photoshop or Photoshop Elements, open the Print Preview dialog (File > Print Preview). Check the thumbnail to ensure that the whole of the picture is located

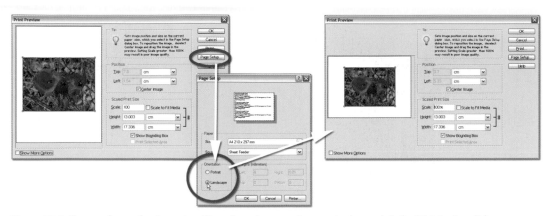

Figure 31.4 You can change the size and position of your image on its paper background via the Print Preview dialog.

within the paper boundaries. To change the paper's size or orientation, select the Page Setup and Printer Properties options. Whilst here, check the printer output settings are still set to the type of paper being used. Work your way back to the Print Preview dialog by clicking the OK buttons (see Figure 31.4). To alter the position or size of the picture on the page, deselect both Scale to Fit Media and Center Image options, and then select the Show Bounding Box feature. Change the image size by clicking and dragging the handles at the edge and corners of the image. Move the picture to a different position on the page by clicking on the picture surface and dragging the whole image to a different area (see Figure 31.5). To print, select the Print button and then the OK button.

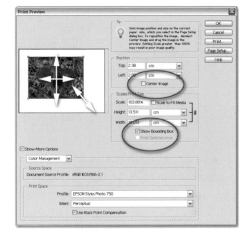

Figure 31.5 Change the size and position of the image on the page with the Print Preview dialog.

Summary steps

1 Select Print Preview (File > Print Preview) and click the Page Setup button. Check the printer Properties options are set to the paper type, page size and orientation, and print quality options that you require. Click OK to exit these dialogs and return to the Print Preview dialog (Figure 31.6).

2 At this stage you can choose to allow Photoshop or Elements to automatically center the image on the page (tick the Center Image box) and enlarge or reduce the picture so that it fits the page size selected (tick the Scale to Fit Media box) – see Figure 31.7.

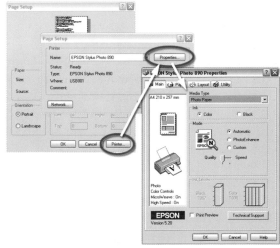

Figure 31.6 Making a digital print – 1.

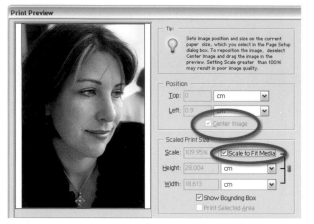

Figure 31.7 Making a digital print – 2.

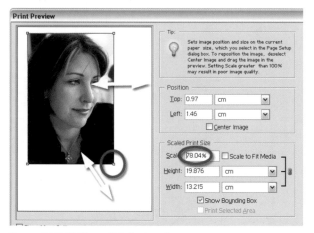

Figure 31.8 Making a digital print – 3.

3 Alternatively, you can adjust the position of the picture and its size manually by deselecting these options and ticking the 'Show Bounding Box' feature. To move the image, click inside the picture and drag to a new position. To change its size, click and drag one of the handles located at the corners of the bounding box. With all the settings complete, click Print to output your image (Figure 31.8).

Producing a digital contact sheet

Digital photographers are not afraid to shoot as much as they like because they know that they will only have to pay for the production of the very best of the images they take. Consequently, hard drives all over the country are filling up with thousands of pictures. Navigating this array of images can be quite difficult and many shooters still prefer to edit their photographs as prints rather than on screen. The people at Adobe must have understood this situation when they developed the Contact Print feature for Photoshop and Elements.

With one simple command, the imaging program creates a series of small thumbnail versions of all the images in a directory or folder. These

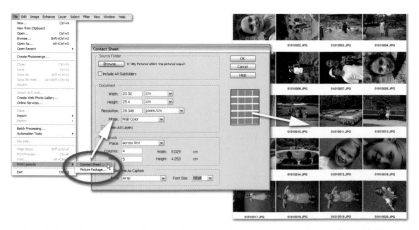

Figure 31.9 The Contact Sheet feature creates thumbnail versions of all the images within a selected folder or directory.

small pictures are then arranged on pages and labeled with their file names. From there, it is an easy task to print a series of contact sheets that can be kept as a permanent record of the folder's images. The job of selecting the best pictures to manipulate and print can then be made with hard copies of your images without having to spend the time and money to output every image to be considered (see Figure 31.9).

The options contained within the Contact Sheet dialog allow the user to select the folder where the images are stored, the page size, and to decide the size and the number of thumbnails that will be placed on this page (see Figure 31.10).

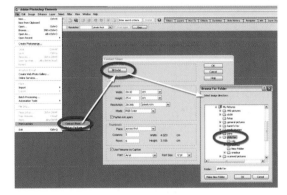

Figure 31.10 The options in the Contact Sheet dialog allow the user to select the image folder, the number of thumbnails per page and the final print size. (1) Images folder (source folder). (2) Print size and resolution (document details). (3) Thumbnail layout. (4) Caption details.

Summary steps

1 Select File > Print Layouts > Contact Sheet (Elements) or File > Automate > Contact Sheet (Photoshop) and use the Browse button to pick the folder or directory containing the images to be placed on the contact sheet (Figure 31.11).

2 In the *Document* area, input the values for width, height, resolution and mode of the finished contact sheet. In the *Thumbnails* section, select the Place or sequence used to layout the images, as well as the number of columns and rows of thumbnails per page. Keep in mind that the more images you have on each page, the smaller they will be. If the folder you selected contains more images than can fit on one page, Elements will automatically make new pages to accommodate the other thumbnails (Figure 31.12).

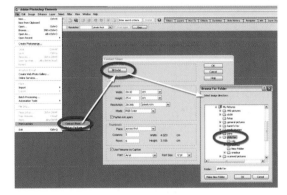

Figure 31.11 Producing a digital contact sheet – 1.

3 In the final section you can elect to place a file name, printed as a caption, under each image. The size and font family used for the captions can also be chosen here. Click OK to make the contact sheet (Figure 31.13).

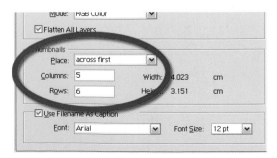

Figure 31.12 Producing a digital contact sheet – 2.

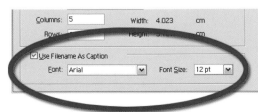

Figure 31.13 Producing a digital contact sheet – 3.

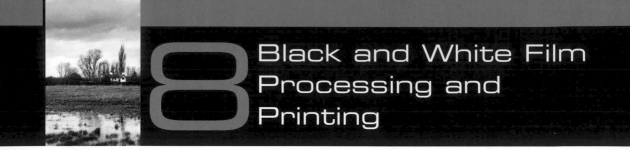

8 Black and White Film Processing and Printing

Doing your own film processing and printing gives you much more control over your results than passing them over to the local laboratory. You probably won't save money, but mastering the skills is enjoyable and will allow you to produce prints just the way you want them to look. This grows more important the further you progress in your photography – aiming for your own style of pictures or perhaps tackling specialized subjects beyond the range of the average commercial laboratory.

By far the best way to start is to process black and white film and make black and white prints (by contact and by enlargement). This will get you familiar with handling chemicals and setting up and working in a darkroom. Later, you can progress to the extra challenge of judging color test prints and working in the near darkness of a color printing darkroom.

32 Processing a film

Processing black and white negatives is in many ways like cooking – you use liquids, and have to control time and temperature quite carefully. You also need some basic equipment. The ten most important items are (see Figure 32.1):

1 *35 mm film-end retrieving tool.* Used to extract the first inch or so of film if wound fully into the cassette, so it can be prepared for tank loading (see Figure 32.2 for the precise steps involved).
2 *Light-tight plastic tank containing a reel.* You push or wind your film into the spiral groove of the reel in the dark; the whole length is held only along its edges, with each turn slightly separated from the next so that processing solutions act evenly over its entire surface. Each solution is poured in through a light-proof hole in the tank lid. You block off the hole and invert the tank at set intervals to agitate the solutions; some tanks have a plastic rod to rotate the reel for the same purpose.

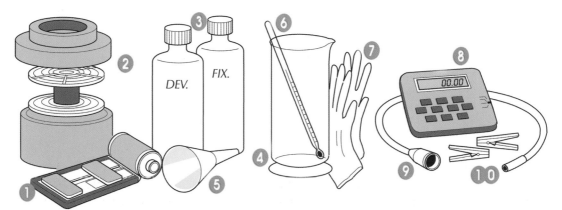

Figure 32.1 Basic equipment for processing film (see text for definitions of numbered items).

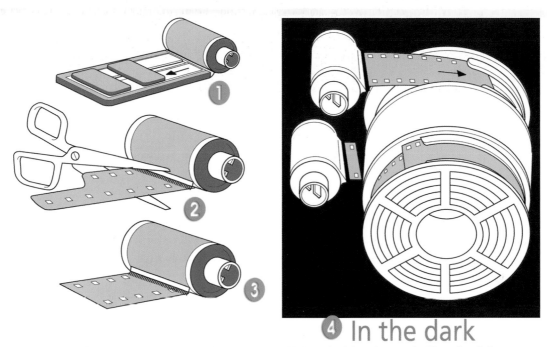

In the dark

Figure 32.2 (Left) Retrieving and trimming the film end, in normal lighting. (Right) Loading into the film reel, in darkness.

3 *Bottles containing developer and fixing solutions*. Start off by using the developer recommended on your film's packing slip. A standard fine-grain developer such as Ilford ID11 or Kodak D76 (made up from powder) is a good choice. You can also buy most developers in liquid concentrate form, which are quicker and easier to prepare. Made-up developer can be stored for weeks in a stoppered container. The acid hardener fixing solution is simpler and cheaper, and is also known by its main constituent 'hypo' (sodium thiosulfate). Unused fixer keeps indefinitely. Never let developer and fixer mix, because they will neutralize each other.

4 *Measure graduate*. A plastic measuring graduate holding sufficient solution to fill your tank.

5 *Funnel*. A plastic funnel for re-bottling solutions.

6 *Thermometer*. A photographic thermometer clearly scaled from about 13°C (55°F) to 24°C (75°F).

7 *Thin plastic gloves* for handling chemicals (see the safe handling recommendations in Appendix O before using any chemicals).

8 *A minute timer*.

9 *A flexible plastic tube* for ducting wash water down into your tank through the lid hole.

10 *Plastic pegs* to attach to the top and bottom of your processed film when it is finally hung up to dry on a nylon cord.

Loading the tank

Before you try using a tank for the first time, practice loading with a scrap film, or an unwanted (and uncut) length of negatives. Do this first in the light, then with your eyes closed, then in a darkened room. It's important not to force and buckle the film during loading, or you may get results as shown on page 119. The shaped tongue must be cut off the front end of the film to give a square shape for loading. If necessary, use a retrieving tool to slip into the cassette without fogging film (Figure 32.2, step 1). Having pulled out the tip, you can then do your trimming in the light (Figure 32.2, steps 2 and 3).

The stage after this – winding a whole exposed film into the reel – only takes a few minutes but must be done in total darkness.

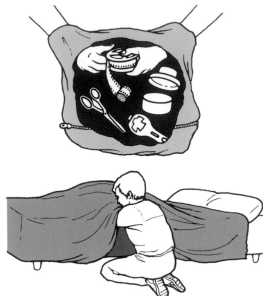

Figure 32.3 A changing bag (top) or just using your bed (bottom) saves having a darkened room.

If you don't have a darkroom use a large cupboard. It is also possible to untuck one side of your bed, pushing your hands in deep under the blankets in between the sheets. Alternatively, buy a light-proof 'changing bag' (Figure 32.3), which pushes onto your arms. Feed film in direct from the cassette (as shown in Figure 32.2, step 4) or use a cassette or bottle opener to take off one end and withdraw the spool of film. The actual way the film slides into the reel grooves depends upon your particular make of tank. Some are cranked in, others just pushed. As soon as the whole film is loaded, place the reel in the empty tank and fit on the lid. After this point you can then do all your processing in ordinary lighting.

Using the solutions

The various stages and typical times of processing are shown in Figure 32.4. Developer solution, waiting in the graduate at the recommended temperature (normally 20°C), is poured into the tank and the clock

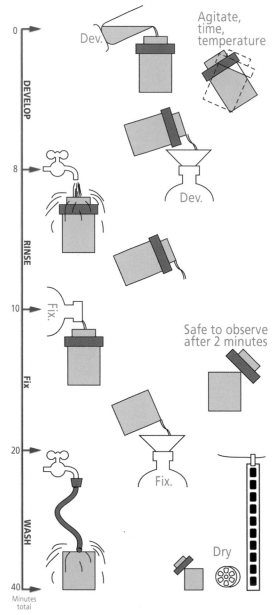

Figure 32.4 Film processing, stage by stage.

started. The time required depends upon the developer and type of black and white film you are processing. The hotter the developer, the faster it will work. Conversely, developer that is cool will take longer to process the negatives. It is critical for you to measure the temperature of the developer and then use the time/temperature/film chart (usually supplied with the developer or film) to calculate the length of time that your specific film must be processed. In addition, you must regularly agitate the solution to avoid streaky development, typically by gently inverting the tank several times during the first 30 seconds, and then for 5 seconds every half minute. At the end of development time you pour the solution out through the light-tight tank top. It is either poured away (if one-shot only) or returned to its bottle for reuse.

Although you cannot yet look, inside the tank the creamy surface of your film now carries a black image corresponding to where it received light in the camera. For the next step, which is rinse, you fill the tank to overflowing with water and immediately empty it again. Repeat this process at least five times. This helps to remove developer from the film (alternatively use 'stop bath' solution, which halts development faster).

Now fixer solution is poured into the tank and initially agitated. Fixer temperature is less critical than developer – room temperature is adequate. The fixer turns creamy silver halides unaffected by development into colorless compounds that can later be washed out of the film. Generally, but depending on your film and developer type, you will need to immerse you film in the fixer solution for about 10 minutes, but after 1–2 minutes most of the film's milkiness will have cleared and you can remove the tank top without having light affect your results. When the film has finished its fixing time, the solution is returned to its bottle.

Next, a 20-minute wash in cold water removes all remaining unwanted chemicals and you can remove the processed film from the reel and carefully hang it up to dry, with a peg attached to each end. A few drops of photographic 'wetting agent' in the final wash water will help the film dry evenly. Always hold film by its edges only. Once it has fully dried, cut it into convenient strips of five or six negatives and immediately protect these in sleeves made for the purpose (see Figure 32.5).

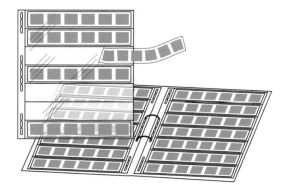

Figure 32.5 Sleeved pages hold strips of processed 35 mm negatives and fit into a ring binder.

Film processing faults

Don't put the fixer in first – this will destroy all your pictures! Check temperatures before and during development, and be careful with timing, otherwise it is easy to under- or overdevelop (see Figure 32.6). Avoid putting finger-marks or splashes of any kind on your film – remember too that the film surface is easily damaged by scratches, dust and hairs when drying.

If your film is clear with no images, check to see if edge printing is present. If the information is there you have either processed an unused film or the camera was faulty – shutter not opening or film not winding on. If the edge data is not present, the fault is almost certainly processing. Perhaps the developer was totally exhausted or solutions used in the wrong order.

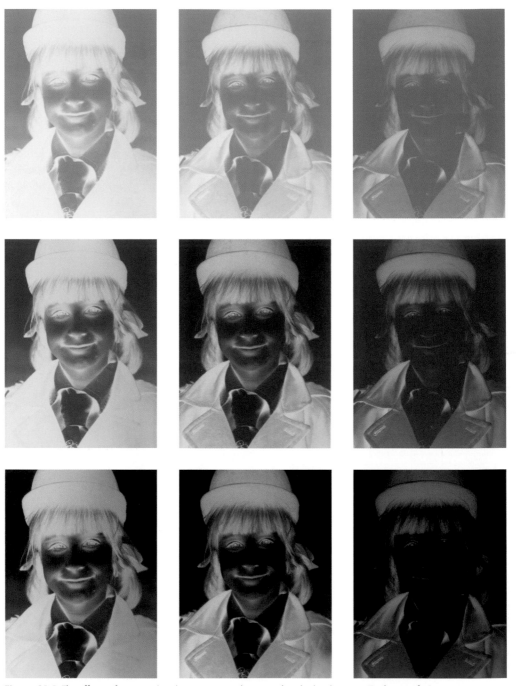

Figure 32.6 The effects of over- and underexposure, and over- and underdevelopment. For key see facing page.

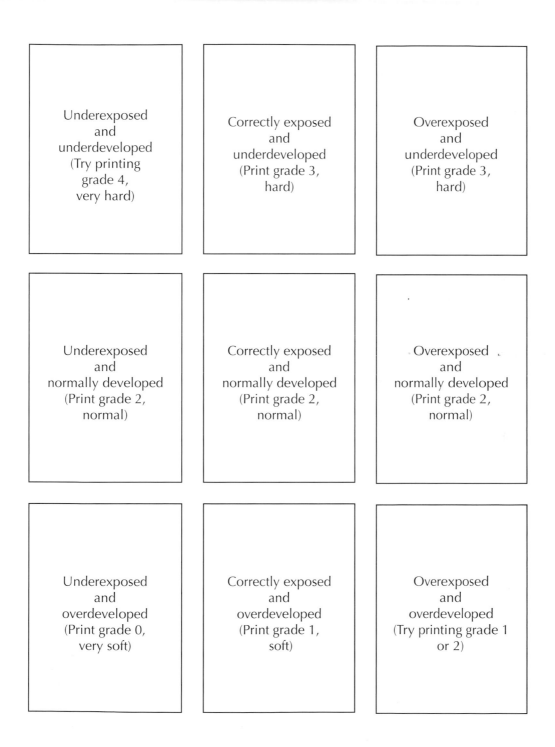

Underexposed
and
underdeveloped
(Try printing
grade 4,
very hard)

Correctly exposed
and
underdeveloped
(Print grade 3,
hard)

Overexposed
and
underdeveloped
(Print grade 3,
hard)

Underexposed
and
normally developed
(Print grade 2,
normal)

Correctly exposed
and
normally developed
(Print grade 2,
normal)

Overexposed
and
normally developed
(Print grade 2,
normal)

Underexposed
and
overdeveloped
(Print grade 0,
very soft)

Correctly exposed
and
overdeveloped
(Print grade 1,
soft)

Overexposed
and
overdeveloped
(Try printing grade 1
or 2)

Film that is still creamy has not been fully fixed; further fixing time, or change to fresh fixer, will probably result in good negatives. Patches of uneven tone usually mean uneven development. Perhaps adjacent coils of film touched each other in the reel. Dark crescent-shaped marks (Figure 32.7) and kinks or creases in the film itself are due to rough handling. The film was most likely buckled after removal from its cassette, when you were trying to load the reel in the dark.

Most of the time, however, faults are concerned with negatives that are a bit too dark ('dense') or too pale ('thin'). At first, it is difficult to tell whether, say, a thin negative is due to underexposure or insufficient development. Of course, if every picture on your film looks thin, the fault was probably development – although it could also be the ISO rating having been incorrectly set on the camera.

As Figure 32.6 shows, though, an underexposed negative is characteristically transparent and empty of detail in subject shadow areas, such as the girl's hair. A correctly exposed but underdeveloped negative (top center) shows more detail here, but looks generally weak and gray ('flat'). A dense negative due only to overexposure records the subject's lightest parts as so solid that finer details are destroyed. Notice how shadows have ample detail, though. Overdevelopment instead gives a negative that is contrasty and 'bright' – dense in highlights but carrying little more shadow detail than a correctly developed film.

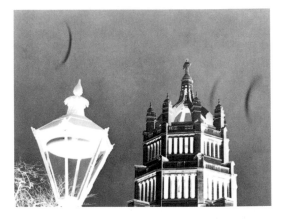

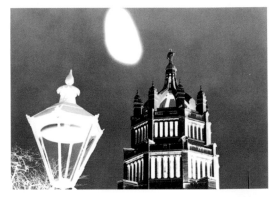

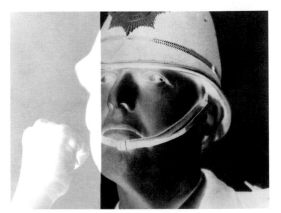

Figure 32.7 Processing faults. (Top) Dark, crescent-shaped kink marks. (Center) Undeveloped clear patch, where this part of the film remained in contact with another. (Bottom) All negatives throughout the film show part of the picture pale. The cause is probably insufficient developer in the tank.

33 Contact printing

Film processing does not really require a darkroom, but before you can print or enlarge your negatives you will have to organize yourself some kind of blacked-out room to work in. This might have to be the family bathroom, quickly adapted for the evening (see Figure 33.2). Maybe you can convert a spare

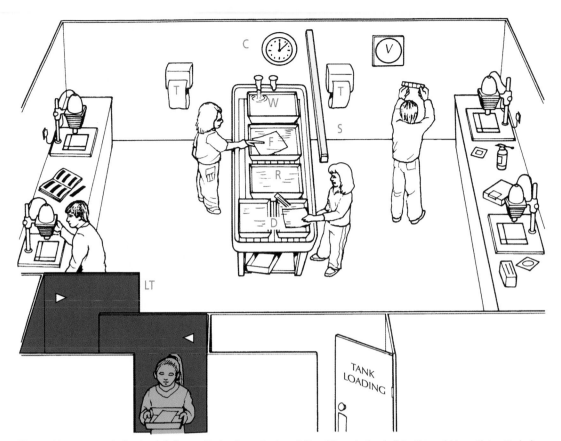

Figure 33.1 Purpose-built school darkroom. D, developer; R, rinse; F, fixer; W, wash; S, safe light; T, towel; V, ventilator; C, clock with large second hand; LT, light trap.

room, or perhaps you are lucky enough to have use of a communal darkroom designed for the purpose at a school or club, as shown in Figure 33.1.

The darkroom

The most important features to consider when you are planning a darkroom are:

- blackout;
- ventilation;
- water supply; and
- electricity.

Excluding the light

Existing windows have to be blocked off – either temporarily using thick black plastic sheeting or paper, or more permanently with hardboard. Alternatively, buy a fabric roller blind blackout. As

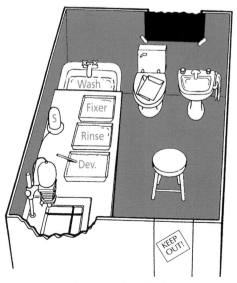

Figure 33.2 Darkroom in adapted bathroom (S, safe light).

long as you have kept out unwanted white light, the walls of the room can be quite pale toned – a matt white finish helps to reflect around the colored illumination from your safe light, designed not to affect the photographic paper.

Ventilation

Working alone for an hour in the darkroom you may not find the air too stuffy, but for groups working for longer times you need a light-tight air extractor fan (V). A communal darkroom also needs a light trap (LT) instead of a door. This helps the circulation of air and makes it easy for people to enter or leave without disturbing others. Wall surfaces inside the light trap are painted matt black, to reduce reflections.

Water supply

In the bathroom, use the bath to wash prints and the hand basin to rinse your hands, free of chemicals. The permanent darkroom has a large, flat-bottomed PVC sink to hold trays for processing solutions, and a tank or tray for print washing. Always separate the wet stages of darkroom work from 'dry' work, such as handling the enlarger and packets of paper. In the larger darkroom, each activity can take place on different sides of the room.

Electricity

Take special care over your electricity supply, needed for the enlarger and safe light, because electricity and water can be a lethal combination. Never let wires or switches come into contact with water or wet hands. Take your supply from a three-pin socket, and include a circuit-breaker of the type sold for garden tools. Metal parts of your enlarger or safe light should be connected to the earth wire ('grounded'). This is especially important in any board-over-the-bath bench arrangement. Take out any temporary wiring as soon as you have finished work, even though you intend to return within a few hours.

Equipment for contact printing
Print processing

Most of the items necessary for contact printing are shown below (Figure 33.3). You need at least three plastic trays (1) big enough for your prints – 12 in ×10 in is a good size. One is for

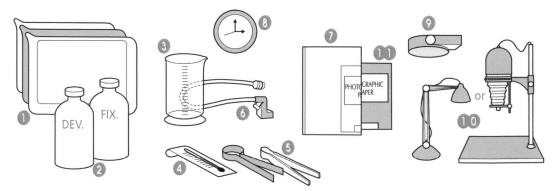

Figure 33.3 Basic equipment for contact printing. See text for explanation of numbered items.

developer, one for rinsing and washing, and the other for fixing. Print developer (2) is similar to, but much faster-acting than, negative developer. It comes as a concentrated solution, diluted just before use and discarded after your printing session. The fixer is a less concentrated form of negative fixer, and can be reused.

You also need the measuring graduate (3) used for films and a photographic tray thermometer (blue spirit or LCD with red display). The thermometer (4) stays in the developer tray to tell you if the solution is too warm or cold. Plastic tongs (5) – one for developer, the other only for fixer – allow you to keep your hands out of solutions. A washing hose (6) connects the cold water tap to the rinse tray and turns it into a print washing device. Have a clock (8) to time minutes during processing and (if you have no enlarger timer) seconds during exposure.

Suitable orange lighting is permissible in the printing darkroom (7), as black and white paper is not sensitive to this color. You can buy a bench or hanging safe light (9), which contains a 25-watt bulb behind dyed glass, or use a fluorescent strip light with a special colored sleeve (10). The safe light is positioned near the developer tray (Figure 33.1) but no closer than specified, usually 1 m (3 ft).

Exposing equipment

To expose your contact print you need an even patch of white light, which will shine through the negatives laid out on the paper. You could use a reading lamp fitted with a 15-watt bulb, but as an enlarger will be needed later for making bigger prints of individual negatives, this can conveniently provide your contact printing light. All you have to do at this stage is raise it to a height where it provides a large enough patch of light for your print, as shown in Figure 33.4.

The negative strips can be held down in tight contact with the light-sensitive printing paper during exposure by a sheet of thick glass. Better still, buy a proper contact printing frame – glass with thin plastic grooves on its underside to hold the film, and hinged to a baseboard.

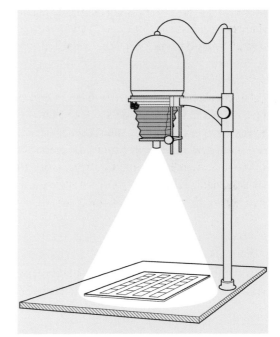

Figure 33.4 Using an enlarger to give a patch of light for exposing a contact print.

The light-sensitive paper

Most black and white photographic paper is known as bromide paper (due to the silver bromide used in its light-sensitive emulsion). It comes in different sizes, surfaces and types of base, and is available in either grades of contrast or the more popular multi-contrast variety. The 10 in × 8 in size just accommodates seven strips of five 35 mm negatives. Start off with a packet this size of glossy, resin-coated (RC), multigrade paper. You will also need a set of simple enlarger filters to adjust the contrast of the paper.

Printing a contact sheet

It is best to make a contact print from every film you shoot. This way you have a visual file of all your pictures from which to choose the ones to enlarge. Prepare the solutions in their trays and bring the developer to its recommended temperature (usually about 20°C). Now you can change the lighting in your darkroom to safe lighting and open your packet of paper. Position one sheet, glossy side upwards, under the switched off enlarger and re-close the packet. Lay out your negatives in rows on the paper with their emulsion (dull) side downwards. Have all the edge numbers running the same way – it is irritating later to discover one row of pictures upside down. Then cover over the negatives with the glass.

Insert a grade 2 (normal contrast) filter into the enlarger lamphouse. Then, with the enlarger near the top of its column and the lens two f settings 'stopped down' from widest aperture (usually about f8), give a trial exposure of about 20 seconds (see Figure 33.6). Remove the glass

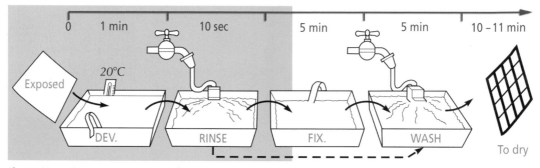

Figure 33.5 Print processing, RC paper. (Rinse tray does double duty as wash.)

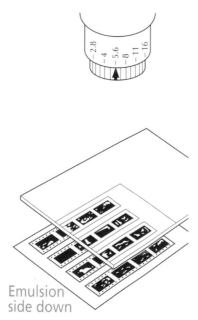

Figure 33.6 Stop down the lens for the first trial exposure.

and put your negatives carefully to one side. As shown in Figure 33.5, slide the exposed sheet of paper smoothly under the surface of the developer. Note the time on the clock and rock the tray gently to keep the paper fully submerged. Magically, the shapes of the frames on your film appear on the paper, then the pictures themselves – growing darker and stronger all the time. But keep one eye on the clock and remove the print when its recommended development time is up (typically 1 minute at 20°C for RC paper).

Maintain the same time in the developer for each successive print no matter how fast or slowly the print darkens – in the printing process you alter the results by exposure, and always keep development consistent. The print next has a quick rinse (approximately 30 seconds in running water) and goes face down into the fixer tray. Full fixing generally takes about 5 minutes, although after 1 minute or so you can switch on normal lighting. In the example (Figure 33.7), the exposure given is correct for most pictures on the sheet.

If results were too dark, you would give a shorter exposure time (less than the original 20 seconds) or reduce the lens aperture (change to a bigger aperture number); if too pale, increase exposure time (more than 20 seconds) or widen the aperture (change to a smaller aperture number).

Prints can be allowed to accumulate in the fixer – for up to half an hour if necessary – before you put them to wash as a batch. Washing also takes about 5 minutes, but keep separating the prints now and again, and prevent any floating face upwards to the surface, where washing will be ineffective. After

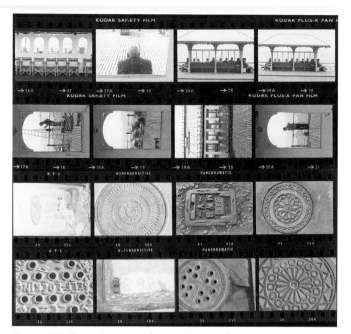

Figure 33.7 The result – correct for most, but not all, pictures.

washing, sponge off surplus water from the front and back surfaces and dry your print by pegging it on a line or laying it out on photo blotting paper. RC plastic paper dries quickly, but the process can be hastened with warmed air from a hair drier.

Often, you find that when exposure is correct for some pictures on the sheet it is too much or too little for others. This occurs because of the way that your original negatives vary. This difference is evident in Figure 33.7, where the four frames at the bottom left are underexposed. The easiest way to solve the problem would be for you to make two sets of contacts, one exposed for dark pictures, one for light. But better still, you can use a shaped card (Figure 33.8) to give 50 per cent extra exposure time to this corner of the sheet. Figure 33.9 shows the improvement that this extra light makes. Note also that an ordinary wooden ruler is about the same width as 35 mm film. You can cover up individual rows or ends of rows of pictures by laying rulers on top of the glass, and then remove them according to the exposure times required.

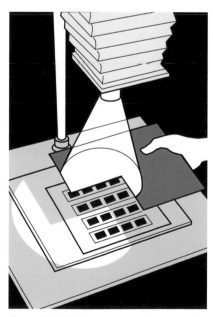

Figure 33.8 Shading to correct unevenness in the set of contact prints.

Color negatives can be contact printed to give black and white results in just the same way as monochrome negatives, but often need about two to three times the exposure (see also the section on photograms).

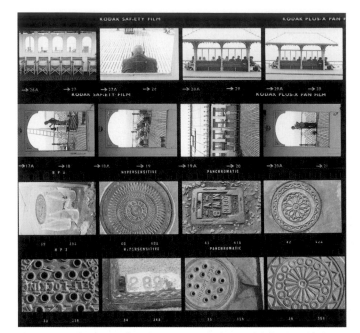

Figure 33.9 The corrected reprint. Compare the bottom left frames with those in Figure 33.7.

Drying prints

The simplest way to dry your washed prints is to first wipe off surplus water with a sponge or a flat (window-cleaning type) squeegee. Then peg them on a line, or lay them face up either on clean photo blotting paper or a fiber-glass drying screen or muslin stretched on a frame (see Figure 33.10). Special hot-air driers are made that accept RC black and white paper and all color papers. They give you dry results in a few seconds, but even when left at room temperature these plastic papers will dry within about 15 minutes.

If you have made black and white prints on fiber-based

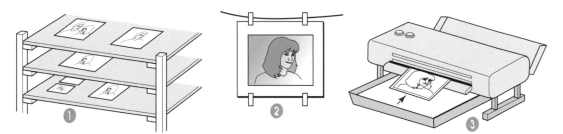

Figure 33.10 Drying prints by muslin rack (1), line and peg (2) or hot-air RC drier (3).

paper, which is more like drawing paper, peg them up in pairs back to back to avoid curling. Never attempt to put fiber paper through an RC drier. A few drier/glazers are designed for fiber-based printing papers. Don't try glazing RC papers of any kind – the face of your prints will become stuck to the equipment! Glossy RC paper air dries with a shiny finish.

When the print is dry, number your contact sheet on the back with the same reference number you put on your set of negatives. Check carefully to see which images are sharp enough to enlarge, what people's expressions look like, whether the composition works, and so on. Using grease pencil drawn on the print surface, mark up your best shots, showing possible cropping (see Figure 33.11). As you will probably be checking these contacts in the darkroom, don't use pencil marks in a color (reds or oranges) that makes them invisible under safe lighting. If you have several very similar images in your contacts, double-check the edge number to ensure you put the negative that you selected into the enlarger.

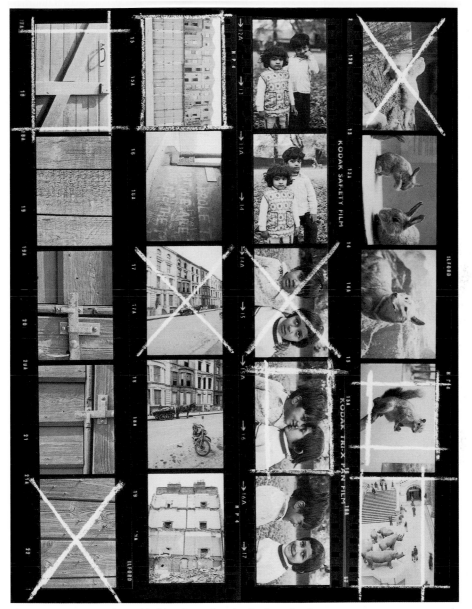

Figure 33.11 Contact sheet with shots chosen for enlarging framed up in wax crayon.

34 Enlarging

Making an enlargement reveals details and gives an impression of 'depth' to your pictures that is lost in a small print. During enlarging you can decide to exclude parts of the negative in order to improve composition, darken or lighten chosen local areas of the picture, and juggle with contrast and density so that (within limits) you can compensate for negatives that are slightly dark (overexposed) or pale (underexposed). It is even possible to construct pictures with the enlarger, by combining parts of different negatives into one print.

The 35 mm enlarger

Up to now, the enlarger has just been a handy source of light for contact printing, but before making enlargements you need to understand it in more detail. Basically, an enlarger is like a slide projector, although it has a much less powerful lamp and is attached to a vertical stand. Inside, to ensure that your negative is evenly illuminated, the light first passes down through large condenser lenses, or a plastic diffusing screen. The negative itself is held flat, its dull (emulsion) side downwards, between two halves of a carrier having a rectangular cut-out the size of one film frame. Alternatively, some models have two sheets of glass in the carrier that sandwiches the negative to keep it in place. The negative carrier pushes into a slot in the enlarger just below the condensers or diffuser.

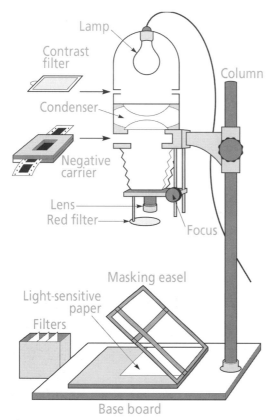

Below the negative is a lens (typically 50 mm focal length), which you can move up or down to focus a sharp image on the enlarger baseboard. Adjustable bellows prevent the escape of any light between carrier and lens. An enlarging lens needs no shutter but has an adjustable aperture, usually scaled in f-numbers. As is the case with our camera lenses, changing from one f-number to another doubles or halves the amount of light, which in turn alters the brightness of the image. (As you can feel and hear the position of each setting by a 'click', it is unnecessary to keep peering at numbers.)

Your enlarger may also contain a filter drawer in the lamphouse, as Figure 34.1 shows, to accept contrast-changing filters for variable

Figure 34.1 Parts of a (condenser) enlarger.

contrast ('multigrade') paper. Alternatively, a filter holder can be attached to the lens or you can 'dial-in' colored filtration using the dials at the top of the enlarger head.

The whole enlarger head can be moved up or down a firm metal column and locked at any height to control the size of enlargement. On the base board, you will need to place a masking easel, which has a white base surface and a hinged frame with adjustable metal strips. You can move the easel around to compose your enlargement, adjusting the side-strips to give a picture of the chosen size and proportions. During exposure, the bromide paper is held down flat and correctly positioned under the strips on all four sides. The strips also prevent light reaching the paper and so give your enlargement neat white borders. Avoid holding paper down by glass – this upsets sharpness and may introduce dust specks and scratch marks.

If possible, have an enlarging exposure timer – a clock-based switch that plugs in between enlarger and power supply. You set the estimated number of seconds needed, press a button and the lamp switches on for a duration of exactly this time. Another useful aid is a focusing magnifier. This is a tool used to magnify a small part of the image to help fine-tune the print focus. You place this on the masking easel and look through it whilst focusing the enlarger.

The printing paper

For making enlargement prints, you use the same type of light-sensitive paper as for contact printing. In other words, it can have a plastic RC base and so be a fast processing type that uses the same process as outlined in Figure 33.5. Or you might prefer a fiber-based paper (better for mounting and retouching, but less readily available and slower to process and dry). The surface may be glossy or semi-matt (again better for any additional handwork later).

Contrast

You can control the contrast of your enlargement – normal, hard (more contrast), soft (less contrast) – in two ways. Either buy packets of graded paper – grade 1 (soft), grade 2 (normal) and grade 3 (hard), or instead use one packet of variable contrast or 'multigrade' paper and buy a range of filters to tint the enlarger light for each of the different grade effects. Using graded papers means you must buy several packets at once and it can mean that you may run out of a particular grade right when it is needed. 'Multigrade' paper is therefore a more economical approach (once you have bought your multi-contrast filters). In addition, you can make prints that differ in contrast between one chosen part and another (see page 199).

Making a test print

Start by picking a negative that has plenty of detail and a good range of tones (see Figure 34.2). Set the masking frame for the size of paper you are using. Position the negative dull side downwards so that the shot you want to enlarge fills the cut-out part of the carrier. Check that there is no dust on the film surface (a can of compressed air is useful here) and then insert your negative into the enlarger. Fit a grade 2 filter (normal contrast) if

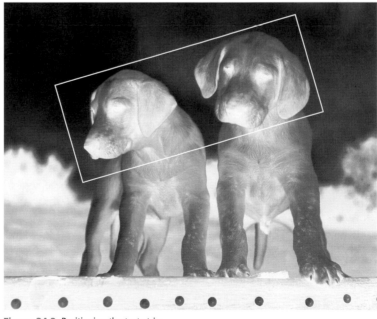

Figure 34.2 Positioning the test strip.

Test strip production

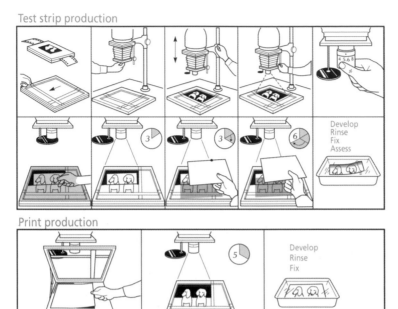

Print production

Figure 34.3 Enlarging. (Top sequence) Making an exposure test strip (see result in Figure 34.4). (Bottom row) Making the final enlargement (see Figure 34.5).

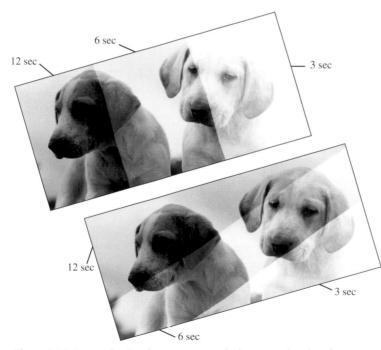

6 sec

12 sec

3 sec

12 sec

3 sec

6 sec

Figure 34.4 Processed series of test exposures – the bottom version gives the most information.

you are using multigrade paper. Open the lens aperture fully. Switch on the enlarger and change the darkroom from ordinary light to safe lighting. You can now visually focus the projected image on the white easel surface, making further adjustment to enlarger height if necessary until the picture is exactly the size you want, and sharp. Close down the lens aperture by about two clicks (three clicks if the negative is pale, or one if rather dark). Switch off the enlarger.

Cut or tear part of a sheet of your printing paper to form a test strip, and lay it face upwards on the easel, where it will receive an important part of the image (the puppies' heads in Figure 34.2). Now, by shading with a piece of card, give the paper three different exposure times, in strips as shown in Figure 34.3. Carefully decide the most informative way for each strip of exposure to run. Don't arrange them like the top test strip in Figure 34.4, which only shows you how the longest exposure affects one puppy and the shortest exposure the

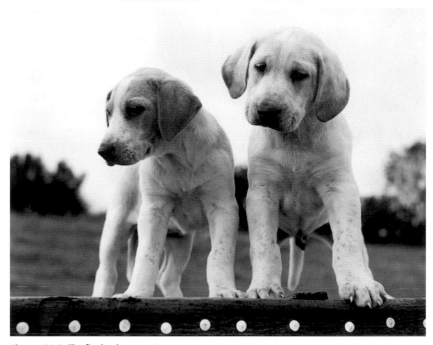

Figure 34.5 The final enlargement.

other. Instead, by making each band run lengthways, it allows you to discover how much each exposure time affects the tone of both the dogs.

To get this result, the whole test piece of paper was first given 3 seconds. Then, holding thick card an inch or so above it, two-thirds of the paper received 3 seconds more. Finally, the card was shifted to give the final third another 6 seconds. The combined effect was therefore to give strips of 3, 6 and 12 seconds. By holding the card quite still, a noticeable line of tonal change records on the print, which helps you pick out the different exposure bands when you judge results.

The test strip is processed in the same way as the contact sheet on the previous pages. You can then switch on normal lighting to decide which is the best exposure. If all three strips are too pale, make a further test using longer exposure times, or a wider lens aperture. In the example picture, an exposure time of about 7 seconds was judged correct for the puppies. So next a whole sheet was given this exposure, and when processed, produced the result shown in Figure 34.5.

Controls in printing

If you look along the middle row of pictures in Figures 34.6–34.17, you see what happens when a normal contrast negative is printed onto different contrast grades of paper. On grade 1 paper (or multigrade paper printed through a grade 1 filter) you get more grays between pure black and white than when using grade 3 paper (or a grade 3 filter on multigrade paper). Grade 1 is your best choice when you are printing a contrasty negative like the one in the bottom row. Similarly, you might use grade 3 for a flat, low-contrast negative. In other words, the contrast grade (or filter) of the paper compensates for negative contrast. Although not shown here, you can buy other graded papers or use further filters for multigrade paper, to give more extreme grades 0 or 5.

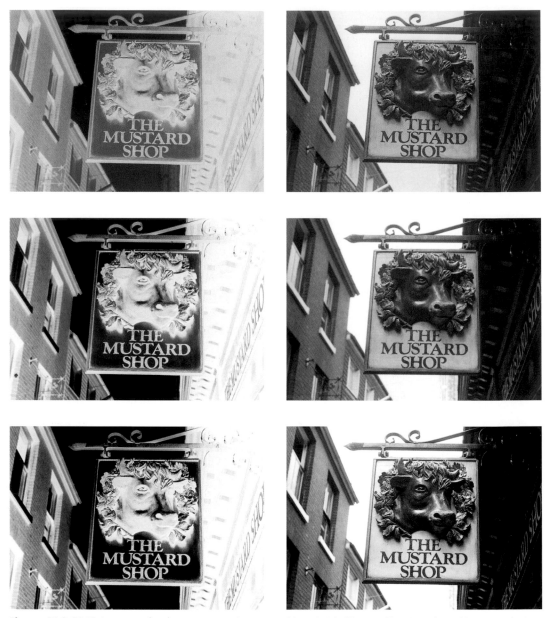

Figures 34.6–34.17 Low, normal and contrasty negatives printed onto:

(a) grade 1 (soft) paper; filter 0 or 1 for multi-contrast paper

To get the best out of a set of negatives, expect to use at least three different contrast grades, or filters. Even with the most accurate film processing the range of subjects recorded on any one film means that differences in lighting and the subjects themselves are bound to result in negatives of differing contrasts. The usual way to decide which grade to use is by simply examining the contrast of the image projected on the white surface of your masking easel, and comparing it with how previous negatives have printed.

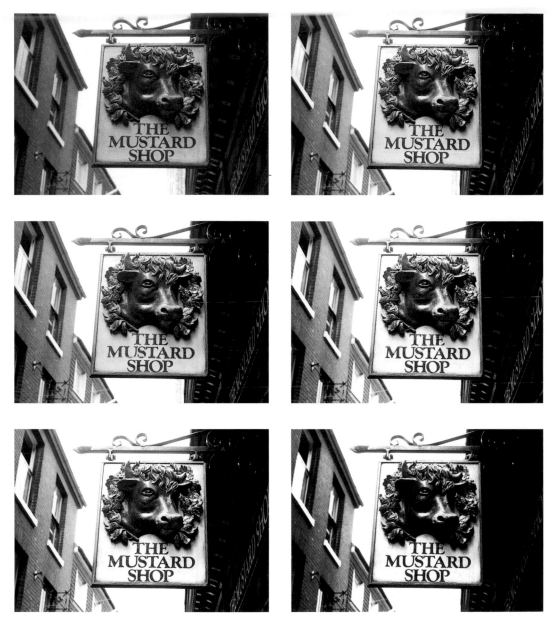

(b) grade 2 (normal) paper; filter 2 or 3 for multi-contrast paper

(c) grade 3 (hard) paper; filter 4 or 5 for multi-contrast paper

Don't expect miracles, however, when your film exposing technique has been faulty. Very pale and flat negatives caused by underexposure and underdevelopment, and dark negatives caused by overexposure and overdevelopment, are both too lacking in shadow or highlight details respectively to be correctable by any contrast grade in printing.

Another reason for grades is to intentionally distort contrast. This may just be to give extra 'punch' and emphasis to a picture. Though the contrast in these types of pictures is not strictly 'correct', relative to the actual subject, manipulation of contrast can help to emphasize both shape and pattern in the final image.

Printing-in and shading

Since a longer exposure gives a darker print, it is possible to give extra exposure time to just part of the paper where you want to darken your picture. You can use this 'printing-in' technique to bring up detail in a pale sky, as in Figure 34.19. Of course, such details have to be present in the negative in the first place, but often cloud information is quite dense on the film and the sky records as white paper when you give your whole print correct exposure for ground details. Figure 34.18 was given a 10-second exposure all over. Figure 34.19 had the same exposure but then the sky alone was exposed for a further 12 seconds while an opaque card prevented light reaching the landscape portion of the picture.

Unlike the making of test strips, you do not normally want a sharp-edged line to show where change of exposure has taken place. So, while you are printing-in, blur the line by keeping the card continuously on the move and holding it nearer to the lens than to your paper

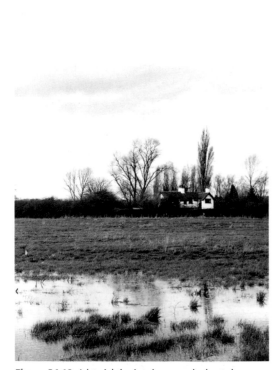

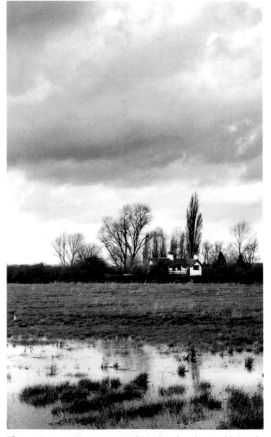

Figure 34.18 A 'straight' print shows washed out sky, although the land detail is reasonably correct.

Figure 34.19 The same negative printed with an additional 12 seconds given to the sky (totalling 22 seconds here) prints in missing detail.

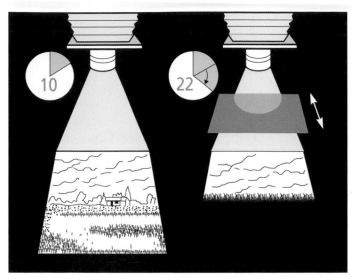

Figure 34.20 Printing-in sky detail.

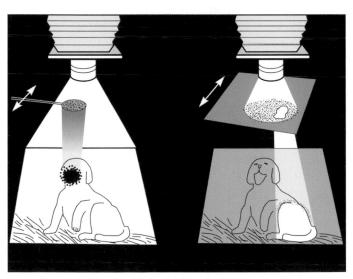

Figure 34.21 Shading with a 'dodger' (left) and printing-in using a hole in a card (right).

(see Figure 34.20). If you use multigrade paper it's also possible to change filters between the main and printed-in parts of the exposure. In this way, landscape ground information can be printed with grade 2 contrast, but dense, low-contrast sky detail can be emphasized by being printed in grade 4.

Printing-in, or 'burning-in' as it is sometimes called, an entire sky is a useful technique, but you will more often want to darken some relatively small, isolated part of a picture – the over-lit side of a face perhaps, or the window part of a room interior. The best way to do this is to add your printing-in exposure with a card carrying a hole about the size of a small coin.

For the opposite effect – making an isolated central area paler, or 'dodging' – use a small disc of card taped to a thin but rigid piece of wire. You can then push this 'dodger' into the enlarger light beam a few inches above the paper during part of the main exposure, to keep back light from the area that prints too dark. Again, keep the dodger moving to ensure a soft edge to the tonal change in the final print.

The enlargement (Figure 34.22) was given a straight, overall exposure of 14 seconds. The result looks correct over most of the image, but the dog's mouth is too dark and its hindquarters too light. The second version (Figure 34.23) also received 14 seconds, but during this time a disc-on-wire dodger was pushed into the light beam about 2–3 inches above the paper, and allowed to cast a shadow over the open mouth for 3 seconds. Then, when 14 seconds had elapsed, a card with a hole in it about the same size as the disc was used to give extra exposure to the dog's hindquarters only, for another 5 seconds. In each instance, the dodger and the printing-in card were kept on the move.

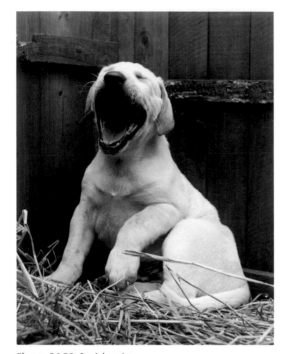

Figure 34.22 Straight print.

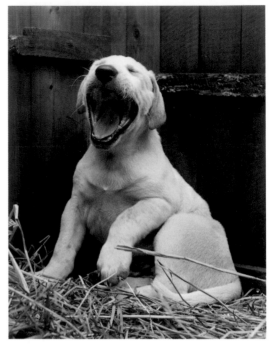

Figure 34.23 Corrected print.

Using this technique of adding and subtracting exposure, you can change the way that the tones in the final print are created. Careful photographers can use this approach to further enhance the appearance of their images and to help direct the viewer's eye to the parts of the picture that are important.

Print faults to avoid

If your printing paper still just looks white after processing or carries a ghost-like pale image, you may have processed an unexposed sheet, or exposed it upside down, or put it in the fixer first . . . or it may simply be grossly underexposed. Perhaps your developer was exhausted, contaminated or much too diluted.

If the print goes dark all over, including its white borders, the whole sheet was fogged to light – maybe the safe light is too bright, or someone has opened the printing paper packet in room lighting? If borders remain white the fault is probably gross overexposure or light reaching the easel other than through the enlarger lens.

A yellowish all-over stain suggests that your print was developed for a very long period (possibly in exhausted developer) or has not yet fixed properly. Yellow or purplish patches are due to uneven fixing – for example, when prints are left face up and allowed to float to the surface of the fix solution.

Your print may show smears or blobs of darker or lighter tone (Figure 34.27) not present on the negative. The most likely cause is odd spots of water or developer getting onto the paper before processing. Perhaps your 'dry' bench was splashed with liquid, or you handled dry paper with wet fingers.

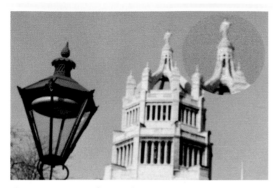

Figure 34.24 Print from unsharp negative.

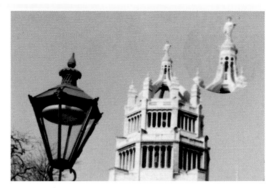

Figure 34.25 Unsharp print from sharp negative.

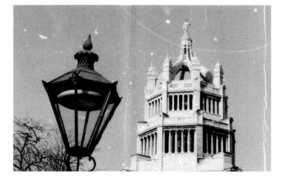

Figure 34.26 Hair and debris on negative.

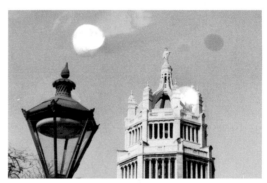

Figure 34.27 Damp finger-marks, solution splashes.

White specks or hairs and other clear-cut squiggle shapes, as in Figure 34.26, are often magnified debris on the negative itself – although they are sometimes due to dirt on the enlarger lamp house condenser or diffuser, which only appears clearly at a small lens aperture.

If your enlargement is not quite sharp, check closely to see if the grain pattern of the negative has printed clearly; if it has (Figure 34.24), then the image shot in the camera was unsharp. But if the grain is also unsharp your enlarging lens is improperly focused (Figure 34.25).

Sometimes a print from a perfect negative reveals a double image – either overall or just some part you have printed-in. This is because you jogged the enlarger or paper part way through exposure.

Constructed prints
Double printing

Shading and printing-in also allows you to combine parts of several negatives into one picture. For Figure 34.28, the mouth negative was enlarged and exposed first, shading the child's tongue and bottom left quarter the whole time. Then the negative was changed and the unexposed parts of the paper exposed to the train shot, this time shading the top and right-hand side of the paper.

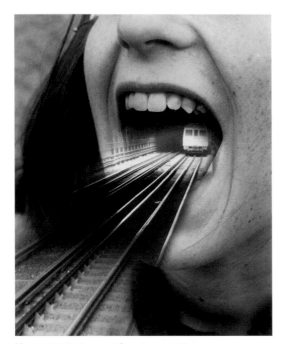

Figure 34.28 One print from two negatives.

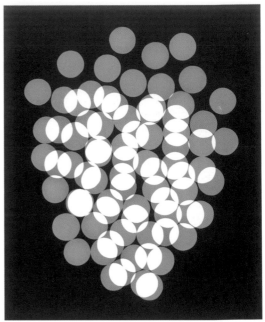

Figure 34.29 Chocolate button photogram.

Photograms

'Photograms' are pictures created from the shadows of objects placed directly on or above the paper. For Figure 34.29, the enlarger was set as if for contact printing, but instead of negatives, chocolate buttons were just scattered on the surface of the paper. Then, after giving half the exposure time needed for a good black, all the buttons were shifted around and the same time repeated. Figure 34.30 goes further, using three pressed leaves in a pile on the paper, two of which were removed in turn after 3 and 6 seconds of a 9-second exposure. After processing, this negative print was contact printed face down under glass onto another sheet of paper to give a positive result.

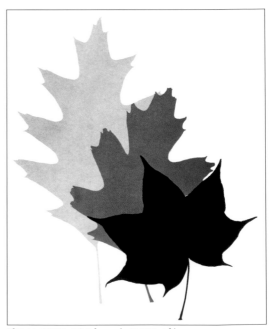

Figure 34.30 Print from photogram of leaves.

1 Create a series of photograms using household objects found in the kitchen or the garden shed. Remember that to create a variety of tones using this technique, you will need to remove objects at different times during the exposure.

2 To see the changes in contrast that different filters produce on multigrade paper, take the same negative and print it with 0, 2 and 5 filters. Keep in mind that most multigraded papers require a change in exposure (usually double) for the filter numbers between 4 and 5. Check the instructions that came with your paper or make a test strip for each print. A similar test can be produced using sheets of different graded papers if your darkroom is not set up for multigrade use.

3 Select a negative with interesting foreground detail that ends neatly at a distant horizon line. Choose another photograph with a good sky. Expose the first negative onto a portion of your photographic paper whilst shielding the upper portion of the print. Change negatives and then expose the second image on the upper section (whilst shielding the bottom).

4 Choose an underexposed negative (too light) that you have previously rejected because of its lack of detail and by using a high filter (or paper grade) number try to make an acceptable print. You can also try to rescue an overexposed negative (too dark) using different filter grades as well.

5 Select a landscape or cityscape picture with good foreground detail and a cloudy sky area that also contains detail but usually prints very pale. Expose the whole of the picture using standard filtration and then change to a higher filter number and print-in (burn-in) the missing detail of the sky with extra exposure. Be sure not to shield the foreground part of the picture from the extra light.

9 Experimental and Constructed Images

Don't become too fixed in your ideas about what makes a technically good photograph. Successful pictures don't necessarily have to be blur-free, full of detail and an accurate record of what was in front of your camera. In fact, sometimes what at first seemed like an error can produce the sort of image that sums up an event or expresses a subject better than a completely controlled photograph that produces a predictable result. Happy accidents or the unexpected result mean that you can then explore this approach further, allowing you another chance to expand your picture-making skills. It's also great fun.

Few of the techniques in this part call for equipment beyond a camera offering a 'B' setting shutter (long exposure), or a couple of small attachments such as lens filters. On the other hand, they are all suggestions for experiments, so you must be prepared to waste film on a trial-and-error basis. Or if you are a digital shooter, expect to shoot many images in order to obtain a couple that are usable.

Don't let this idea worry you, as even professionals expect to shoot many frames for one good result. This is often called the 'shooting ratio'. Areas like wildlife photography and sports journalism typically have high numbers of wasted photographs for every one or two acceptable pictures. For your experiments take a range of versions of your subject, making notes of the settings used. This way you can match the results with the techniques used to produce them. You can then, if necessary, make further experimental shots based on your best results.

Remember too that even after the shooting and processing stages there is still plenty you can do to alter and reconstruct pictures. This can be done by joining prints, combining slides, and hand-coloring black and white prints. A wider range of manipulative possibilities opens up if you are working with digital photographs and some of the special effects features of one of the many image editing software packages on the market.

35 Letting the image move

The painter Paul Klee once said that 'a line is a dot that has gone for a walk'. In photography, as soon as you allow the image to move, while it is exposing every dot, the highlights of the picture are drawn onto the photograph as a line. This image movement might be the result of shifting your camera during a long exposure, in which case the subject remains static and fixed and the camera moves (see Figure 35.1). Alternatively, the camera might remain still and the subject move, as in Figures 35.3–35.5. Or thirdly, interesting pictures can result when both the camera and subject are on the move, as in Figure 35.7.

We are all used to experiencing blur as a symbol of movement, from close objects rushing past the car window, to the streaks drawn behind characters in comic strips. A photograph can exaggerate speed by showing the subject with lengthy blur trails, created by allowing considerable image movement during a long exposure time. Your subject can appear to have bumpy or smooth motion too, according to the shape of the lines – something you can control by jerking or gliding

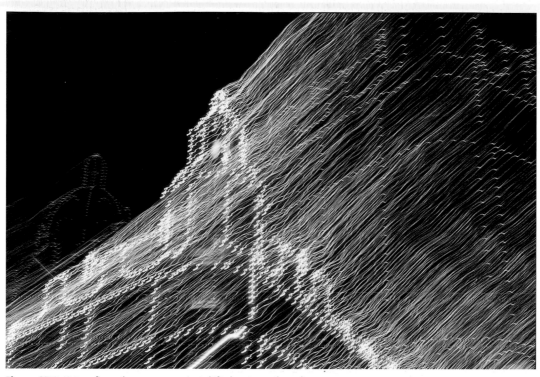

Figure 35.1 Not on fire – the camera was just shifted part way through exposure.

the camera with its shutter open. In extreme instances (Figure 35.2, for example), the nature of the subject gets lost and what you create is an abstract pattern of color and light.

General technique

The best way to start experimenting is to shoot at night, picking scenes containing plenty of pinpoints of different colored light. Street lights, illuminated signs; decorative lamps on buildings or at the seaside; and moving traffic during the rush hour are all good raw material. Try to pick a clear night with intensely black sky. You will need a camera allowing timed exposures up to several seconds and/or a 'B' setting. A tripod and a cable or remote shutter release are also essential. If your camera doesn't have the option for a cable release, try activating the self-timer option before the long exposure. This will give the camera time to stop moving before the shutter opens.

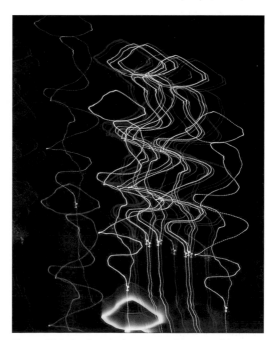

Figure 35.2 An abstract picture created from small lamps in a multi-colored sign. The camera was kept moving for 8 seconds.

Set a low ISO value (digital cameras) or load slow film and then select a small lens aperture. If your camera offers aperture priority, then choosing this mode should result in the slowest possible shutter setting without overexposing. If you have a manual camera, try exposures around 10 seconds at f16 for ISO 100 film or setting, or be guided by what was used for pictures on these pages.

Be careful, though, as some cameras do not measure exposure when set to 'B' – in which case, open the lens aperture fully until your camera indicates a timed exposure, then return the lens setting to f16 and double the time for each change of f-number as you go. For example, if opening the lens to f2 makes the meter respond with 1/8 second, then at f16 you should give 8 seconds held open on 'B'.

Static subject, camera moved

One simple way of creating 'drawn' light patterns is to move around the street at night with your camera with the shutter open. In the example photograph (Figure 35.2), eight small groups of different colored bulbs in a sign were focused small in the frame. Then, as soon as the shutter was locked open, the camera was panned upwards and downwards, swaying side to side to form the tangle of shapes.

Interesting results happen with a lit subject at night when you give part of a (long) exposure with the camera first still and then moving. The 'still' part of the exposure records the general shape of your subject, avoiding total abstraction, and the moving part shifts all the highlights. In Figure 35.1, for example, the camera was loosely attached to a tripod. It was held firm for the first half of a 3-second exposure at f22, and then panned left at 45° throughout the final 1.5 seconds.

Static camera, subject moved

With night subjects like fairgrounds or busy highways, long exposures with the camera kept absolutely still can record static parts of a scene clearly but elongate bright moving subjects into streaking light trails. The nearer a particular light (or the slower its movement) the wider its trail will appear. Figures 35.3 and 35.4 show how two 5-second exposure pictures shot a minute or so apart record different patterns traced out by a fairground ride. Dusk shots of city lights

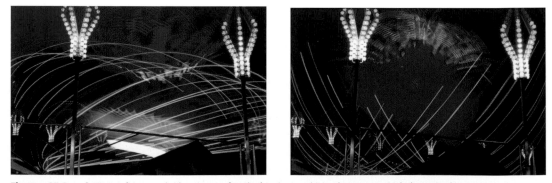

Figures 35.3 and 35.4 A fairground ride acts as a frantic drawing machine. Always try to include static elements too.

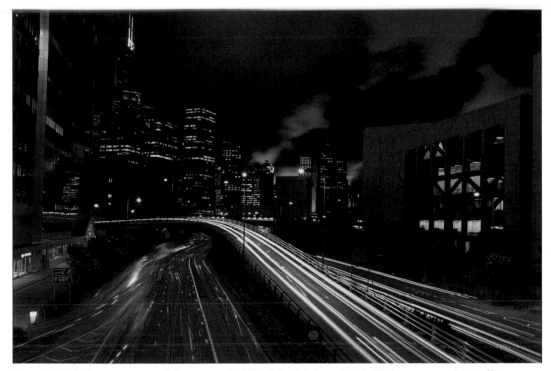

Figure 35.5 The long exposure needed to capture the falling light of dusk, combined with the movement of the traffic, creates streaking light trails against the city sky. Image courtesy of www.ablestock.com.

combined with the remainder of the daylight can combine both the movement and color, as shown in Figure 35.5.

This 'drawing with light' can be developed further into 'writing with light' provided you have a steady hand. You will need to work outdoors at night or in a darkened room with a black background. Secure the camera to a tripod and mark out, on the ground, the left- and right-hand limits of your picture area. Your 'performance' must not exceed these extremes. Focus on something such as a newspaper, illuminated by a hand torch, held midway between the markers. Set the shutter for 'B' or an exposure of several seconds.

To produce the example in Figure 35.6, someone wearing dark clothes stood between the markers, facing the camera. Keeping on the move, they 'wrote' in the air with a lighted sparkler firework whilst the shutter remained open. A small, handbag-type torch makes a good light pen too, provided you keep it pointed towards the camera as you write. Torches with built-in color filters allow the lines to change color, or you can organize someone to use a series of filters over the camera lens.

Exposure varies according to the strength of light and speed of drawing. Test at about f16 for a total writing time of 10 seconds (ISO 100 setting or film). Write at a consistent speed – slower lines thicken through overexposure, fast lines record thin. Words and numbers will appear the wrong way round to the camera, so you should have the negative printed, or slide projected, through the back of the film (unless you can write backwards).

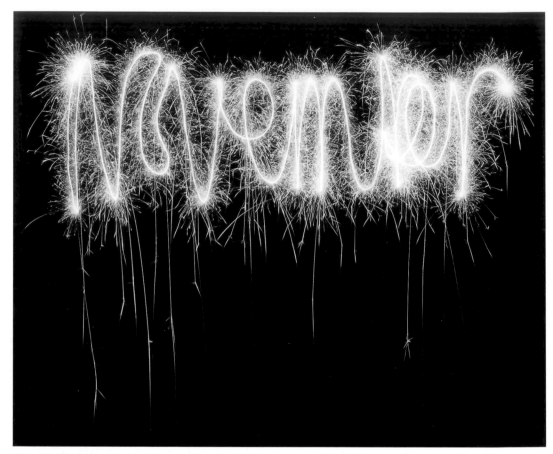

Figure 35.6 Writing in the air with a sparkler in the dark. Image courtesy of Frank Thurston.

Moving camera and moving subject

If you pan the camera whilst photographing a fast-moving subject, you can capture the subject as sharp against a blurred background. This technique is often used by motor sports photographers to isolate cars or bikes against distracting backgrounds. Panning is best attempted at a shutter speed of about 1/30 second, and is therefore within the capabilities of even quite simple cameras. As Figure 35.7 shows, the technique is that you hand-hold the camera, pivoting your body so that its movement is in a smooth sweep, then release the shutter halfway through the pan. If your camera has automatic exposure options, set these to

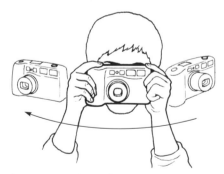

Figure 35.7 Technique for camera panning. Follow the subject with a smooth camera movement. Fire the shutter halfway through.

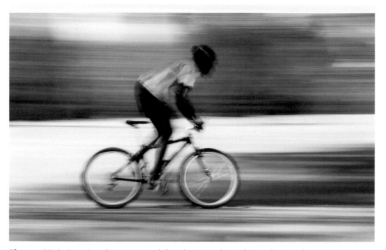

Figure 35.8 Panning the camera whilst photographing this cyclist produces a very characteristic photograph that is full of blurry movement but still retains enough detail that we can recognize the subject matter. Image courtesy of www.ablestock.com.

shutter priority mode so that you can control the shutter speed (see Figure 35.8).

Static subject, static camera

Zooming is a way of making the image move and blur during exposure, while both your subject and the camera itself are completely stationary. You need a camera with a zoom lens, low ISO setting (or slow film) and a subject sufficiently dimly lit to need an exposure time of at least 3 seconds. Then, from beginning to end of the exposure time, you smoothly zoom the lens through its full focal length range. Figure 35.9 depicts a scene looking down on the lights of New York from the Empire State Building. The picture was shot in this way using the zoom-in technique.

Whether you zoom from wide to long or the reverse makes little difference, but check out both ends of the range before shooting. Digital shooters can practice smooth lens handling and can preview the amount of blur in each photograph, adjusting settings and zoom speed for different effects. For all zoom-motion work, a firm tripod is essential.

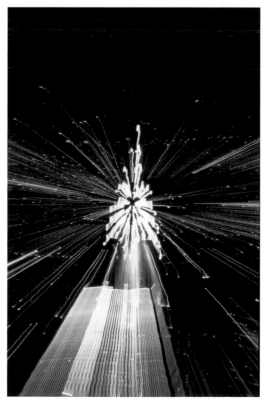

Figure 35.9 City at night. The camera's lens was steadily zoomed during a 3-second exposure. The 'Christmas tree' shape resulted from a group of buildings more brightly lit than the rest, and imaged center frame.

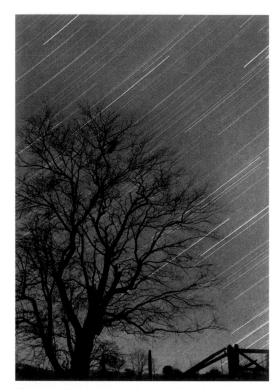

Figure 35.10 Star tracks recorded at night during a 90-minute exposure.

Since all blur lines radiate from the precise center of the frame, it is this 'bull's-eye' part of the scene that should contain a point of focus.

Star tracks

Stars in the night sky look quite static, but only because they move too slowly for us to notice. The sky in Figure 35.10 was exposed for 90 minutes at f16 on a setting of ISO 125. The camera was left on its tripod, pointing generally towards the pole star (around which all other stars appear to rotate). Pick a clear moonless night, and shoot somewhere well clear of light-polluting roads and towns. Open country or a coastal area is ideal. Be sure to include some landmark, such as the tree shown here, to counterpoint the star tracks. If you are using a digital camera make sure that you are careful not to place a light source in the frame, as the extended exposure can cause permanent damage to the image sensor.

36 Exploring reflections

Some unusual and experimental pictures are possible without special know-how or any out-of-the-ordinary gear. They involve straightforward photography of what you can see in front of the camera, but by careful choice of viewpoint and framing you can create a picture with strange optical appearances. Results include distorted shapes, images with detail broken up in unfamiliar ways and combinations of two or more separate picture elements that form dream-like effects. All of these types of picture are based on photographing something either reflected or refracted. Everyday reflective surfaces include still water, glass windows and mirrors. Refraction alters the way things look when your subject is observed through things like patterned glass or clear or disturbed liquid.

Using water

Pictures like Figure 36.1 are best shot looking down into the clear water of a swimming pool, preferably outdoors, where light is plentiful. Using the long focus extreme of a zoom lens helps to fill up the frame. The appearance of this underwater swimmer changes every second due to the swirl of water altering refraction effects and the swimmer's movements, so it is best to work at 1/250 second or faster (using shutter priority mode on an AE camera) and pick the right moment carefully. Auto-focus is helpful here, provided it does not accidentally pick up on the pool's floor pattern some distance below the subject.

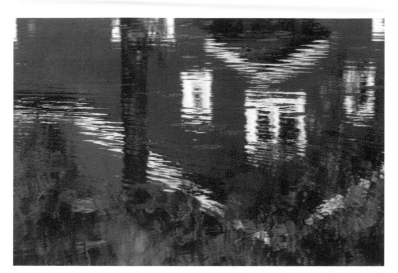

Figure 36.1 Distorted appearance due to reflection of light from the water surface. Image courtesy of www.ablestock.com.

Still water creates an almost mirror surface. By including only the far bank and sky reflected in a river and presenting this upside down (Figure 36.2), an impressionistic landscape image is formed. Remember that the reflection itself requires a lens focus setting different from the much nearer reflective surface. In a shot like this, focusing on the tree's reflection and then setting a small lens aperture would have brought detail on the surface of the water into focus too. Specks of floating flotsam would break the dreamy illusion. This picture was therefore exposed at f2.8, taking great care to (manually) focus so that only tree and clouds were included within the depth of field.

Using glass

Large glass-fronted buildings, including shops, are good locations for mixing one element (behind the glass) with another (reflected from its surface). Lighting is important here. People passing in the street may be sunlit and so dominate over figures inside the building. But later in the day, the balance reverses as internal lighting comes on behind the glass.

Often, reflected images like this include things happening on three different planes.

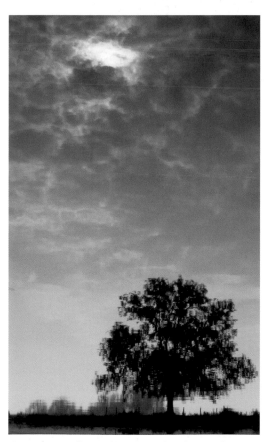

Figure 36.2 Reflection of the far bank in the smooth surface of a river. The result was turned upside down to make this picture.

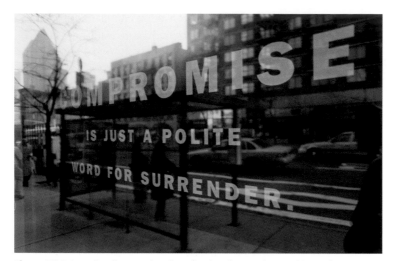

Figure 36.3 Intentionally capturing the reflections from a glass or shiny surface gives you the ability to combine both the two different scenes together. Here a slogan painted onto a shop window is combined with the reflection of the New York city street.

People might be sitting directly behind the window inside the building; others may be a reflection off the glass surface of action outside; and finally there may be those subjects directly included in the viewfinder (not reflected at all). Working with effectively three images like this allows you to make use of interesting mixtures of scale, and can fill up a frame of what would be sparsely occupied scenes if shot individually.

Figure 36.3 mixes an advertising slogan in a New York city window with the reflection of people and traffic in a typical street. The lonely scene seems to give life to the consequences of living your life as the slogan suggests.

Similar possibilities apply to mirrors hung on walls or buildings clad with mirror-finished surfaces – these all allow you to relate two or more quite separate elements together in the same picture. Remember to set a small aperture (large DOF) if reality and reflections are all to appear sharp. You will probably have to set focus (manually) for somewhere between the two and, to prevent you and your camera appearing in the picture, shoot at a slight angle to the reflective surface. Where a square-on view is essential, use a long focal length lens. This will mean that you can shoot from well back from the surface and so appear as a small reflection in the final scene.

37 Using lens attachments

Another way of experimenting with the appearance of subjects is to fit a special effects attachment or filter over the front of your camera lens. This has the advantage that you can create strange results – repeat patterning, abstractions, offbeat coloring – from almost any scene, rather than work with long exposures or reflective surfaces. Some attachments optically soften or diffuse detail or split up the image whilst others, such as colored filters, tint all, or part, of your picture.

Typically, a lens attachment is a circular or square piece of optical plastic sufficiently large enough to cover the lens. Circular types may screw into a thread on the lens rim, or for cameras without this option, they fit via a clip-on holder (Figure 37.3). Failing this, you can also just hold the filter over the lens. For most types, it is important to be able to rotate the attachment freely because this is the way you alter how it interacts with the image. This means that you can

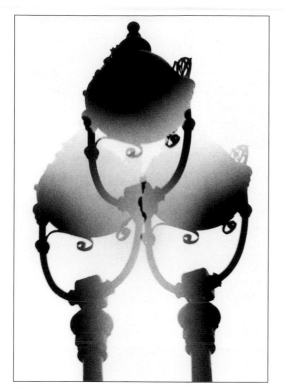

Figure 37.1 A single lamp-post against white sky, turned into overlapping shapes by a three-faceted prism lens attachment.

alter the effect for each particular shot. Using an SLR camera will allow you to forecast exactly the effect produced. Digital users can shoot and then review the picture. When using a compact camera, first look directly at the subject through the attachment by eye, turning it to find the best effect, and then transfer it without further rotation to the camera's lens.

Special effects attachments

Some optical attachments are made of clear plastic with faceted surfaces to give a multiple image of your subject. This way, you can repeat whatever is composed in the center of the frame into three or more separated but overlapping images, like Figure 37.1. Some filters work by having a parallel fluted pattern, which turns one narrow strip of the image into a row of repeats. Strips may run vertically (Figure 37.2) or at any angle you choose to rotate the attachment. When you are making

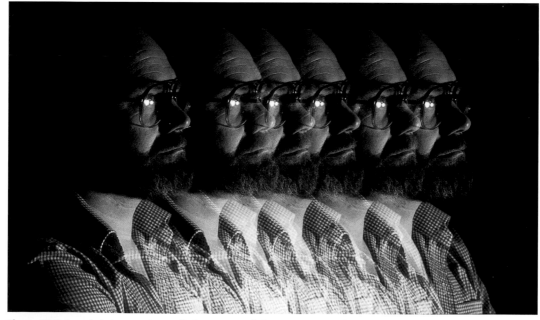

Figure 37.2 A reeded glass attachment, fluting set vertically here, repeats a single portrait profile.

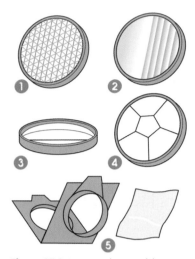

Figure 37.3 Lens attachments. (1) Starburst. (2) Fluted glass. (3) Half-lens (focuses a nearby object in part of the picture). (4) Five-facet prism. (5) Holder for filters.

multiple image shots, pick a subject with a strong, simple shape and plenty of plain background.

Another attachment, known as a starburst and made of etched or moulded clear plastic (Figure 37.3), spreads bright highlights in a scene into star-like patches with radiating 'spokes'. Much used in the 1970s and 1980s, the starburst filter was seen as a good way to glamorize shots that contained brilliant but well-separated pinpoint highlights – for example, direct sunlight sparkling on water, disco spotlights and tight groups of lamps in dark interiors or at night.

As you rotate the attachment spokes rotate, so you can position them at the most interesting angle. Results from a softly lit scene, however, are disappointing, as the starburst just gives flat, slightly diffused results.

Almost all optical-effect attachments alter in their image changes according to lens focal length and aperture you set. An SLR camera with aperture preview button is the best way to make an exact check of image appearance at the f-number you will be using. There are dozens of different effects attachments made. They include types which just give soft focus around the edges of the picture. Others are bifocals containing a portion of close-up lens you can rotate to coincide with some small close object so it appears sharp when the camera's main lens is focused on a more distant part of the background scene. This way, a foreground flower may record with as much detail as a landscape filling the other half of a shot.

Though all of these special effects filters are still readily available, much of their popularity has waned with the advance of digital photography. Many of the effects that were once only available as attachments for the camera lens can now be reproduced digitally via any good image editing package. Software packages like Adobe Photoshop and Photoshop Elements contain many of these style of effects filters for you to experiment with (see Figures 37.4 and 37.5).

Filters

'Filters' are so called because they remove some of the light that would enter the lens:

- *Neutral density*. A simple gray 'neutral density' (ND) filter just dims the whole image, useful for avoiding overexposure when you have fast film loaded but want to use a slow shutter speed or set a wide lens aperture.
- *Polarizing filter*. A polarizing filter offers this same advantage but, like Polaroid sunglasses, also subdues reflections at some angles from surfaces such as glass or water. The filter is also used to darken areas of blue sky at right angles to the direction of sunlight.
- *Light-colored and gradient filters*. A pale-colored filter will 'warm up' or 'cool down' the general mood of a scene. Both these and ND filters are available as 'graduates' – meaning their color or tone fades off in the lower half of the filter to tint or darken just sky and clouds in a landscape.

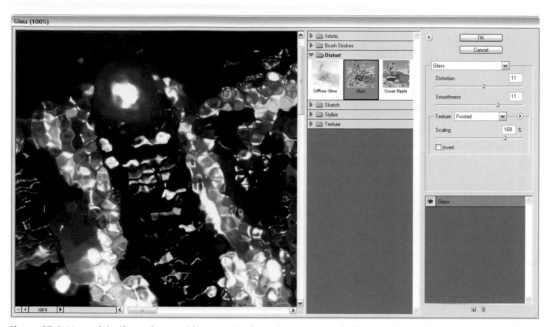

Figure 37.4 Many of the 'front of camera' filters previously used to create visual effects in photographs have been replaced by digital versions, which are applied to the images back at the desktop. Here a Glass filter is added to a picture, producing a similar effect as if the original picture was photographed through a piece of rippled glass.

- *Filters for black and white*. Stronger, overall color filters have a special role in black and white photography, allowing you to alter how a particular subject color translates into a darker or paler gray tone. The rule here is that a filter lightens the appearance of colors closest to itself and darkens opposite or 'complementary' colors. An orange or red filter, for example, darkens blue sky, so that white clouds in a landscape record more clearly (see Figure 37.6).
- *Color-correcting filters*. In color photography, especially when using film, you may want to use a strong overall color filter to compensate for a fluorescent or other artificial light source when using daylight balanced film – instead of hoping the lab can do corrections in printing (see Table 25.1). Some special effects color filters, 'tobacco' hue for example, are made as graduates to tint as well as darken the sky area alone. They produce results suggesting dusk or dawn.
- *Multi-color filters*. 'Dual color' filters are split into contrasting halves. Often, good results depend on you composing a picture with the horizon in a straight line, located about halfway across the frame. The smaller your lens aperture, the more abrupt the division between the two colors appears.

Most filters call for an increase in exposure. This is automatically taken into account, though, if you are using a camera that reads the light through the lens and therefore the filter as well. If this isn't the case, you should override the suggested exposure by the maker's rating on the filter.

There are no set ways of using most lens attachments, so experimenting is always worthwhile. For example, deep color filters intended for black and white work can produce strong effects in color photography. Try jazzing up the light trails from a moving camera or moving traffic at night by holding a filter over the lens during part of a long exposure.

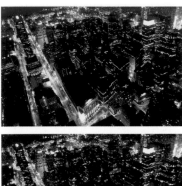

Original

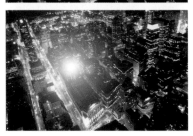

After
Glass
filter

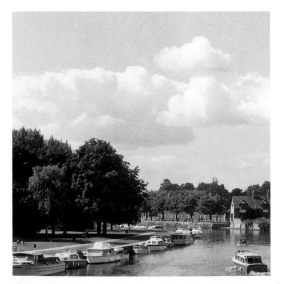

After
Lens
Flare
filter

Figure 37.5 Hundreds of different digital filters can be found supplied as part of your favorite image editing package, such as Photoshop or Photoshop Elements. Some of these replicate existing traditional filter effects and others provide changes that have only become available with the advent of digital photography. Image courtesy of www.ablestock.com.

For Figure 37.7, red, green and blue squares of filter were taped edge to edge to form one long continuous strip. Then, throughout a 30-second exposure of distant highway traffic, the strip was kept moving its full length several times across the lens.

38 Combining pictures

Photography allows you to combine records of separate scenes or subjects taken at quite different moments in time, place and scale, into one picture. This fact gives you the freedom to construct images that never existed in reality. Results can be bold and eye-catching, like a poster, or haunting and strange, often making a statement in a visually more convincing way than something that is drawn or painted. Constructed images may differ radically from normal vision – or at first glance look normal but contain an odd and disturbing feature, like Figure 38.7.

As far as equipment is concerned, you will need a tripod and a cable release. Some

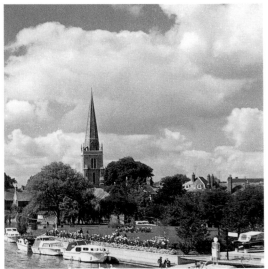

Figure 37.6 Darkening blue sky. (Left) No filter. (Right) Orange filter.

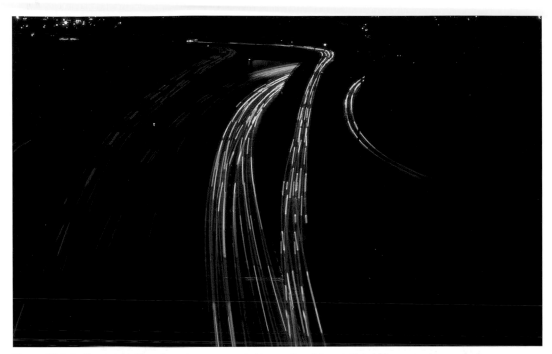

Figure 37.7 Traffic at night. Changing colors were created by a series of strongly tinted filters passed across the lens.

techniques call for access to a slide projector and a filter; for others, you will need to use a camera that has a 'B' setting.

One way of combining images is by projecting a slide onto a subject, which is then photographed. Another is to sandwich two slides together, or make two exposures on the same frame of film. Other methods include the basic cutting and sticking together of photographic prints, or the popular (and some say easiest) method of using a computer and image editing software to cut and paste picture elements together.

Combining by projection

Using a projector, you can make a slide (or negative) image appear on the surface of any suitable light-toned object; the scene can then be photographed, with the result being recorded exactly as it appears to the eye. Work in a blacked-out room and if you are using daylight film add a bluish 80A filter on the camera to correct for the orangey light from the projector. In Figure 38.1, a slide of brickwork is projected onto a hand. By using a distant, black background, no brickwork appears elsewhere (see Figure 38.2). Your image-receiving surface could be flat or curved – one or more eggs perhaps, paper cups, wooden blocks or any object painted matt white especially for the purpose. Be careful not to make the result too complicated, though – if the image you project has a strong pattern then pick a receiving object that is simple in shape.

Strips of black card held about halfway between projector and receiving surface will restrict the image to where you want it to appear. Other lighting is needed to just suggest surroundings and the forms of your still life objects, provided you keep the light off the projected image. Keep in mind that the fill light can't be too strong, otherwise it will obscure the projected image.

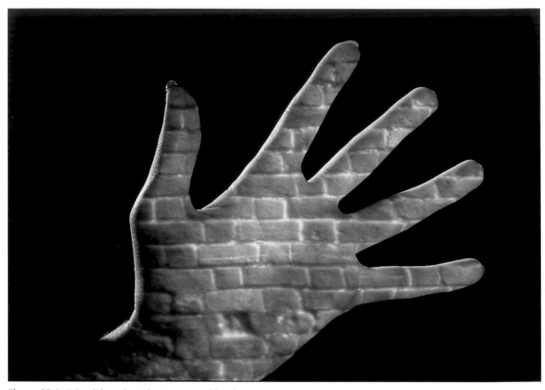

Figure 38.1 Color slide projected onto an actual hand.

Combining by sandwiching

'Sandwiching' simply means placing two slide film images together in face-to-face contact within the same (glass) mount. Details of one appear in the lighter parts of the other. You can then project your result, or send it for a print or scan the picture ready for use on the computer.

Be careful that the relative size of each image, as well as its positioning in the frame, suits the other slide. You don't have the same flexibility to adjust size here as you do when projecting a slide onto an object. Another point to watch is that each slide should be slightly pale – overexposed by about one stop – otherwise your sandwich will be too dark. It is worth keeping a selection of reject slides for this possible purpose.

Quite often, one existing slide suggests another that needs taking to complete an idea. In this way, you can also ensure that size,

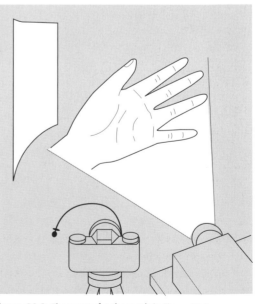

Figure 38.2 The set-up for the result in Figure 38.1.

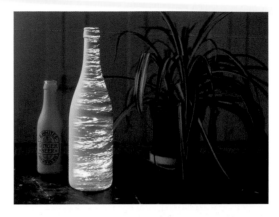

lighting and subject placing are tailored convincingly. The sandwiched picture (Figure 38.6), for example, started as an experimental night shot of a distant town, the camera being tilted downward and wiggled for the second half of a 4-second exposure. The result seemed to suggest chaos and stress. Then another slide was planned and shot of a man with his hands to his head and silhouetted in front of white sky (Figure 38.5). This silhouette was slightly overexposed, so that

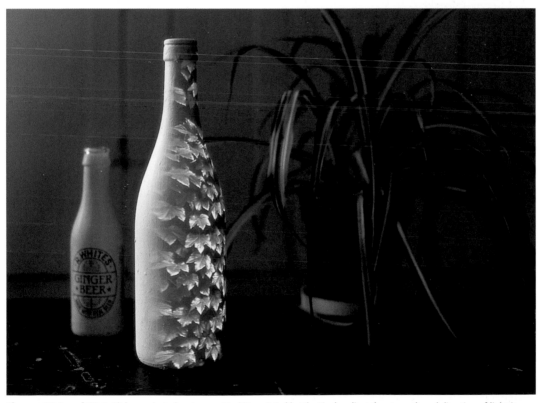

Figures 38.3 and 38.4 Slides projected onto a matt white-painted bottle. Finely adjust the strength and direction of light in the room.

when sandwiched it was not impenetrably black and some of the light trails could be seen 'penetrating' his head.

The seaside is an ideal location for shooting several picture components because of the large plain background offered by ocean and sky. Figure 38.7 is a sandwich combining two 'throwaway' slides. One is a shot of the seashore with a blank, overcast sky. The other contains

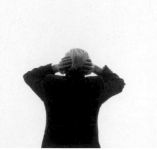

Figure 38.5 Man against white sky – a component of the picture in Figure 38.6.

only blue sky and clouds, but sandwiching this film upside down creates a slightly unsettling, surreal effect.

Bear in mind that results similar to the combining of two pictures by sandwiching are now possible by digital means, using cloning or 'layering' software. Sizing and subject orientation problems are less of an issue when digital is used for composition, as this technology allows for the separate resizing and positioning of each image part.

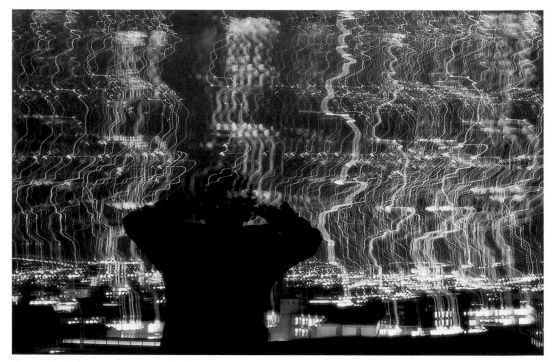

Figure 38.6 'Chaos and stress'. Sandwich of the slide in Figure 38.5 and camera-moved street lights.

Multiple exposures

Another way of mixing images together, involving only your camera, is to make several exposures onto one frame of film. When sandwiching slides, the details of one picture appear most strongly in the light parts of the other, but multiple exposures work the opposite way, one picture showing up most in the dark areas of the other (see Figure 38.8). Keep this idea in mind when you plan out your picture.

Making two or more exposures is easiest if your camera has a superimpose button. This disengages the wind-on mechanism so that the film stays still and only the shutter resets after each exposure. Superimpose ('multiple exposure') controls are provided on a number of compact and SLR cameras. On the other hand, any camera with a 'B' shutter setting can be used for this work provided it accepts a cable release, preferably with a locking screw. You will need to work with slow film, probably indoors, in order to make a time exposure necessary. A tripod is essential. Both Figures 38.8 and 38.9 were taken with a manual SLR camera, with the shutter set at 'B'.

For the picture in Figure 38.8 the girl sat in the chair for half the exposure, then got up (taking care not to shift the chair itself) so that the second half recorded it empty. Working indoors with dim light from a window and at smallest aperture, f16, the exposure required was 4 seconds. So, with the girl in place and keeping very still, the shutter was held open on 'B' for 2 seconds. Then, keeping the cable release pressed and locked, the lens was covered with a black card while the girl left. Next, it was uncovered again for a further 2 seconds before the shutter was finally closed.

It is important to plan pictures like this in terms of where 'lights' and 'darks' will overlap. In Figure 38.8, the girl wore a plain dark dress and the chair was chosen for its lighter tones and patterned design, which would therefore 'expose through' her clothing. The cardigan, face and hands had the opposite effect – dominating over the shadowy part of the room behind.

The man looking two ways at once (Figure 38.9) is also the result of two superimposed exposures. If you cover up vertically half of the picture at a time you will see that, between exposures, he has simply moved his eyes. For the first exposure only, the left half of his face was illuminated (while he looked that way), then that light was switched out and another, illuminating the right half, was switched on instead.

For this technique you need a darkened room, or work outdoors at night. Have two lamps you can control from the camera, set up well to the left and right, or use a flashgun you fire manually on its 'open flash' button, holding it first at arm's length to the left and then

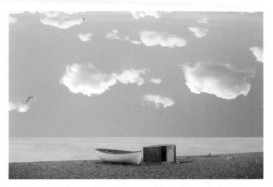

Figure 38.7 Surrealism at the seaside – via sandwiched slides.

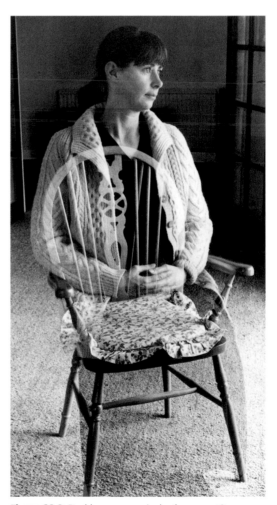

Figure 38.8 Double exposure – is she there or not?

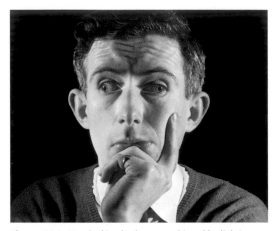

Figure 38.9 Man looking both ways, achieved by lighting change and double exposure.

to the right. Only half of the face must be seen at a time, leaving the other totally shadowed. Give the full measured exposure to each half of your picture, since quite different parts of the head are illuminated at a time.

In Figure 38.10, the exposure needed was 1/60 second at f11. To achieve this effect, the shutter was fired three times at this setting onto the same frame of film, rotating the camera a few degrees about a horizontal axis between each one.

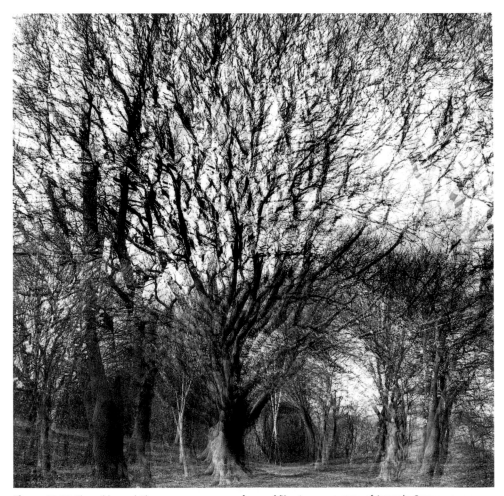

Figure 38.10 The wild wood. Three exposures on one frame of film. Image courtesy of Amanda Currey.

Combining images digitally

Using a home computer of sufficient power, your photographic images can be combined and manipulated on screen (see Figure 38.11). In only a few minutes it is possible to digitally combine two separate images to create a new constructed photograph. In Figure 38.12, the artichoke has been cut and pasted onto the shaven head and then blended into the skin of the skull. To add extra realism, the toning on the artichoke was altered to fit with the lighting of the head and shoulders photograph.

The first step is to input ('capture') chosen negatives or slides into your computer system by converting them into digital data. An inexpensive way to achieve this is to get your photographic lab to transfer them all onto a CD, which you then insert into the computer's CD player. Alternatively, use a desk scanner designed to capture prints or films/slides. If your shots were taken with a digital camera, this may be connected directly to the computer to download its pictures, or the camera may contain a memory card that you remove and slot into a card reader.

The computer also needs an image manipulation software program such as Photoshop Elements or Photoshop, which is initially installed from a CD. With pictures and software installed, you can then load the images into the program, which in turn displays them on your monitor screen (negatives being electronically converted into positive form). Using the mouse, or better still a graphics tablet and stylus, you may manipulate the pictures with 'tools' offered on screen by your software program.

Two or more images can be slid as 'layers', one on top of the other, to superimpose wholly, or in part, with great precision (see Figure 38.13). Tools like the 'eraser' can be used to remove sections of the upper image to reveal the detail from beneath. Using the selection tools, you can combine the main subject in one shot with the background of another. Any chosen elements in a picture can be multi-cloned, changed in size or color, reversed in tones or switched left to right, then returned to the shot. In fact, it's tempting to overdo these and many other image-distorting controls just for their novelty value.

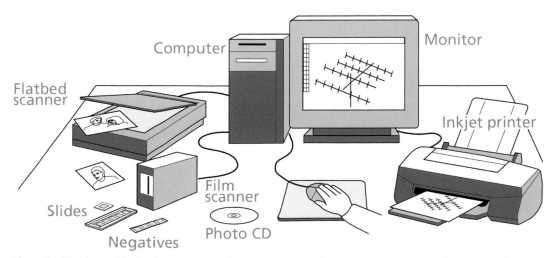

Figure 38.11 A home digital workstation. Films and prints here are input by scanning, or via bureau-made Photo CD. After onscreen changes pictures print out by inkjet.

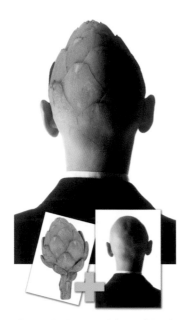

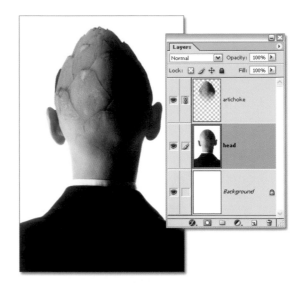

Figure 38.12 Many of the traditional techniques used to combine different images have been superseded by digital photography techniques. Here an artichoke is combined digitally with a portrait to create a new photograph. Such a task would take an experienced photographer about half an hour to complete. Producing the same image traditionally (non-digitally) would take considerably longer. Images courtesy of www.ablestock.com.

Figure 38.13 Montaging separate images digitally is made easier because a single photographic document can contain multiple layers, each with different content. In the example, the artichoke, head and white background are all stored on separate layers, but are seen as one complete picture in the final photograph.

These types of image editing programs have even greater usefulness for improving and 'fine-tuning' results in more subtle ways. Retouching out any spots, disguising joins or removing obtrusive items from backgrounds is made easy by enlarging the image on screen and working on it pixel by pixel. Done well, changes are almost imperceptible and the results are easily accepted as straight and natural pictures.

The final stage, when you are satisfied with what you have put together on the screen, is to print it out onto paper. This requires a photo-quality digital printer such as a four- or six-color inkjet. You then need to save your manipulated image on the hard drive of the computer, where it will be ready for future prints (see Part 7 for more details on digital photography).

39 Manipulating prints

Even with the advent of such digital technologies, there is still plenty of scope for physically experimenting with images after you get your prints back from the processing lab. If you are good at handwork and have an eye for design, there are various possibilities of montage – pictures constructed from different paper prints arranged so that they join, overlap or blend with each other. Your aim may be simply an original form of pattern and decoration, or the assembly of a panorama otherwise impossible to shoot 'straight' without special equipment. You can construct a picture of a crowd of people or a fantastic landscape, create a caricature or a visual pun.

Similarly, the hand coloring of monochrome photographic prints opens up possibilities of color pictures in which every individual hue is under your control. Realistic or bizarre, colored in full or limited to just a suggestion here and there, you have a free hand. Watercolors, retouching inks and translucent oil paints can all be applied to the surface of black and white prints to give a hand-colored effect. Despite its heritage as a way to record color in a picture before color films were invented, this technique is best used for interpretive effect.

Assembled, montaged or colored, once your handworked print is complete you can copy it – either using your camera (as shown on page 140) or through a high-quality photocopying machine or scanner. Results will then be free of joins or irregular surface finish.

Montaging

Like slide sandwiching and multiple exposure work, a print montage can combine elements or events that did not in fact occur together in real life. One person with eyes shut in a group can be pasted over with a cut-out print from another negative that is bad of everyone else. A strong foreground lead-in to a landscape can be combined with a distant main subject, when they were really hundreds of miles apart and shot on different days.

Again, most of these forms of manipulation are now handled digitally, but there is still plenty of scope for those who prefer to work in a more handcrafted manner.

Another form of reconstruction is to carefully dissect a single print into a regular pattern of slices, concentric discs, squares, etc., and then reassemble them in some different way, like the church architecture shown in Figure 39.2. In Figure 39.1, four prints have been butt-mounted to create one pattern. Look at the bottom left-hand quarter only and you will find that the subject is simply the inside of a shed door, including the shadow of the handle. It was constructed using two normal prints and two printed through the back of the negative.

The landscape (Figure 39.3) shows a more subtle form of repeat patterning – two butt-joined prints, one enlarged through the back of a negative and one from another negative, straight. Notice that having the dog on only one half breaks up the symmetry of the final result, making you wonder if the scene is real or constructed. Pictures like this need to be planned out before they are shot. If possible, make them pose a question or express some point of view. Figure 39.4, for example, says something about the fact that we work with hard edges to our pictures, unlike scenes observed by eye. A print of the man was pasted onto a seascape print and the shadow by his feet painted in with watercolor.

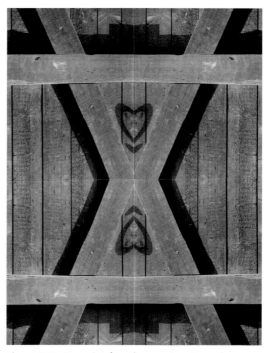

Figure 39.1 Four prints from the same negative make up a pattern montage.

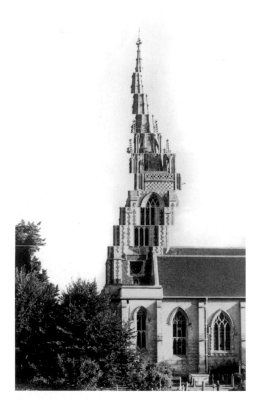

Figure 39.2 With slice and reassembly you can redesign any building.

Hand coloring

Hand-tinting monochrome prints allow you to choose to leave some parts uncolored and suppressed, others picked out strongly like the girl's eyes in Figure 39.5, irrespective of original appearance. Have your print made on fiber-based paper (if possible, make the print yourself and sepia tone it). The print should be fairly pale because underlying dark tones desaturate your colors. Choose paper which is matt, not glossy – the latter's extra gelatin top coat often gives uneven results. Remember too that big prints take longer to color than small ones. Begin with a size you know you can finish in one session.

Work with either transparent photographic dyes or ordinary watercolors. Dyes give stronger hues and you can build them up by repeated application, but unlike watercolors they are hard to blend and mistakes cannot be washed off. (A dye remover pen will erase small color areas.) Start off by slightly damping your whole print surface to swell the gelatin, and firmly attach it on all four sides to hardboard with gummed brown tape. Work on the largest areas first, with a

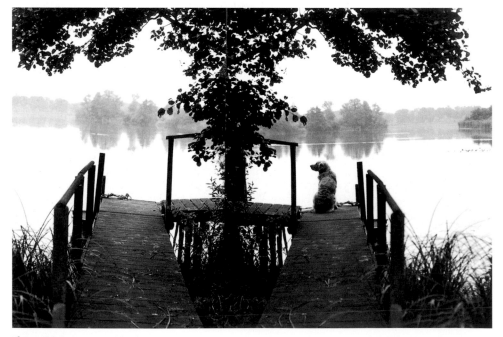

Figure 39.3 Constructed landscape.

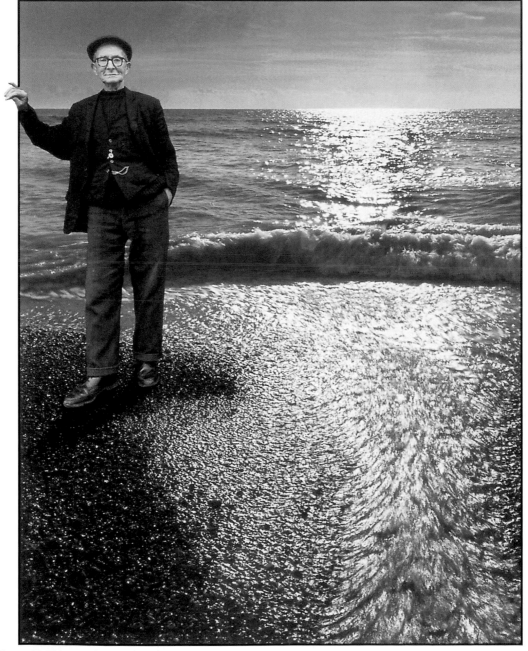

Figure 39.4 Montage (courtesy Graham Smith).

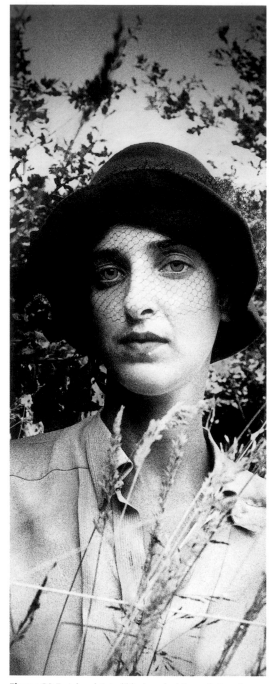

Figure 39.5 A hand-tinted black and white sepia toned enlargement. A set of photo-coloring dyes is needed for this. Image courtesy of Sue Wilkes.

color wash on cotton wool. Then color in smaller parts using a brush, size 0–4, or a hand-coloring dye pen. Explore local coloring by computer too.

Panoramas

A panorama can consist of two, three or more prints joined up to form one uninterrupted picture. This is a very successful way of showing an architectural interior or a landscape when you do not have a sufficiently wide-angle lens. Building up a panorama also gives you an impressively large image from what were only quite small images (see Figure 39.6).

For the most accurate-looking result you must work carefully at the shooting stage. Expose each picture for a panorama from exactly the same spot. Pick a viewpoint giving some kind of start and finish to your vista – perhaps trees at one end and a building at the other. Avoid showing objects close to you in the foreground and shoot with a normal or long focal length lens – otherwise it will be difficult to join up both the near and the far details in the prints. In any case, try to overlap the contents of each frame by at least 30 per cent so you need only use the central zone of each shot.

Expose your series of pictures as quickly as possible in case figure movements or fluctuating lighting conditions upset your results. A camera with motor drive will allow you to keep your eye to the viewfinder. If the panorama features a prominent continuous line, such as the horizon, keep your camera dead level. Pointing the camera slightly upwards or downwards results in prints that only join up to show this line curved (Figure 39.7).

Auto-exposure cameras will change the exposure settings according to the different subjects entering the frame of the various source images. If this happens, then individual photographs then show continuous elements like sky as too dark or light, and they will not match up. So ensure that exposure remains unchanged by keeping to one manual setting or applying AE exposure lock. This same advice should be applied to the focus and zoom settings as well. Lock these both at the beginning of the shot sequence to avoid changes during the series of images.

For digital shooters, make sure that the white balance option is set to the dominant light source in the scene, such as 'Daylight'. Leaving this option on 'Auto' can cause changes in color from one photograph to the next as the camera tries to eliminate color casts from a range of different subject-filled scenes.

Finally, if you are working with film and prints you can lay out your panorama images so that, when they overlap, details and tone values join up as imperceptibly as possible. Next, tack them down onto card with masking tape. Then, with a sharp blade, cut through each print overlap – either in a straight line or following the shape of some vertical feature. Discard the cut-off pieces and either tape together or butt-mount the component parts of your panorama. If necessary, trim or mask off the top and bottom as straight lines.

Those readers who have shot their source images digitally can use a stitching program to blend the edges of their photographs together. Image editing software like Photoshop Elements, as well as Photoshop itself, now contain a dedicated stitching feature, called Photomerge, built into the main program. Photomerge imports, sequences and positions the source images automatically, producing a stitched panorama. For problem picture sequences where adjacent images don't quite match up, the user is able to fine-tune these blending areas with a series of manual controls. The end result is a new picture file that is compiled of all the stitched source files (see Figures 39.8 and 39.9).

Joiners

Not every set of panorama images needs to marry up imperceptibly into one image. Another approach is to be much looser, abandon strict accuracy and aim for a mosaic that just suggests general appearance. The painter David Hockney explored composite image making this way by 'spraying' a scene with dozens of shots, often taken from more than one viewpoint and distance. The resulting prints, which he called 'joiners', both overlap and leave gaps. They have a fragmented jigsaw effect that suggests the passage of time and movement around the scene, concentrating on one thing after another.

Figure 39.10 is a rough mosaic in the form of a single sheet of contact prints. It was made by contact (page 184) from a film of 20 consecutive exposures. The individual pictures, all shot from one position using a hand-held camera and 50 mm lens, collectively make up something approaching a fish-eye view (page 76). For this kind of result, pre-plan how many exposures are needed per row. Don't overlap pictures – in fact, compose trying to leave gaps where the black horizontal bars (rows of perforations and film edges) will stretch across the final picture. The way that inaccuracies in a mosaic such as this restructure the architecture gives it individuality and life, but try to pick a camera position giving a symmetrical view to help hold it all together as one picture.

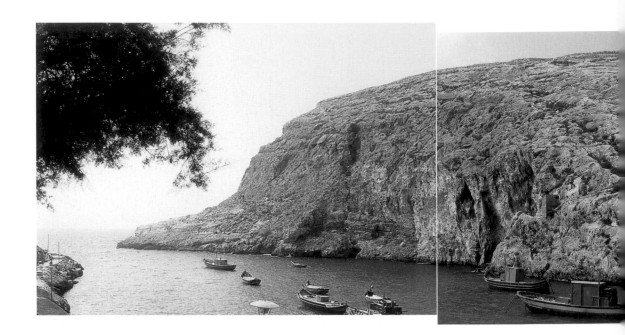

Figure 39.6 Panoramas are a quick, cheap way of making a big picture of a scene you cannot get in completely with one shot.

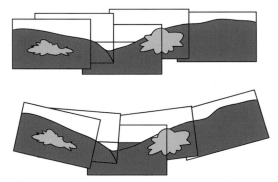

Figure 39.7 Avoid tilting the camera or pictures only join up in a curve.

A similar technique can be employed when working digitally, but instead of composing the images as a contact sheet, simply create a large blank picture document onto which all the source photographs can be placed. Each picture can be imported as a separate layer, allowing the user to move, size and crop the images to suit the composition. Many image editing programs also have the option to display a grid on the picture surface to help

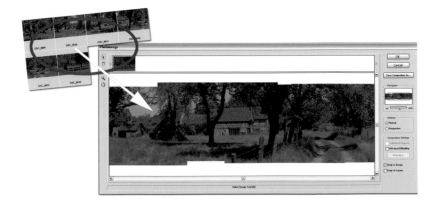

Figure 39.8 The Photomerge feature found in both Photoshop and Photoshop Elements programs stitches together a series of overlapping images to form one complete panoramic photograph.

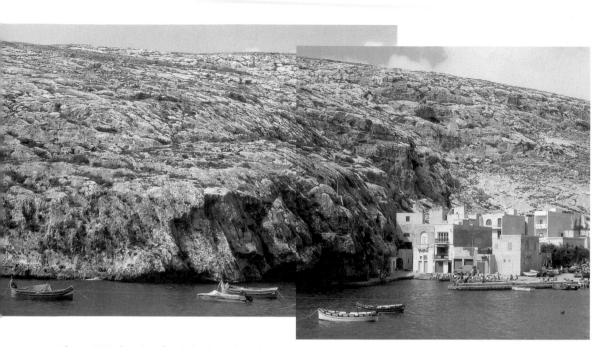

Figure 39.6 (Continued) Include plenty of overlap.

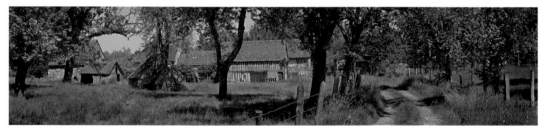

Figure 39.9 Photomerge, like other stitching software, matches and seamlessly blends the edges of adjacent images to form the final wide vista composition.

with more precise alignment. Once the composition is complete, the grid can then be hidden from display.

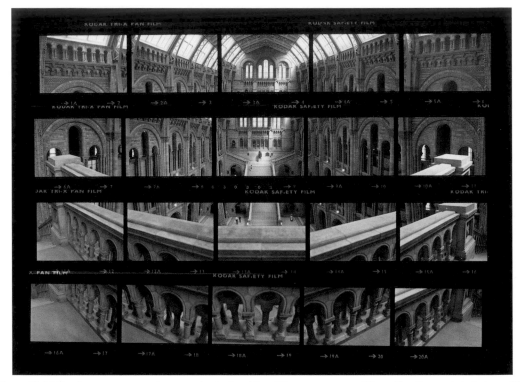

Figure 39.10 Mosaic-type panorama. A contact sheet printed from 20 exposures on one 35 mm film. Always start photographing at top left and finish bottom right.

1 Using a sequence of pictures, create a visual diary of '5 minutes' in the life of a friend or relative. Try to make sure that each image is linked to the next so that the story flows more like a collection of stills from a movie rather than a bunch of individual pictures.

2 When shooting hand-held in low light, try using your flash together with a long shutter speed. The flash will freeze part of the frame and the long exposure time will create a sense of movement. This technique is often called 'flash-blur'.

3 Shoot a series of architectural details concentrating on strong shapes, textures and colors. Then, select a single image and, if you are a film user, print it several times the correct way round as well as reversed. Arrange the prints to form a reflecting kaleidoscope composition. Digital users can achieve the same results by copying the original picture several times and then flipping several of the photographs so that they are mirror reflections. The various pictures can then be arranged into position to form the kaleidoscope.

4 When next on holiday, try making a 'joiner' of a famous landmark. Instead of trying to capture all of the texture, color and detail of the site in a single image, use a series of pictures that focus on various aspects of the scene. After returning home, montage the pictures together,

(continued)

PROJECTS

either as prints or via the computer, to produce a rich visual description of the landmark.

5 Produce a series of pictures showing: (a) slow subjects – elderly people, milk floats, tortoises, fat animals, etc., apparently whizzing along; (b) fast subjects made to appear stationary or moving very slowly.

6 Walk around a fairground or lighted traffic-filled street at night, holding the camera with its shutter open for 3–5 seconds (at f16, ISO 100 film or setting). Include plenty of pinpoint lights. Keep the camera still for part of each exposure.

7 Make a series of abstract images of the human figure. Consider the possibilities of focus, movement, blur, reflection, refraction and shooting through various semi-transparent materials.

8 Create 'physiogram' patterns. In a darkened room, rest your camera on the floor facing upwards, focused for 1 m and set for f8 (ISO 100 film or setting). Suspend a pen torch pointing downwards so that it hangs 1 m above the lens, on nylon cord firmly anchored to the ceiling. Make the torch swing freely in various directions within an area about 1 m square for 30 seconds with the shutter open.

9 By combining two or more images, construct a photograph of a fantastic landscape.

10 By means of a double exposure, produce either a double profile portrait or show the contents of a household appliance (crockery in a dishwasher, for example) inside its closed opaque unit.

11 Make an imaginative series of five pictures on one of the following themes. Either: (a) the tree as a dominant element in a landscape; or (b) railway and/or road patterns as a visual design feature.

12 Using three consecutive frames, carefully shoot an accurate panorama showing part of the interior of your room. Then use all the rest of the film, or space on the memory card, to shoot a loose 'joiner' of the whole room. Assemble the two results appropriately.

13 Create an interpretive photographic sequence of four to six pictures illustrating your concept of either: (a) transformation; or (b) harmony.

14 Shoot several interior scenes and landscapes, then use montage to combine the foreground of one with the background of another to give an inside/outside fantasy scene.

15 Using a montage of images, illustrate one of the following themes: the mob; stairs and entrances; family ties; street-wise; ecology rules!

Presenting and Assessing Your Work

The final stage of photography is to present your results in the most effective way possible. If you made your own prints, either digitally or traditionally, they must be dried and finished, but even if you have received back work from a processing and printing lab, several decisions still have to be made before proceeding to the presentation stage.

Shots need to be edited down to your very best, cropped to the strongest composition, and then framed as individual pictures or laid out as a sequence in an album or wall display. Slides can similarly be edited and prepared for projection either traditionally or viewed as a digital slide show on a computer or television screen. At the same time, negatives, slides, contact prints and digital files deserve protective storage and a good filing system, so that you can locate them again when required.

Now you have the opportunity to review what has been achieved and assess your progress in picture making since starting photography. But how should you criticize the work . . . and also learn to listen to the criticism of others?

40 Finishing off

Final cropping

This is the final stage in deciding how each picture should be cropped. What began as the original framing up of a subject in the viewfinder concludes here by your deciding whether any last trims will strengthen the composition further. Don't allow the height-to-width proportions of photographic paper to dictate results. Standard size enlargements from a processing lab, for example, show the full content of each negative – and however careful you were in the original framing, individual pictures are often improved now by cropping to a squarer or a more rectangular shape. Placing L-shaped cards on the print surface (Figure 40.1) is the best way to preview any such trim. Then, put a tiny pencil dot into each new corner to guide you in either cropping the print itself before mounting, or preparing a 'window mat' cut-out the correct size to lay on top (see Figure 40.2).

Mounts and mounting

If your finished print is to be shown mounted with a border, choose this carefully, because pictures are strongly affected by the tone or color of their immediate surround. Compare the two identical black and white prints (Figure 40.3). On a white mount dark parts such as the shadows form a strong comb shape, whereas on a black mount the pools of sunlight become more emphasized. Even a thin white border left from the masking easel can change the picture by enclosing and separating it from a dark mount – just as a black edge-line drawn on it would do the same on the white mount.

Don't overdo colored mounts or they may easily dominate your pictures. Color prints usually look best against a mid-gray or a muted color surround in harmony with the picture. If the dominant color scheme of the shot is, say, green, try a gray–green mount. Always use

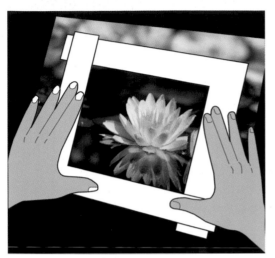

Figure 40.1 Using L-shaped cards to decide trim.

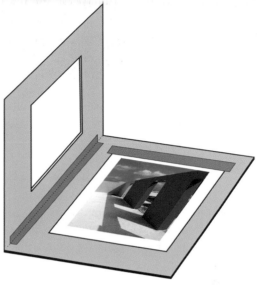

Figure 40.2 Print taped along one edge to card and covered by a cut-out window mat.

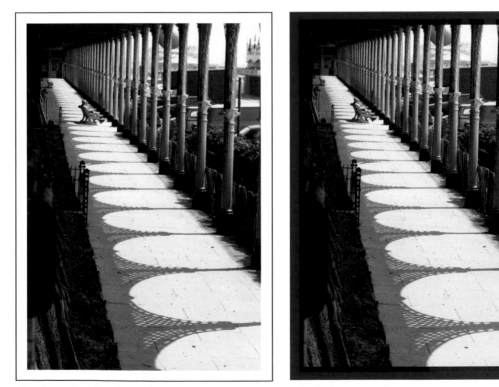

Figure 40.3 How final picture appearance is influenced by a light or dark mount.

archival quality photographic display board – other card may contain chemicals which in time will stain your picture.

A window mat form of presentation is relatively simple and effective. You attach your (untrimmed) print to the mount along one edge only with high-quality adhesive tape and then secure another card with a correctly measured cut-out 'window' on top. Use a firm, really sharp blade when cutting the window – make sure corners are left clean and free from bits.

If, instead, you simply want to mount directly onto board (surface mount), trim the print first and coat the back with a spray-on or paint-on photo-adhesive, or use wide double-sided self-adhesive sheeting. Then, position your picture accurately on a mounting board, allowing the same width of surround at the top and sides. Some spray adhesives are designed to allow repositioning after mounting and so are useful if you need to adjust the position of the picture.

For the cleanest, flattest most professional-looking mounted result, it is difficult to beat dry mounting. However, to do this job properly you need access to a dry-mounting press and an electric tacking iron.

As shown in Figure 40.4, there are four main steps:

1 Cover the back of your print with an oversize sheet of heat-sensitive mounting tissue. Briefly touch the center of the tissue with the heated iron, to tack them together.
2 Trim print and tissue to the exact size you need.
3 Position your print accurately on the mount, then carefully lifting each print corner, tack the tissue to the board. Keep one hand on the print center to keep it steady.
4 The mounting press must be set to the recommended temperature for your mounting tissue. This may be between 66 and 95°C, according to the type of heat tissue that you are using. Cover your print and board with a sheet of non-stick silicon release paper, insert the whole sandwich into the heated press and close it for about 15 seconds.

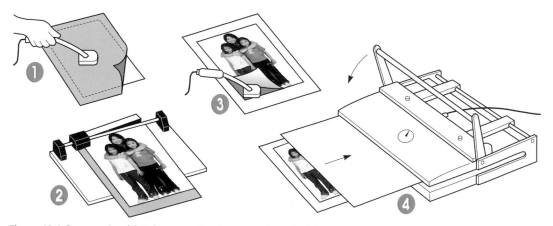

Figure 40.4 Dry mounting. (1) Tacking mounting tissue onto the back of the print. (2) Trimming print plus tissue. (3) Tacking onto mount. (4) Inserting into heated press.

As the image quality of some digitally produced prints will deteriorate when heat mounted, always test a scrap of the printing paper first to make sure that the image is unaffected by the process.

Spotting

Sometimes, otherwise perfect enlargements show one or more tiny white dust spots. The simplest approach is to spot these in with black watercolor applied almost dry on the tip of a size 0 sable brush. You can also buy spotting dye in gray and sienna, as well as neutral black.

Alternatively, use a retouching pen that has a brush tip and contains its own dye (pens come in different shades of gray). Checking through a magnifier, stipple tiny gray specks into the white area until it disappears. Gray is successful for tiny spots on color prints too, but multi-color sets of pens are also made for this purpose.

Digital photographs should never be printed until the whole image is checked carefully on screen (magnified to at least 100 per cent) for dust and scratch marks. Any such problems should be removed from the file using either the Dust and Scratches filter or the Clone Stamp tool. The same approach can be used when spotting a marked print or slide. Start by scanning the original into a computer system and then use retouching software to correct the fault. You can then print out the mark-free result through any high-resolution digital printer.

Mounting and display tips

For most photographers, the final result of their picture making activities is the print. The origins of the picture may be digital, or film, but the end product is very similar. The print is the culmination of all your skill and hard work, and if you are like me then you like to show it off. Good presentation is about showcasing the photography not the presentation.

Some new photographers spend a lot of time and money putting together elaborate mounts or frames that contain bright colors, strong textures and/or a high degree of decoration. The net effect is that the picture is overwhelmed by the visual power of the frame. The following tips have been collated to help you present your images in such a way that the viewer will be left in no doubt that the picture is what is important, not the framing.

1 *Try to create a visual space between the picture and the wall.* This is usually achieved by surrounding the image with a neutral mat board. This is a device that professionals use all the time. Even when they are working with small prints they make sure that the photograph is surrounded by plenty of visual space. This device draws the viewer in towards the picture and makes sure that his or her attention is not distracted by the surroundings.

2 *Provide more space at the bottom than the top and sides.* When positioning your image on a backing or mat board, place it in the center from side to side but move it slightly higher than center from top to bottom. It is an optical illusion, but when pictures are placed absolutely in the center there will always appear to be less space at the bottom than on the sides and the top; counteract the illusion by adding more space to the bottom.

3 *Choose colored surrounds carefully.* Though very attractive when admiring them in the arts supply shop, choosing a vibrantly colored board to surround your picture is a very risky business. It is very easy for the color to dominate the presentation and in some cases make the photograph's colors seem strange in contrast. Neutral tones tend to recede and therefore provide a better presentation platform for your pictures.

4 *Don't' use black or white without good reason.* As we have already seen, our eyes automatically adapt to the spread of tones in a scene. Placing your pictures against a brilliant white or deep black background can make them seem too dark, too light, too contrasty or not contrasty enough in comparison to their surrounds. Instead, try to choose light or midtoned hues so that the rich black and delicate white tones in your picture can really shine.

5 *Keep your pictures flat.* There is nothing worse than trying to appreciate the quality of a well-produced photograph if it has become rippled in its frame. As the humidity changes throughout the year, the moisture content of your mounted print will change also. In the more humid months your print will absorb extra moisture from the air and will grow slightly in dimension. When the picture has been mounted by securing the

photograph on all four sides, this change will result in the wrinkling of the print's surface. To stop this occurring either:

- surface mount the picture (so that all the print surface is adhered to the board) to a sturdy backing board; or
- loosely tack the photograph at the top edges only and then cover with a window mount (this gives the picture three sides to expand).

6 *Protect the images from deterioration*. To fully protect you pictures from the ravages of time, use a framing sandwich of glass, window mat, picture and backing board. These layers are then sealed into the frame using framing staples and tape on all edges. All the parts of the sandwich should be acid free and the picture should be loosely attached to the backing board (on one edge only remember) with acid-free tape (or a couple of 1 penny stamps).

7 *Use the same frames and mounts for a series*. To help unify a group of pictures, use the same size, type and color frame and mounts on all images. The pictures within the frames can change in orientation (portrait or landscape) and size within the frame, but the external dimensions of the frames should remain the same.

41 Presenting pictures in sets

Print sequences and photo-essays

I f you have shot some form of narrative picture sequence, you must decide the minimum number of prints needed to tell your story. Perhaps the series of pictures was planned right from the start, set up and photographed like scenes from a movie. Sometimes, though, it evolves from part of a heavily photographed event or outing, which becomes a narrative story once you begin to sort out the prints.

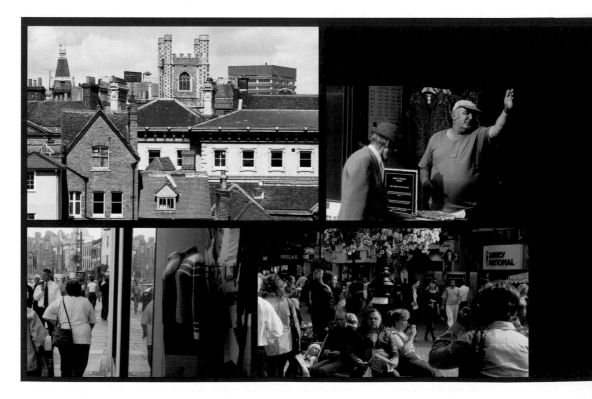

Often, the only way of making a documentary-type story is simply to photograph an event from beginning to end. All the images taken on the day are then laid out (or viewed on screen) and the best group of six or seven selected. Make your choice based on how well each picture tells the story individually and as part of the greater series. Ensure that all the technical aspects of the images (focus, exposure, depth of field, lighting) are suitable as well. Once you have made a selection, check the sequence of the images. Make sure that each links to each other and they logically fit all together. Be prepared to add, subtract and replace pictures from the group that you originally started with until you are sure that you have the strongest mix of photographs.

When it comes to presenting the series, it may help with the continuity of the group if all the prints are trimmed to the same shape and size. Then, you can present them in rows on one mount so that they read like a cartoon strip, or run them one to a page in a small album or a handmade book, or even hang them as an exhibition at a local library or café.

If you want to caption the photographs, be sparing in what you write. As a photographer it is often best to let your pictures speak for themselves, even though some viewers may differ slightly in the story they read from the sequence. People don't like to have ideas rammed into their heads; unless you can write brilliant copy you will probably only be repeating what can be seen anyway and this can seem precious or patronizing.

Sets of pictures that share a common theme but are not based on a narrative often don't need to be read in a set order. This approach offers you much freedom of layout. Follow some of the layout ideas on the pages of picture magazines and display your work more as a 'photo-essay', presenting half a dozen prints on an exhibition board or page of a large format album.

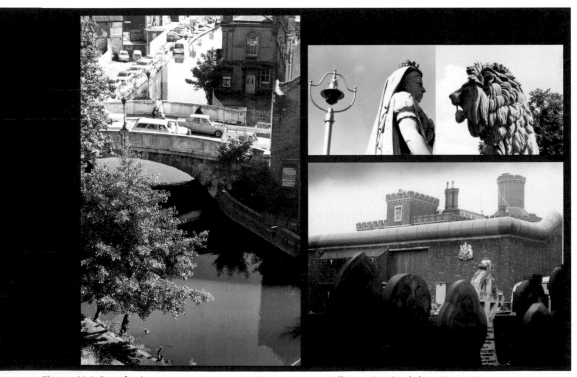

Figure 41.1 Part of a documentary series on a British country town. Differing print sizes help to give variety.

As Figure 41.1 shows, you can make all the picture proportions different in a documentary series, to give variety and best suit each individual composition.

Don't be tempted to slip one or two dull or weak pictures into a photo-essay just because their subject content ought to be included. Every shot should be good enough to stand on its own and each should add strength to the whole series. If you feel that there are gaps in the sequence, then it may be necessary to take some more pictures. Similarly, if one print is a bit too small or large relative to others, be prepared to print it again at a different size.

When laying out your set of pictures, take care over the way you relate one print to another – the lines, colors, textures and shapes, as well as the subject matter they contain, should flow together well, not conflict and confuse.

Storage options
Digital images

One of the real advantages of working digitally is that there is little cost (after your initial equipment purchase) involved in shooting as many images as you like. So, obviously, with no film and printing costs to worry about, many digital photographers are amassing hundreds if not thousands of images each year. This is great for the photographer, but once you have saved your pictures to the hard drive, locating an individual image later can be a major drama.

Recently, editing programs like Photoshop and Photoshop Elements have included image browsing features that make searching for specific photographs as simple as hunting through an

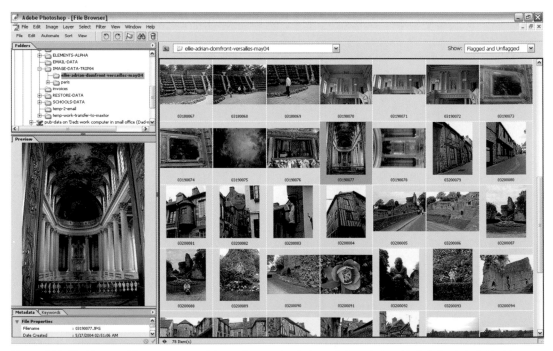

Figure 41.2 Most image editing programs contain special browsing features that are designed to help locate individual images amongst the thousands stored on photographers' hard drives.

electronic 'contact sheet' displayed on screen (see Figure 41.2). The trick to taking full advantage of these programs is making sure that the sets of images taken for different occasions are stored in aptly named folders. Do not just load all the photographs that you make into the one folder tilted My Photographs, as very quickly you will find that searching for images will become a tedious process of scrolling through hundreds of thumbnails. Instead, make a new folder for

Where does my image file go when I save it? (see Figure 41.3)

One of the most difficult concepts for new computer users is the fact that so much of the process seems to happen inside a small obscure box. Unlike traditional photography, where you can handle the product at every stage – film, negative and print – the digital production cycle can seem a little unreal. Knowing where your image goes when you store it is one such part of this mysterious process.

■ *Windows machines.* All devices that are used to store digital information are usually called drives. In Windows computer terms they are labeled with letters – the 'A' drive is for your floppy disk drive and the 'C' drive your hard disk. It is possible to have a different drive for every letter of the alphabet, but in reality you will generally only have a few options on your machine. If, for instance, you have a CD or DVD drive, then this will probably be called the 'D' drive, with any card readers attached to your machine being labeled 'e'.
■ *Macintosh computers.* If your platform of choice is the Macintosh system, then you need not concern yourself about the letter names above. Each drive area is still labeled but a strict code is not used.

Within each drive space you can have directories (Windows) or folders (Macintosh). These act as an extra way to organize you files. To help you understand, think of the drives as drawers within a filing cabinet and the directories as folders within the drawers.

When you save your files from inside an image editing program, the picture is held within a folder on a specific drive. To locate and open the picture again, you must navigate to this place and select the image that you want to edit, so make sure that when you are making folders and naming files that you use labels that make sense.

each shooting occasion. Name the folder with a title that makes sense and include a date – 'Bill's Birthday, October 2004'.

Most new computers have very large hard drives that can store many thousands of digital photographs, but even with this amount of space, if you are a dedicated photographer there will come a time when you will need to add extra storage. The simplest option is to have another hard drive added to your machine by a technician at the local computer store.

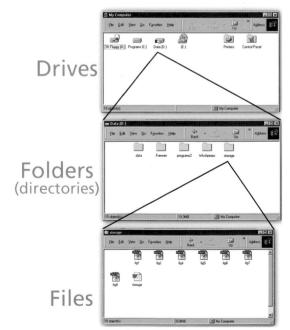

Figure 41.3 Your digital photographs are stored as individual files in folders on drives in your computer. You can aid the location of individual pictures by creating new folders for each photographic session and labeling these with titles that reflect their contents.

Backing up of important images is another consideration that many new digital photographers need to make. Unlike the situation with traditional photographic images, where new prints can be easily made from the original negatives if the first ones are damaged or misplaced, digital files, once lost, damaged or accidentally overwritten, are gone forever. From the moment that you start making digital photographs you should ensure that your best pictures are always stored in a second place other than your computer's hard drive. This can be as simple as copying your pictures to a data CD or DVD, or even saving them on an external hard drive. Any of these options will guarantee that you pictures are preserved if you main hard drive fails or is infected with a computer virus.

Negatives and prints

Smaller family albums give you less scope for layout ideas but they are a quick, convenient way to sort out your best shots. Most albums are geared to the print sizes produced by the photo labs, laying out two or three to a page. The type that have a 'cling film' overlay on each page

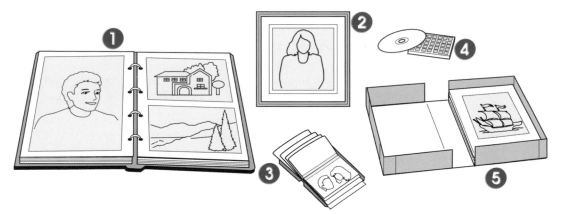

Figure 41.4 Some ways of showing work. (1) Cling film album. (2) Glass frame. (3) Pocket file. (4) Photo CD. (5) Print box.

allow you to insert, reposition or remove prints at any time without adhesive or mounting equipment. A pocket file (Figure 41.4) is also a handy way of carrying around small prints.

Unframed enlargements on individual board mounts are most safely stored in boxes made of archival material. You can keep to one standard mount size and buy or make a box that opens into two halves so that anyone viewing your pictures can move them from one half to the other.

Don't overlook the importance of filing negatives and contact prints efficiently too – otherwise you may spend hours searching for an important shot you want enlarged. A ring file with loose-leaf sleeved sheets (negative sleeves), each accepting up to 36 negatives, is ideal. If you make a contact sheet off all your pictures, punch each one and file it next to its set of negatives.

Slides

Processed slides are normally returned to you in plastic, glassless mounts. For maximum protection from finger-marks and scratches it is advisable to transfer your best slides into glass mounts. If you have your own projector, these selected shots can be stored in a magazine, ready for use. Each slide should have a large spot stuck on its mount at the bottom left when you hold the picture correct way up, exactly as it should look on

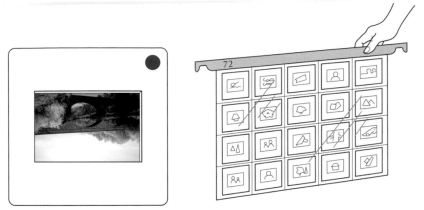

Figure 41.5 (Left) Spot the slide mount top right (image upside down) when loading the projector. (Right) Clear plastic hanging sheets have individual pouches for slides and can be numbered for filing.

the screen. This gives you a visual guide for loading the slide into the projector. Always make sure that the image is loaded with this spot in the top right facing the lamp. To store a large slide collection, keep them in pocketed clear plastic sheets (Figure 41.5), which can be numbered and hung in any standard filing cabinet.

When projecting slides pick a matt white surface for your screen, as even a slightly tinted wall will distort colors. Slight presence of light will dull colors and turn blacks into flat grays, so make sure that you room is darkened.

42 Non-print-based presentation

As well as the traditional way of presenting your work, such as albums, boxes or exhibitions, the world of digital has opened up a whole new range of display options for the photographer who wants to share his or her work. Some, like the computer slide show, mimic traditional techniques whilst others such as web presentations offer completely new ways of presenting and viewing your photographs.

Slide shows without the slides (see Figure 42.1)

I'm sure that it wouldn't take too much prompting for many readers to recall the dreaded family slide shows that seem to occur regularly on lazy Sunday evenings in many households around the country. Everyone's favorite uncle would present a selection of the family archives, and we would all sit around amazed at how much we had changed and try not to make rude comments about clothing styles and receding hairlines.

Well, the days when most photographers recorded the family history on slide film are slowly going, but the slide show events that accompanied these images are starting to make a comeback – thanks, in part, to the ease with which we can now organize and present our treasured digital photos on new media like CD and DVD discs. Gone too are the dusty projectors, being replaced instead by DVD players linked to widescreen 'tellies'.

Companies like Roxio provide easy-to-use CD and DVD writing software that handle both the initial image editing (via Photosuite) and then the picture sequencing and recording to disc

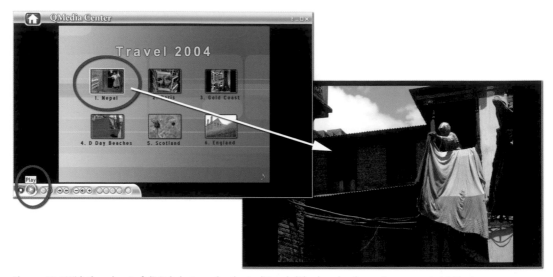

Figure 42.1 With the advent of digital photography, the traditional slide show has been given a new twist. The images are sequenced on the computer and then recorded to CD or DVD ready for showing on a computer or television.

all in the one program suite. Using the following steps, you can produce a CD-based slide show complete with main menu that can be shown on TV or computer screen.

Step by step

Program: Roxio Easy Media Creator

1 First of all, make sure that all the images that you intend to use in the slide show have been enhanced for color, contrast, brightness and sharpness. Next, to create a menu-driven slide show, start by opening the DVD builder application from the Easy Media Creator 7.0 home page. Click the Add New Title button and choose an image that will act as a menu image for one of the slide shows on the disc. Click on the text beneath the menu image to change its label. Do the same for the heading for the menu. Repeat the process of adding titles till you have all the menu items you need (see Figure 42.2).

2 Now select a menu item in the Preview screen and then click on the Add to Selected Title option from the list on the left side of the screen. Select the images to add to the slide show from the browser that appears and then click Add. Next click the Transition Themes button and choose a scheme from those listed. Click OK to apply the scheme to all the transitions between the pictures in the slide show (see Figure 42.3).

3 Repeat the addition of images to the menu items and the selection of transitions schemes until all the slide shows are built. Now click the Burn button to create the disc-based slide show (see Figure 42.4).

Disc types explained

Most CD and DVD writing (recording software) can produce your slide show in a variety of disc formats. In the example, we created an SVCD or Super Video Compact Disc, but many programs can also produce slide shows as a DVD (Digital Versatile Disc) or standard VCD. Most DVD players can read and display the content of any of these formats, but to be sure that your machine is compatible, check the equipment's manual.

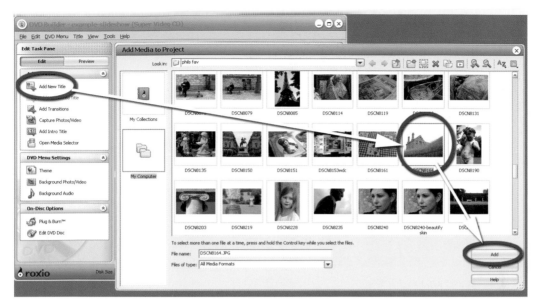

Figure 42.2 Setting up a slide show – 1.

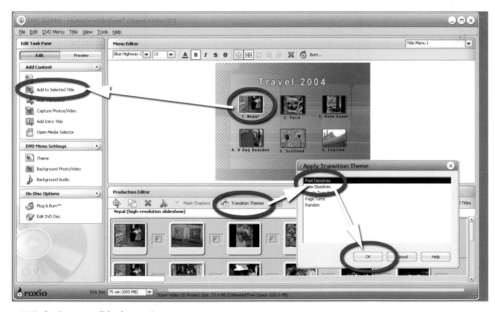

Figure 42.3 Setting up a slide show – 2.

E-mail photocards (see Figure 42.5)

Sending e-mails is nothing new, but adding your favorite pictures as attachments is a great way to share your photographs. Add some true spice to your next e-mail message by adding a picture postcard featuring images of a recent party or sites from your latest holiday. Or why not combine your love of photography with the speed and convenience of e-mail to produce the twenty-first century equivalent of the 'carte de visite' showcasing the latest family portrait.

Many software packages now make the process of making the photograph suitable for the task by playing around with pixel dimensions, compression settings and special web file formats a simple affair. Operating systems like Windows XP allow you to e-mail pictures

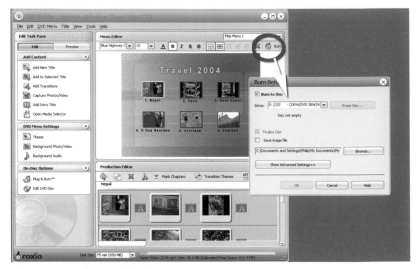

Figure 42.4 Setting up a slide show – 3.

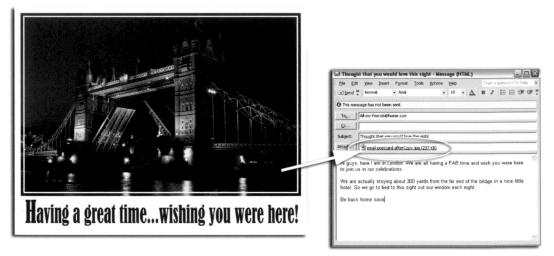

Figure 42.5 With the aid of programs like Photoshop Elements you can quickly and easily create e-mail postcards featuring your favorite pictures. Image courtesy of www.ablestock.com.

(as attachments) directly from the folder they are stored in. If you want a little more control, then many of the image editing packages provide this level of flexibility too.

Photoshop Elements, in fact, has a special feature, Attach to E-mail, designed just for this purpose. To send a photocard using Elements, start with your candidate photograph open in the program, add some text and maybe a border and then click the Attach to E-mail button (nestled about midway along the shortcuts bar). Click to Auto Convert to adjust the image to the right size, compression and format for web work and then Elements will automatically open a new e-mail message with your picture attached. The only task left for you to do is to address the e-mail, type in a suitable subject and add a few comments into the body of the e-mail. Clicking the Send button will 'post' your work of art and pithy words along to the lucky recipient. If you want a 'picture only' e-mail then just add the address and a subject and send away.

Step by step

Program: Photoshop
Elements – File > Attach to
E-mail

1 Start by opening the picture to
   be used as the base image for
   the card. With white selected as
   the background color, choose the
   Crop tool and click and drag a
   rectangle around the whole of
   the image. Next, grab the corner
   handles for the crop marquee
   and drag them outwards beyond
   the edges of the picture. Double-
   click inside the marquee to apply
   the crop. This creates a white
   border around your photograph
   (see Figure 42.6).

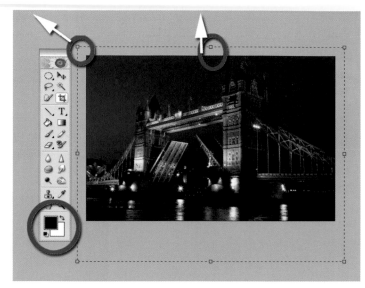

Figure 42.6 Creating an e-mail photocard – 1.

2 Now select the rectangular
   selection tool and click and drag a marquee that is
   slightly smaller than the dimensions of the
   photograph. Move the selection by click-dragging the
   selection until it is positioned an even distance from
   the edges of the picture. Now edit stroke the
   selection with a thin white frame (see Figure 42.7).

3 Use the Type tool and a fancy font to add a message
   to the bottom of the card in the white space created
   by the crop in step 1. To match the type color with
   the hues in the picture, use the Eyedropper tool to
   select a suitable foreground color from the image
   before adding the text (see Figure 42.8).

4 With the card picture now complete, it is time for
   Photoshop Elements to do its magic. Click onto the
   Attach to E-mail button in the shortcuts bar. Select
   the Auto Convert option from the Attach to E-mail
   dialog that pops up. This option adjusts the size, file
   type and size (compression) so that it can be e-mailed
   easily (see Figure 42.9).

5 The Choose Profile dialog appears after clicking the
   Auto Convert button. Select the profile of the
   program that you use to create and send e-mails and
   then select OK (see Figure 42.10).

6 A new e-mail message appears with your picture
   already neatly included as an e-mail attachment. All
   you need to do is add an address, a subject heading
   and then type in a message into the body of the
   e-mail. Now click Send to 'post' your digital postcard
   (see Figure 42.11).

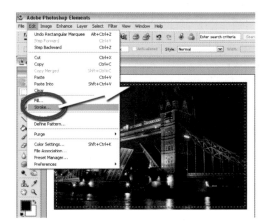

Figure 42.7 Creating an e-mail photocard – 2.

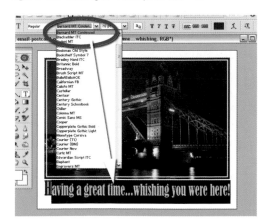

Figure 42.8 Creating an e-mail photocard – 3.

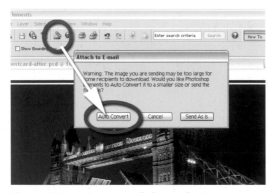

Figure 42.9 Creating an e-mail photocard – 4.

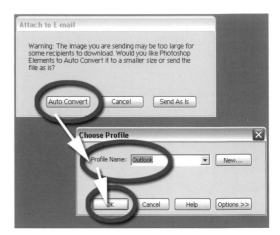

Figure 42.10 Creating an e-mail photocard – 5.

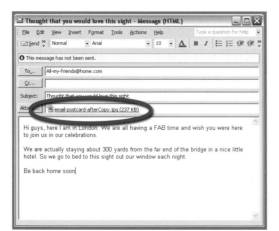

Figure 42.11 Creating an e-mail photocard – 6.

E-mail photocard tip (see Figure 42.12)

If you want a little more control over the process used to make the picture ready for e-mailing, try adjusting the size of the picture manually using the Image > Resize > Image Size feature. The dimensions should be no bigger than 800 × 600 pixels, with most e-mail pictures being as small as 640 × 480 pixels.

You will also need to change the file format to JPEG and add some compression to make sure that the picture is not too big to send. For the best results, use the File > Save for Web feature.

With dimensions, file format and size all manually adjusted, you can attach the postcard to the e-mail using the Send As Is option in the Attach to E-mail dialog (rather than Auto Convert).

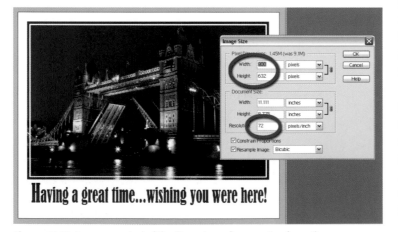

Figure 42.12 For more control of the dimensions of your postcard, use the Image > Resize > Image Size feature to set the exact proportions of the document before using the Attach to E-mail feature.

Web gallery (see Figure 42.13)

Putting your pictures onto the web is a great way to create a permanent, 'open all hours' gallery of your work. For many photographers new to the web, the steps involved in putting together a series of linked web pages seems a little daunting, but there are many software packages on the market that can help make the process easier.

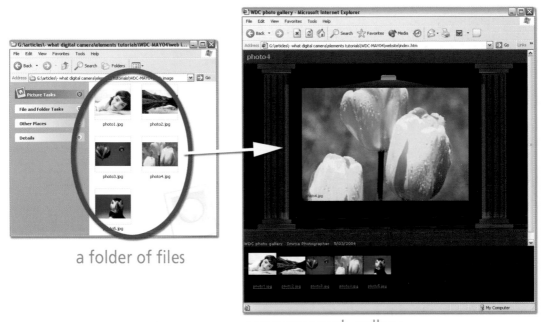

a folder of files

your own web gallery

Figure 42.13 Many photographers now use the web as a way to permanently display their photographs. Photoshop and Photoshop Elements both contain a feature (Web Photo Gallery) designed to quickly and easily convert a folder of files into a working website. Image courtesy of www.ablestock.com.

Lurking, almost hidden, in the File menus of both Photoshop and Photoshop Elements is one such little-known feature that will save you loads of time, effort and frustration when making your first website.

Adobe's Web Photo Gallery tool is a purpose-built feature designed to take a folder full of images and produce a multi-page, fully linked, gallery site in the matter of a few minutes. The process is as simple as navigating your way through a series of choices, inputting some text, selecting some pictures and pressing OK.

The result is a website that contains both thumbnails (small index images) and gallery photographs (larger versions of your pictures). Each of the thumbnails is hot linked and, when clicked, opens a larger version of the image or transports the viewer to one of several gallery pages. You can choose to include file name, titles or even security watermarks for each image and viewers can navigate between pictures with a few simple button clicks. Overall, not bad work for a few minutes spent selecting folders and inputting text.

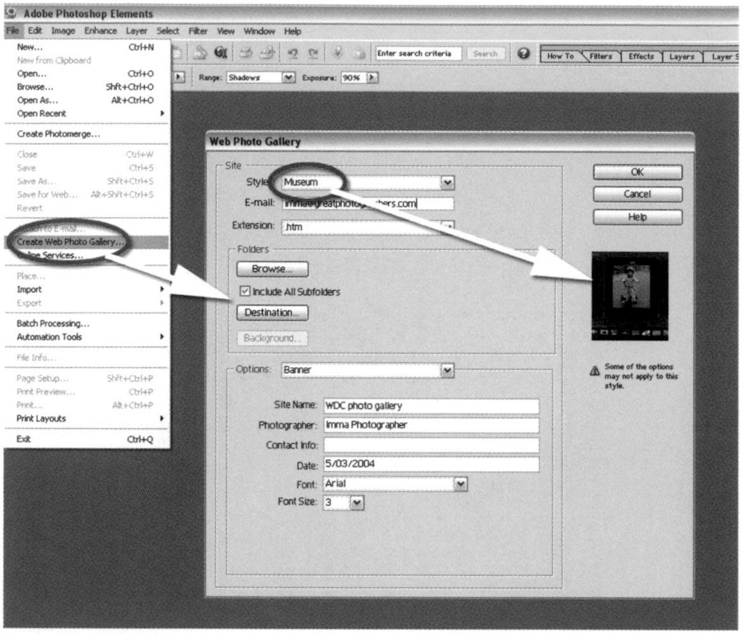

Figure 42.14 Putting your pictures on the web – 1.

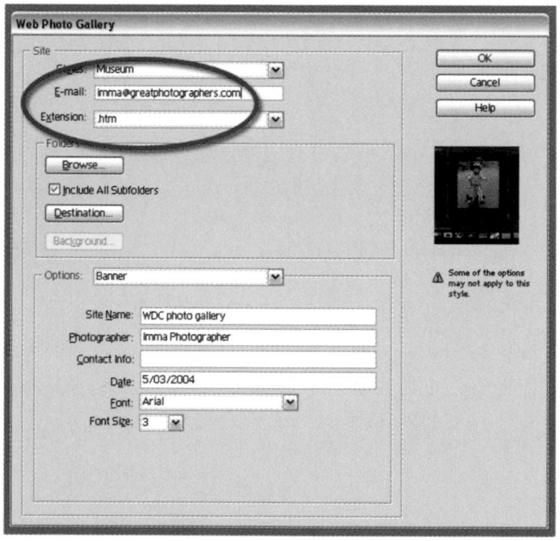

Figure 42.15 Putting your pictures on the web – 2.

Step by step

Programs: Photoshop Elements 2.0 –
File > Create Web Photo Gallery
    Photoshop CS –
File > Automate > Web Photo Gallery

1 Select the Web Photo Gallery feature from the file menu and choose the look that you want for your website from the options available in the Style section of the dialog. Here we selected Museum (see Figure 42.14).

2 Input your e-mail address and select the extension settings preferred by the company who will host your site. Most will work with the default '.htm' setting (see Figure 42.15).

3 Browse for the source folder that contains the images that you want to use for the site. Select the destination folder that will be used to store the files and folders created during the process (see Figure 42.16).

4 Select the *Banner* item from the Options drop-down menu. Input the details for the site using the text boxes provided. Select the *Large Images* item from the Options drop-down menu. Adjust the size and compression settings to suit your images. Add a border to your pictures by inputting a border size and choose any image-related text to be included (see Figure 42.17).

5 Continue adjusting the site settings by selecting the *Thumbnails* item from the Options drop-down menu. Indicate if you want the File Name or File Info included with the thumbnails. Select the font style and size. Select the *Custom Colors* item from the Options drop-down menu. Double-click on each of the swatches to activate the color picker. Sample the new color from the dialog and click OK to set (see Figure 42.18).

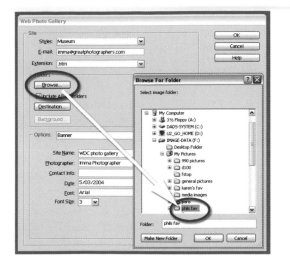

Figure 42.16 Putting your pictures on the web – 3.

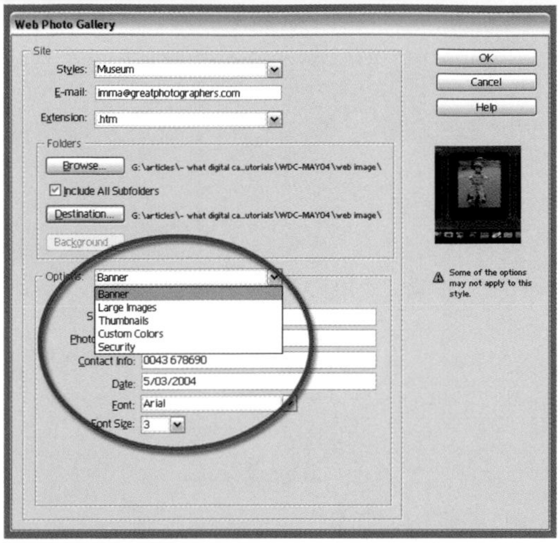

Figure 42.17 Putting your pictures on the web – 4.

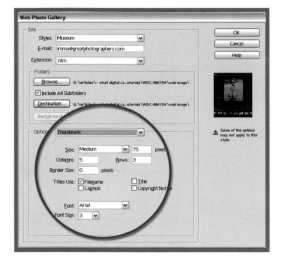

Figure 42.18 Putting your pictures on the web – 5.

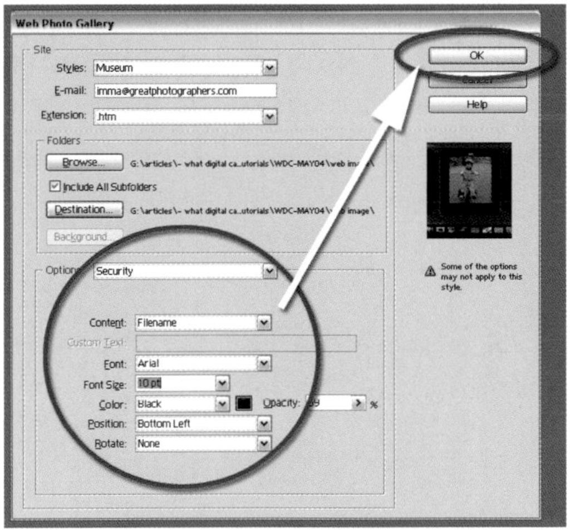

Figure 42.19 Putting your pictures on the web – 6.

6 Finally, make changes in the *Security* section to apply copyright or caption text directly to the image. Click OK to start the site construction process. When completed, the finished website will be displayed in your default browser (see Figure 42.19).

Where to from here?

With the site completed, the next step is to transfer all the files to some server space on the net. Companies called ISPs, or Internet Service Providers, provide or host the space. The company that you are currently using for 'dial-up' connection to the net will probably provide you 5 – 10 MB of space as part of your access contract. As an alternative, there are a range of hosting businesses worldwide that will store and display your gallery for free, as long as you allow them to place a small banner advertisement at the top of each of your pages.

Whatever route you take, you will need to transfer your site's files from your home machine to the ISP's machine. This process is usually handled by a small piece of software called an FTP or File Transfer Protocol program. Your service provider or hosting company will be able to guide you systematically through this process.

Website tips (see Figure 42.20)

When Photoshop or Elements creates your site, the program makes three folders or directories, titled 'images', 'thumbnails' and 'pages'. These are placed in your designated Destination folder along with one or two extra files (depending on the style of site you choose) – index.html and thumbnailFrame.html. Together, these are the core components of your website.

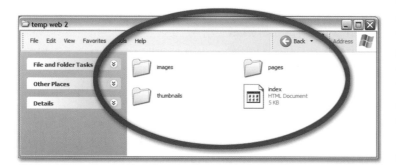

To ensure that your site works without any problems, all of these components need to be uploaded to your ISP. You also shouldn't move, or rename, any of the folders, or their contents, as this will cause a problem when the pages are loaded into a web browser. If you want to add extra images to your site, or change the ones you have, then it is easiest to make a completely new site to replace the old version.

Figure 42.20 The files produced by the Web Photo Gallery feature need to be uploaded to the web in exactly the same arrangement (folder and files) as they were created in order for your site to function correctly.

43 Evaluating your results

Is your photography improving, and if so, on what basis can you tell? It's important to develop some way of assessing the success of picture making. One very practical approach is to put prints up on the wall at home for a while and see if you can keep on enjoying them – perhaps seeing something new each time you come back to look.

Another way is to discuss your pictures with other people – both photographers and non-photographers. By this route you may also discover if and why others reach different interpretations of the same photograph, and how these vary from what you aimed to express.

Discussion is easiest if you are a member of a group, club or class, putting up several people's latest work and then getting everyone to contribute comments. At worst, it allows you to see your own pictures afresh and also discover what others have been doing. At best, you can get down to learning why pictures are taken and the reaction and influence they can exert on others.

But how do you criticize photographs, deciding what is 'good' and what 'bad'? There are at least three aspects to consider, each varying in its importance according to the stage you have reached and the type of photography you undertake.

Technical quality

This has greatest importance when you are a beginner, needing to gain experience in the use of equipment and processes. It involves questions of whether exposure and focusing were correct. Could the print have better color, be darker or less contrasty, and is there too much grain (or digital noise)? As well as improving your technical ability, this form of criticism is especially valid in photography used for accurate record-making. It is mostly concerned with facts (the negative is either sharp or unsharp, grainy or grain free), but if overdone the danger is that you apply the same rules to every picture, irrespective of subject and approach. This in itself can be a problem.

For instance, some photographs more concerned with expression than strict accuracy should be dark and gray or light and contrasty, to strengthen and carry through the emotional content of the particular image. To criticize these images heavily because of 'incorrect' printing technique would be to miss the point of the photographs in the first place.

Communication of ideas

Here results are judged mainly in terms of the approach you have used to express your ideas. This means establishing (or imagining) the purpose of the picture – factual, persuasive, etc. – and then deciding whether your result succeeds in this visual intention.

Maybe it is concerned with expressing the relationship between two people. Perhaps the picture is making a broader comment on society in general . . . or captures the peak of some action or event. Again, most of the interest may be in the content of the photograph and what can be read into a picture.

Formal structuring

Another concern is how effectively the visual 'building blocks' of pictures have been used. Your photograph's overwhelming strength may lie in its design – compositional aspects such as framing, use of perspective, color, pattern, tonal values and so on. Relative to these imaginatively used elements, the precise nature of the subject itself might take second place. On the other hand, you may have chosen to allow the subject to remain a key element but made much stronger (in dramatic appeal, for example) through the way you planned and constructed your picture.

Developing a critique

Whatever approach to criticism you adopt, and, of course, several can be used at once, your photograph is a sort of catalyst. On the one hand, there is you the photographer with your own attitudes and interests, and the physical problems you remember overcoming to get this result. In the middle is the photograph itself, which may or may not communicate the facts and ideas. On the receiving end, there is the viewer with his or her interests and background experience, the way they feel at that particular moment and the physical conditions under which your photographs are seen. All these elements contribute to the judgement of just how successful the photograph is deemed to be.

Discussing photography as a whole area, as well as individual photographs, is very much a part of studying the subject. What things can photography do well, and what can painting or drawing do better? How many ways might a particular theme or type of subject be approached? Educate yourself and make your 'eye' more visually literate by looking at the work of other photographers, in exhibitions and collections of their work printed in books.

Photography is essentially a medium, like writing or speaking, for expressing ideas and communicating information. In the hands of an artist, it provides an outlet for personal feelings and offers almost as much freedom as drawing or painting. Used by a scientist, it can report and measure in a detailed, factual way. Thanks to modern technology, everyone can now take photographs which 'come out' – giving unfettered opportunities to develop visual skills and so make pictures with an individual, personal style.

Appendices

Computer connection types

Lurking at the back of most computers or hidden beneath a front flap are a series of connections used to attach external devices to your machine:

- *USB* is the standard used for attaching most cameras, scanners and printers.
- *Firewire* is a faster scanner and camera connection than USB.
- *Screen/video* port connects the computer to the screen.
- *Mouse* port is color coded to match the mouse plug.
- *Keyboard* connects to the computer using a similar color-coded plug to the mouse.
- *SCSI* ports are sometimes used to connect scanners and external hard drives.
- *Printer* or *parallel* port connections are not used as much as they used to be. Most printers are now connected via USB.
- *Serial* used to be the connection port for mice and some digital cameras, but now is largely unused.
- *Network* connections are used to link several computers so that they can share files.
- *Modem* ports connect into the telephone socket, allowing you to dial up Internet access from your computer.

Camera memory cards

(see Figures B.1 and B.2)

Memory cards, or digital film, as they are sometimes referred to, are used to store your camera's pictures. There are five main types, listed in Table B.1.

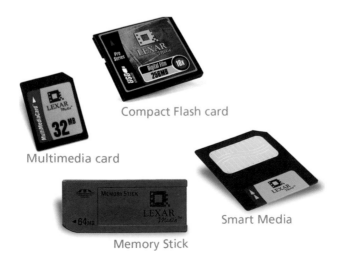

Compact Flash card

Multimedia card

Memory Stick

Smart Media

Figure B.1 Digital cameras use memory cards to store the pictures they take. There are several different card types on the market, with each camera manufacturer preferring one design or another.

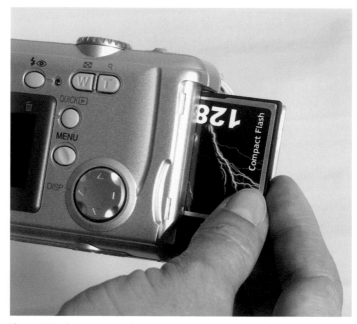

Figure B.2 The memory cards are inserted into the camera via an access flap so that full cards can be replaced with empty ones.

Table B.1 Main types of memory card

Camera memory card type	Merits	Camera makes
Compact Flash	• Most popular card • Matchbook size	Most Canon, Nikon, Hewlett Packard, Casio, Minolta and pre-2002 Kodak
Smart Media	• Credit card thickness • Usually colored black • Matchbook size	Most Olympus and Fuji digital cameras, Sharp camcorders with digital still mode, and some MP3 players
Multimedia (MMC) or Secure Digital (SD)	• Postage stamp size • Credit card thickness • SD are second generation MMC cards	Most Panasonic camcorders with digital still mode, some MP3 players, and the Kyocera Finecam S3, KB Gear JamCam, Minolta DiMAGE X and most Kodak digital cameras produced after 2001
xD Picture Card	• Smallest of all cards • About the size and thickness of a thumbnail	Newly released Fuji and Olympus cameras
Memory Stick	• Smaller than a stick of chewing gum • Longer than other card types	Used almost exclusively in Sony digital cameras, camcorders, hand-helds, portable music players and notebook computers

Appendix C Digital camera sensor sizes and resolution (megapixels)

The best cameras have chip resolution approaching 8.0 megapixels and, as you now know, the more pixels you have, the better quality the final prints will be. This said, cameras with less pixels still are capable of producing photographic prints of smaller sizes. Use Table C.1 to help give you an idea about what print sizes are possible with each resolution level (also see Figure C.1).

Table C.1 Print sizes and resolution levels

Chip pixel dimensions (pixels)	Chip resolution (1 million = 1 megapixel)	Maximum print size at 200 dpi (inches) (e.g. photo print)	Maximum image size at 72 dpi (inches) (e.g. web use)
640 × 480	0.30 million	3.2 × 2.4	8.8 × 6.6
1440 × 960	1.38 million	7.4 × 4.8	20 × 13.2
1600 × 1200	1.90 million	8 × 6	22 × 16
2048 × 1536	3.21 million	10.2 × 7.58	28.4 × 21.3
2304 × 1536	3.40 million	11.5 × 7.5	32 × 21.3
2560 × 1920	4.92 million	12.8 × 9.6	35.5 × 26.6

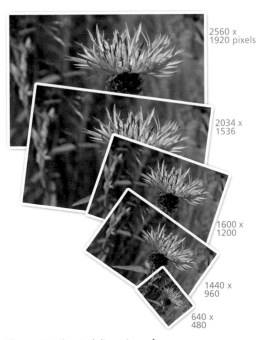

2560 x 1920 pixels

2034 x 1536

1600 x 1200

1440 x 960

640 x 480

Figure C.1 The pixel dimensions of a camera sensor determine the final print size of the photographs produced.

Appendix D Suggested starting speeds/apertures for difficult night scenes

Table D.1

Location	Shutter speed, aperture (with ISO 200 setting)
Street scene at night	1/60 second, f4
Very brightly lit street scene at night	1/60 second, f5.6
Floodlit football stadium	1/125 second, f2.8
Fairground at night	1/30 second, f2.8
Theatre stage, fully lit	1/60 second, f2.8
Boxing ring	1/60 second, f4
Floodlit factory at night	1/4 second, f2.8

Appendix E Scanner connections

The connection that links the scanner and computer is used to transfer the picture data between the two machines. Because digital photographs are made up of vast amounts of information, this connection needs to be very fast. Over the years, several different connection types have developed, each with their own merits. It is important to check that your computer has the same connection as the scanner before finalizing any purchase.

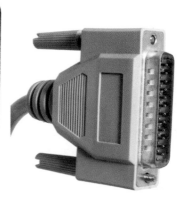

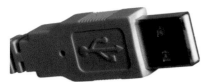

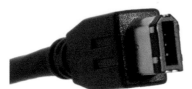

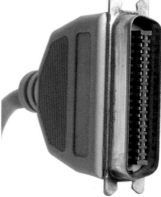

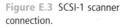

Figure E.1 USB 1.0 scanner connection.

Figure E.2 Firewire scanner connection.

Figure E.3 SCSI-1 scanner connection.

Figure E.4 Parallel scanner connection.

Table E.1 Scanner connections

Scanner connection type	Merits	Speed rating
USB 1.0	• No need to turn computer off to connect (hot swappable) • Can link many devices • Standard on many recent computers • Can be added to older machines using an additional card	Fast (1.5 Mbytes per second) See Figure E.1
USB 2.0	• Hot swappable • Can link many devices • Standard on some new models • No need to turn computer off to connect (hot swappable) • Can link many devices • Standard on many recent computers • Can be added to older machines using an additional card	Extremely fast (60 Mbytes per second)
Firewire	• Hot swappable • Can link many devices • Not generally standard on Windows machines but can be added using an additional card • Standard on newest Macintosh machines	Extremely fast (50 Mbytes per second) See Figure E.2
SCSI-1	• Can link several devices • Standard on older Macintosh machines	Fast (5 Mbytes per second) See Figure E.3
SCSI-2 (Fast SCSI)	• Not generally standard but can be added to machines using an additional card	Fast (10 Mbytes per second)
SCSI-3 (Ultra SCSI)	• Not generally standard but can be added to machines using an additional card	Very fast (20 Mbytes per second)
Parallel	• Standard on most Windows-based machines	Very slow (0.11 Mbytes per second) See Figure E.4

Appendix F What resolution should I pick?

Knowing what is the best resolution, or scanning quality, for a particular task can be a daunting task. Some scanning software allows users to pick from a list of output options such as 'web use', 'laser print' and 'photo quality print'. The program then selects the best resolution to suit the selection.

For those of you without these choices, use Table F.1 as a guide.

Table F.1 Guide to scanning quality (resolution)

What your scan will be used for	Scan quality (resolution) (dpi)
Web or screen	72
Draft quality prints	150
Photographic quality prints	200–300
Magazine printing	300

Appendix G ISO settings and their uses

Table G.1 summarizes the benefits and disadvantages of different ISO settings. Use it as a guide when selecting which value to use for your own work.

Table G.1 Benefits and disadvantages of different ISO settings

	ISO and ISO equivalent setting		
	100	**200**	**800**
Benefits	• Low noise (fine grain) • Good color saturation • Good tonal gradation	• Good noise/sensitivity balance • Good sharpness, color and tone • Can be used with a good range of apertures and shutter speeds	• Very sensitive • Can be used with fast shutter speeds, large aperture numbers or long lenses • Good depth of field
Disadvantages	• Not very sensitive • Needs to be used with fast lens or tripod	• Not the absolute best quality capable by the camera • May not be fast enough for some low light or action scenarios	• Obvious noise throughout the picture • Poor picture quality
Best uses	• Studio • Still life with tripod • Outdoors on bright day	• General hand-held shooting	• Sports • Low light situations with no flash • Indoors

Appendix H Minimum shutter speeds to stop camera shake

Table H.1 illustrates a simple rule to help eliminate camera shake. It uses the principle of not using shutter speeds that are longer than the reciprocal of the focal length of the lens being used.

Table H.1 Eliminating camera shake

Focal length (millimeters)	Reciprocal	Slowest usable shutter speed without camera support (seconds)
28	1/28	1/30
35	1/35	1/60
50	1/50	1/60
100	1/100	1/125
200	1/200	1/250
300	1/300	1/500

Appendix I Settings to control depth of field

Use Table I.1 as a quick guide for setting up your camera for either shallow or large depth of field effects.

Table I.1 Settings to control depth of field

DOF effect required	Best aperture numbers	Best focal lengths	Best subject-to-camera distance
Shallow	Low (e.g. f2.0, f2.8)	Longer than standard (e.g. 120 mm)	Close
Large	High (e.g. f22, f32)	Shorter than standard (e.g. 28 mm)	Distant

Appendix J Suggested starting speeds to freeze the action of different events

Table J.1

Location	Shutter speed (seconds)
Motor sport – straight towards the photographer	1/1000
Motor sport – turning a corner panning	1/125
Athletics – running	1/250
Athletics – long/high jump	1/500
Football	1/250
Ballet dancer leaping – fully lit stage	1/250 (non-pan)
Ballet dancer – fully lit stage	1/125
Pole vault	1/500

Appendix K Flash guide numbers, apertures and distance

Use Table K.1 as a quick reference for the relationship between guide number, aperture, ISO and subject-to-camera distance.

Table K.1 Flash guide numbers, apertures and distance

Guide number of flash	Aperture					
	f2.8	f4.0	f5.6	f8.0	f11	f16
	Distances from camera to subject for good exposure (m)					
10	3.50	2.5	1.78	1.25	0.90	0.62
20	7.10	5.0	3.57	2.50	1.81	1.25
30	10.71	7.5	5.37	3.75	2.72	1.87
40	14.28	10.00	7.14	5.00	3.63	2.50
50	17.85	12.50	8.92	6.25	4.54	3.12
60	21.42	15.00	10.71	7.50	5.45	3.75

NB: This table assumes you are using an ISO of 100, that you are not bouncing, diffusing or zooming the flash, and that the distance measurement is in meters.

Appendix L **Rollfilm and sheet film cameras**

The great majority of modern cameras use 35 mm or APS film, but other cameras are made to accept larger picture format rollfilm or individual sheet films. You will also find many older, second-hand cameras needing films of this kind.

Unlike 35 mm material in its light-tight cassette, *rollfilm* comes on an open spool attached to lightproof 'backing paper' (Figure L.1). Film and backing paper are rolled up tightly together so that light cannot reach the sensitive surface during loading. Inside the camera they wind up tightly onto an identical take-up spool after exposure, ready for unloading. No rewinding is therefore required.

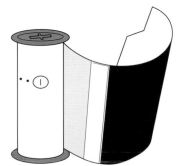

The main rollfilm still in general use is 120 size, which allows pictures 6 cm (2 ¼ in) wide. Rollfilm cameras (often termed *medium-format* cameras) may give twelve pictures 6 × 6 cm to a film; others give ten pictures 6 × 7 cm or sixteen 6 × 4.5 cm.

Negatives this size need less enlargement than 35 mm film so you can make big prints which are relatively grain free.

Figure L.1 How the start of a 120 rollfilm is attached inside its lightproof backing paper.

A few large-format cameras use individual sheets of film, typically 4 × 5 in. Each sheet has first to be loaded into a film holder in the dark (see page 264). Using *sheet film* allows you to process each exposure individually, and the still larger negative gives even finer grain and detail.

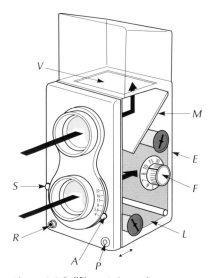

Figure L.2 Rollfilm twin lens reflex camera. S, shutter speed control; R, release for shutter; A, aperture control; V, viewing and focusing screen; M, mirror (fixed); E, exposure counter at back of camera; F, focusing control; L, light-sensitive film.

Twin lens reflex (TLR) cameras

Some rollfilm cameras are designed as twin lens reflexes. As Figure L.2 shows, the camera body has two lenses – one for viewing and focusing, the other for shooting. The upper or 'viewing' lens reflects off a fixed mirror and forms an image on a ground-glass screen on top of the camera. The lower lens is the one which takes the photograph, and is fitted with a shutter and a diaphragm within the lens. To use a TLR camera you load it with a rollfilm, set shutter speed and f-number according to the light and then look down onto the focusing screen to see what you are photographing.

Turning the focusing knob moves both lenses backwards and forwards, so that when your subject is sharply imaged on the ground glass screen the taking lens is also correctly positioned to give a sharp image on the film inside the camera. Pressing the release fires the bladed shutter, exposing the picture. The image on the focusing screen does not disappear at the moment of shooting like a single lens reflex. It is easy to shoot from low viewpoints and still see to focus. However, since viewing and taking lenses are separate, the camera suffers parallax error (page 31) especially in close-up work. It is also bulky, and you lack the ability to change lens focal length. The picture on the focusing screen appears reversed left to right – irritating when trying to follow a moving subject.

View cameras

These sheet film cameras (Figure L.3) look large and professional but are basically of simple construction. They are designed always to be used on a tripod. The front panel carries a lens with a diaphragm and a shutter; the back has a full size 4×5 in ground-glass focusing screen. Focusing controls allow the two panels to be moved towards or away from each other along a rail, and flexible square-shaped bellows between the panels keep out the light. Other knobs allow sliding or swinging of the front and back panels. These are known as 'camera movements' and used to help control depth of field or shape distortion.

The large focusing screen is especially helpful for carefully composing still-life subjects in the studio, although you must get used to checking an image which is seen upside down. The long bellows make it possible to focus very close subjects. However, these cameras are large, slow and cumbersome to use. The step-by-step sequence in Figure L.4 shows how you

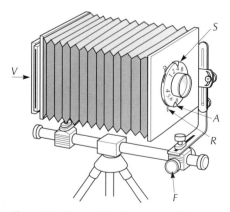

Figure L.3 Monorail 4×5 in camera. V, viewing and focusing screen; S, shutter speed dial; A, aperture setting control; R, shutter release; F, focus controls.

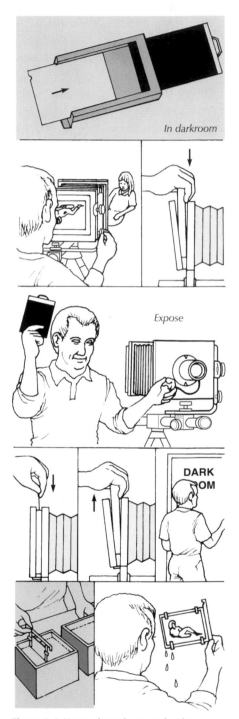

Figure L.4 How a picture is exposed with a 4×5 in camera, using a sheet film holder.

start off in the darkroom where each sheet of film is loaded into a special holder. When the film holder is slipped into the camera it replaces the focusing screen, taking up the same position. A panel or 'darkslide' in the holder is then removed to reveal the emulsion side of the film to the (light-tight) inside of the camera. Then, after the exposure has been made using the shutter on the lens, the darkslide must be replaced. The entire film holder is then withdrawn from the camera and taken to the darkroom, where the film is removed and processed.

Limitations for beginners

Far fewer medium- and large-format cameras are made than 35 mm types. They are mainly aimed at professional photographers, and include single lens reflex and direct viewfinder types. Kits of this kind are expensive – with the exception of one or two basic twin lens reflexes intended for beginners. You must also remember that these cameras are bulkier to carry around, and mostly lack features such as built-in exposure meters and auto-focus common to smaller cameras. You will need more costly enlarging equipment too, able to accept the larger negatives.

Appendix M Using a hand-held meter

Modern small-format cameras have a light meter built into the camera to measure the subject and calculate exposure. But you will not find this feature in older cameras, or in most cameras taking larger formats (Appendix L). You then have to buy a separate, hand-held exposure meter. Used properly this will measure your subject and read out the appropriate combination of f-number and shutter speed to set for the film you are using.

A small hand-meter simplifies the making of local readings of highlight and shadow parts as it is easier to bring near to the subject than moving the whole camera. In fact, you can measure exposure without taking out the camera (an advantage for candid work). However, since the meter does not measure light through the camera lens you must be prepared to adjust the exposure settings it suggests when shooting close-ups (see page 266).

A traditional hand-meter (Figure M.1) as a light-sensitive cell at the front to measure the light reflected from your subject. You first set the ISO rating of your film in a window on a large dial, point the meter, note the number shown under a moving needle, and set this against an arrow on the dial. Suitable combinations of lens aperture and shutter setting, all of which will result in correct exposure, then appear lined up in the upper part of the dial. You choose the one giving the depth of field or movement blur effects you need, and set the camera accordingly.

Different ways of making readings

Any hand-meter pointed generally at your subject from the camera position will give an exposure reading based on the assumption that the subject has roughly equal areas of light and dark. Some hand-meters have a white plastic diffuser, which slides over the cell. You then hold the meter at the subject, its cell facing the camera, when taking your reading. This 'incident light' single measurement scrambles all the light reaching parts of the subject seen by the camera, ignoring light or dark unimportant background.

A very accurate way of working is to take two undiffused readings, pointing the meter direct at the darkest important shadowed area, and then at the brightest important highlight area. You

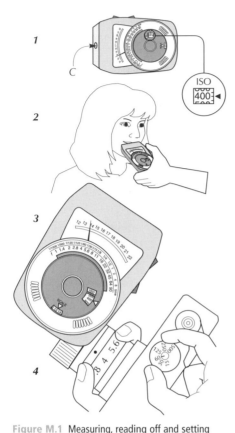

Figure M.1 Measuring, reading off and setting exposure.

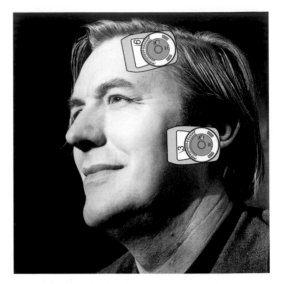

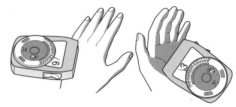

Figures M.2 and M.3 Making highlight and shadow readings. (Top) Direct from subject itself. (Above) From substitute hands in direct light and shadow. (Meter calculator was then set midway between 3 and 6.)

then split the difference between the two. For example, for Figure M.2, readings were taken about 15 cm (6 inches) from the lightest and then the darkest parts of the man's head. The dial was set to midway between the two readings – in this case 4½ – and the camera settings needed then read off.

When a subject cannot be approached so closely try taking readings from nearby substitutes under the same lighting. For example, in Figure M.3 the photographer is reading off the matching skin of his or her own hands – first turned towards, then away from, the same lighting received by the face. In landscapes you can read off the grass at your feet for grass on a distant hill – provided both are under the same lighting conditions. Remember, though, when taking any form of reading, not to accidentally measure your shadow or that of the meter.

Exposure increase for close-ups

When you are shooting subjects very close up (using extension rings or bellows to get a sharp image), the image is less bright than with distant subjects – even though lighting and f-number remain the same. Inside the camera the effect is like being in a darkened room with a slide projector being moved away from the screen (the film). As you focus the camera lens for an ever-closer subject the image becomes bigger but also *dimmer*.

If your camera measures exposure through the lens itself this change is taken into account by the metering system, but when using a separate meter you must increase the exposure it reads out. In practice the increase starts to become significant when you focus on a subject closer than about five times the focal length of the lens you are using, growing greater as you focus on subjects closer still, e.g. something 250 mm from a 50 mm lens needs only 1½ times the normal exposure; at 170 mm it requires twice, and at 100 mm four times the exposure the hand-meter shows. To calculate exposure increase multiply the exposure shown on the meter by $(M + 1)^2$, where M is magnification, meaning height of image divided by height of subject.

For example, photographing a 30 mm high postage stamp so that it appears 12 mm high on the film. As magnification is 0.4 you must multiply exposure by 1.4^2 which is 2. You can increase exposure either by giving a slower shutter speed, or by opening up the aperture – one f-number for a $\times$ 2 increase, one and a half for $\times$ 3, and so on.

Appendix N Batteries

Practically every modern camera relies on some form of battery to power its auto exposure or focus systems, film wind-on, flash, etc. When a camera fails to operate, or functions in a sluggish way, the cause can almost always be pinned down to exhausted battery condition or poor contacts.

There are four main battery types. Relatively low cost *alkaline* batteries are common for powering small wind-on motors, flash and general camera circuitry. They are not rechargeable but have a good shelf life and are virtually leak proof. Tiny *silver oxide* batteries are often used for camera or hand-meters, and for light emitting diode viewfinder displays. They provide constant voltage over a long life. *Nickel cadmium* ('Ni-Cad') batteries are rechargeable, and together with their recharging gear are more expensive than other battery types. They are most often used in accessory flashguns. One problem with Ni-Cad is 'memory fatigue', meaning that a battery will not charge to full capacity as it gets older, and therefore needs recharging more often. *Lithium* type batteries are increasingly used in modern equipment designed for this power source. They have a long powered-up storage life but to avoid any danger of leaking always remove a lithium battery from your equipment immediately it is exhausted.

In general, remember that batteries are affected by temperature. Low temperatures slow down their chemical reaction, resulting in erratic or sluggish camera operation. On the other hand, batteries stored bagged in a refrigerator have a greatly extended shelf life. Make sure batteries are inserted with the polarity (+ or −) marked on their contacts matching the terminals in your equipment.

Safety points

Keep batteries away from young children – some tablet types look like sweets. Never allow anyone to try opening a battery or throw it on a fire. Do not attempt to recharge batteries other than nickel types marked as suitable, and always recharge through the recommended transformer.

It is good practice to remove the batteries from photographic equipment you will not be using for some months. Changing non-rechargeable batteries once a year is also advisable – especially before going to a location where the correct replacements might be difficult to buy.

Appendix ○ Health and safety in photography

The equipment and processes used in photography are not particularly hazardous, provided you take one or two (mostly common sense) precautions. For example, the use of electrical equipment in the studio, or within the darkroom in the presence of water and dim lighting, clearly requires care. Similarly, when you are using photographic chemicals it is best to adopt working habits which pay due regard to your health.

Electrical equipment

Remember that studio spotlights and floodlights produce heat as well as light. The *bottom* of the lamp head is always cooler than the *top*, so only grip the bottom when tilting the light. Never drape any diffusing or filtering material you may be using over a lamp head. Instead, arrange to support it a foot or so in front of the lamp (even just hold it there when you take the picture). Keep lamps and curtains well apart for similar reasons, and don't leave lamps on in an empty room.

Each lighting unit needs a plug fitted with an appropriate fuse. Lamp wattage divided by the supply voltage tells you how many amperes are drawn. Fit a fuse rated just slightly above this figure, e.g. use a 5 A fuse if the lamp draws four or less amperes. Just fitting a 13 A fuse in every plug reduces your protection. All lighting equipment should be earthed ('grounded') through a third wire.

Watch out, with items like lamps which you move about, that the cable does not fray where it enters the lamp head, and that the connections at each end have not worked loose. Never try to remove a bulb from its socket whilst it is still hot, and make sure your lighting unit is disconnected before fitting a new lamp. Be careful not to have the power cable stretched between socket and lamp head so you can trip over it, or have the unit set up in a way that makes it unstable and top heavy.

Most flashguns have two circuits – a trigger circuit to the shutter which uses a very low and harmless current, and an internal higher powered circuit to the flash tube. Never try opening up the internal electrics to repair your unit. Even though battery operated it may be storing enough electricity to give you a powerful shock.

In the darkroom, where water is present, it is even more important to have your electrical equipment – enlarger, safe light, ventilator – properly fused and earthed (see page 186). Avoid having sockets or switches where someone might grasp them with a wet hand – near the sink, for example. If possible, have all switches fitted to the ceiling and operated by non-conductive pull-cords. Avoid running wiring under, or close to, sinks, metal drying cabinets, etc. Your power supply outlets should be at benchtop height, never at floor level in case of flooding.

Care with chemicals

Handle photographic chemicals with the same care as other chemicals used around the home. Always read any warning on the label, especially if you are unfamiliar with what you are about to use. If any contents are hazardous the container will have first aid measures labeled.

Avoid splashing chemicals into your eyes or onto your skin, particularly skin that is dry and chapped. A few people may have an adverse reaction to chemicals such as developers, resulting in skin irritation. Waterproof gloves are then essential when film processing or printing. It is always a good idea to wear simple eye protectors and gloves (rubber or plastic) when preparing chemicals, especially if you are dissolving chemicals in powdered form. Never use a punctured glove though – it can give your hand prolonged contact with trapped liquid chemical.

Wearing gloves can be uncomfortable and impractical if you are working for long sessions, constantly moving from wet to dry bench operations, as in printing. At least keep your hands out of solutions by using tongs or paddles to move chemical-covered prints.

Always try to mix chemicals where the ventilation is good and there is running water nearby to dilute any splashes. If you spill any chemical clean it up as soon as possible. Spilt solution soon evaporates, leaving behind a chemical dust that blows about. This is easily inhaled or accumulates in odd corners of your darkroom.

Don't have food or drink in any room where chemicals are used. Make sure all your storage containers are accurately labeled, and *never store chemicals in food or drink containers*. Someone else may assume they are for consumption. For similar reasons keep all photographic chemicals out of the reach of children. Don't store chemicals, or solutions, in a refrigerator or freezer.

Appendix P Chemically treating black and white prints

Even after you have made a black and white bromide print, there are still several ways you can alter the image by chemical means. You can decide to make your picture lighter in tone or bleach away parts to white paper, or tone it so that the neutral black image turns into a color. All these chemical treatments are carried out in trays, working under ordinary room lighting.

Start off with a fully fixed and washed print. If it has already dried re-soak it in water for 2–3 minutes, then blot it or wipe off surplus liquid. Working on a damp print helps to allow the chemicals to act evenly.

Reducing (lightening) the image

Farmer's reducer is a mixture of potassium ferricyanide and hypo (see formula, page 271). This forms a yellow solution which you apply on a cotton wool swab to over-dark parts of the picture. Then immediately hold your print under a cold water tap to halt the reduction. Examine the effect carefully. Repeat the process – just a little at a time – until the part of the print (or the entire image) is sufficiently lightened. If you go too far there is no way you can bring back the image again. Finally re-fix and wash the whole print.

Farmer's reducer has its most rapid effect on the palest tones in an image, so it is excellent for the overall 'brightening up' of pictures with veiled-over (gray) highlights. Don't expect to rescue a really dark print this way, however – if overdone the reducer leaves a yellowish stain and brownish-black tones. Farmer's reducer can also be used to lighten very dense, low contrast negatives; i.e. overexposed and underdeveloped. At the same time it greatly exaggerates the graininess of the image.

Bleaching to white with iodine

By using an iodine bleacher you can erase chosen parts of your print right down to white paper, without leaving any final stain. It is ideal for removing an unwanted background to a subject, leaving it with a 'cut-out' appearance. Two separate solutions are needed – the bleacher itself, and a tray of print-strength fixer.

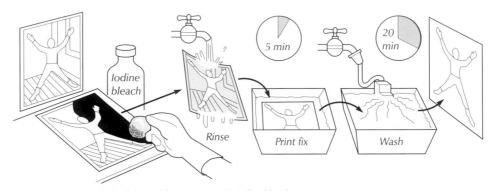

Figure P.1 Erasing the background from a print with iodine bleach.

As Figure P.1 shows, paint over the unwanted area of your print with a swab of cotton wool (changing to a watercolor brush when working close to the edges of fine detail). A strong brown stain immediately appears, with the black image fast vanishing beneath it. Wait until the unwanted parts have lost all their black silver, then rinse the whole print in water for at least 30 seconds. Next put it in the fixer solution for 5 minutes or so until the brown stain has completely disappeared, leaving clean white paper. Finally, wash the print for the same time recommended for your printing paper after regular fixing.

Sepia toning

Changing the print image from black into sepia is the simplest and most popular toning process. It gives a rich sepia or chocolate color, like a nineteenth-century photograph. Sepia toning is also advisable before hand coloring (see page 226).

You need two spearate solutions, bleacher and toner. Slide the print into the tray of bleacher, face up, and rock it for a minute or so until the once black image is bleached to a pale straw color. You then rinse it under the cold water tap and place it in a tray of toner solution. The picture reappears in a sepia color within a few seconds, but needs 2–3 minutes to reach full richness and depth. You fininsh off by washing and drying in exactly the same way as when making the print in the first instance.

The image now consists of brownish silver sulfide instead of the usual black metallic silver. This is very permanent – you cannot return a sepia print to black. Remember too that with toners of this kind bleaching is essential before the black image can become sepia. You can therefore

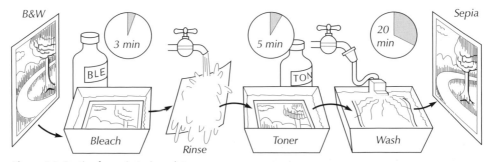

Figure P.2 Routine for sepia toning prints.

selectively bleach, say, just the background to your main subject by carefully applying bleacher on a brush or swab. Only this area then becomes sepia in the toner, leaving the main image black.

Another alternative is to dilute the bleacher with an equal volume of water to slow its action. You then immerse the whole print but remove it before darkest grays and shadows have lost their black appearance. After completing the toning stage of the process as normal your picture consists of a mixture of sepia and black. Results have deeper brown-black shadows than given by full toning. And if you don't like the result just re-bleach your print to affect the remaining black parts and tone the print again to get a fully sepia image.

You can also buy kits of multi-toner chemicals, typically consisting of a bleacher and a range of toners, each of which will result in a different color image. A kit with yellow, magenta and blue toners permits you to mix them in varying proportions (blue and yellow to get green, for example) and so form a wide choice of image hues. Most results are rather garish; some are not very permanent and alter with time.

Chemicals required

Farmer's reducer and most toners can be bought as packs of ready-weighed powders and liquids from manufacturers such as Tetenal. This is the most convenient and, in the long run, cheapest way of working. To make up your own solutions, however, prepare them from the following chemicals. Follow the handling precautions described on page 268.

Iodine bleacher

Warm water	400 ml
Potassium iodide	8 g
Iodine	2 g
Water up to	500 ml

Farmer's reducer

(a) Potassium ferricyanide	5 g
Water	500 ml
(b) Sodium thiosulfate	
(hypo crystals)	80 g
Warm water	500 ml

Mix equal quantities of (a) and (b) just before use (does not keep as a single solution).

Sepia toning

Bleach in:

Potassium ferricyanide	20 g
Potassium bromide	20 g
water up to	1 liter

Tone in:

Sodium sulfide	20 g
Water up to	1 liter

The sulfide in this formula gives off a 'bad eggs' smell, especially when diluted. Use it in a well-ventilated area, away from films and papers.

Glossary

AE Automatic exposure metering, i.e. the camera measures the light and sets shutter and aperture (either or both).

AE lock (AE-L) Locks an automatic exposure setting in the camera's memory.

AF Auto-focus.

AF lock (AF-L) Locks an auto-focus lens in its present focus setting.

Aliasing The jaggy edges that appear in bitmap images with curves or lines at any angle other than multiples of 90°.

Angle of view The extent of the view taken in by the lens. It varies with focal length for any particular format size. The angle made at the lens across the image diagonal.

Aperture (of lens) Size of the lens opening through which light passes. The relative aperture is calibrated in f-numbers, being the diameter of the beam of light allowed to pass through the lens, divided into its focal length. Widest relative apertures therefore have the lowest f-numbers. All lenses set to the same f-number give images of a (distant) scene at equal brightness.

Aperture preview Button on some SLR cameras to close the lens to the aperture set for photography. Allows you to visually check depth of field in the viewfinder.

APS Advanced Photographic System. Easy-load cameras and film cartridges 30 per cent smaller than 35 mm (see page 48).

ASA Stands for (obsolete) American Standards Association. The initials were once used for a film speed rating system. Now replaced by ISO.

Aspect ratio This is usually found in dialog boxes concerned with changes of image size and refers to the relationship between width and height of a picture. The maintaining of an image's aspect ratio means that this relationship will remain the same even when the image is enlarged or reduced.

Auto-focus (AF) System by which the lens automatically focuses the image of a selected part of your subject.

Av Aperture value. AE camera metering mode by which you choose aperture, and the metering system sets shutter speed (also called aperture priority).

'B' setting Brief or bulb. On this setting the camera shutter stays open for as long as the release button remains depressed.

Background printing A printing method that allows the user to continue working whilst an image or document is being printed from a computer.

Batch processing Refers to a function or a series of commands being applied to several digital files at one time. This function is useful for making the same changes to a folder full of images. In Photoshop Elements, this function is found under the File menu and is useful for converting groups of image files from one format to another.

Bit Stands for 'binary digit' and refers to the smallest part of information that makes up a digital file. It has a value of only 0 or 1. Eight of these bits make up one byte of data.

Bitmap or 'raster' The form in which digital photographs are stored, made up of a matrix of pixels.

Blend mode   The way in which a color or a layer interacts with others in a digital photograph. The most important after the Normal blend mode are probably Multiply (which darkens everything), Screen (which adds to the colors to make everything lighter), Lighten (which lightens only colors darker than itself) and Darken (which darkens only lighter colors than itself). Both the latter therefore flatten contrast. Color maintains the shading of a color but alters the color to itself. Glows therefore are achieved using Screen mode, and Shadows using Multiply.

Bracketing (exposure)   Taking several pictures of your subject at different exposure times or aperture settings, e.g. half and double as well as the estimated correct exposure.

Brightness range   The range of brightnesses between shadow and highlight areas of an image.

Bromide paper   Light-sensitive photographic paper for enlarging or contact printing. Carries a predominantly silver bromide emulsion. Must be handled in appropriate (usually amber or orange) safe lighting.

Burning-in   Giving additional exposure time to one selected area, during printing.

Burning-in tool   Used to darken a digital image, can be targeted to affect just the Shadows, Midtones or Highlights. Opposite to Dodge. Part of the toning trio, which also includes the Sponge.

Byte   This is the standard unit of digital storage. One byte is made up of 8 bits and can have any value between 0 and 255; 1024 bytes equal 1 kilobyte; 1024 kilobytes equal 1 megabyte; 1024 megabytes equal 1 gigabyte.

Camera obscura   A dark chamber to which light is admitted through a small hole, producing an inverted image of the scene outside, opposite the hole.

Cassette   Light-tight container for 35 mm camera film (see page 48).

CCD   Charge-Coupled Device. Electronic light-sensitive surface, digital replacement for film.

CD-ROM   Compact disc with read-only memory.

Clone Stamp or Rubber Stamp tool   Allows a user to copy a part of a digital image to somewhere else. It is therefore ideal for repair work, e.g. unwanted spots or blemishes. Equivalent to Copy and Paste in a brush.

Close-ups   Photographs in which the picture area is filled with a relatively small part of the subject (e.g. a single head). Usually photographed from close to the subject, but may be shot from further away using a long focal length lens.

Close-up attachments   Accessories which enable the camera to focus subjects that are closer than the nearest distance the lens normally allows.

Color balance   A color photograph that closely resembles the original subject appearance is said to have 'correct' color balance. Mismatching film type and lighting (wrong color temperature) gives a cast most apparent in gray tones and pale tints.

Color mode   The way that a digital image represents the colors that it contains. Different color modes include Bitmap, RGB and Grayscale.

Color temperature   A means of describing the color content of a 'white' light source. Based on the temperature (absolute scale, expressed in kelvin) to which a black metallic body would have to be heated to match the light, e.g. household lamp 2800 K, photoflood 3400 K.

Complementary colors   Opposite or 'negative' colors to the primary colors of light (blue, green and red). Each is made up from the full spectrum less the primary color, e.g. the complementary of red is blue plus green = cyan.

Composition   The activity of positioning the various subjects in a picture within a frame or viewfinder. Photographers often aim to create a visual balance of all the elements within their photographs. They do this via careful composition.

Compression   Refers to a process where digital files are made smaller to save on storage space or transmission time. Compression is available in two types: lossy, where parts of the original image are lost at the compression stage; and lossless, where the integrity of the file is maintained during the compression process. JPEG and GIF use lossy compression, whereas TIFF is a lossless format.

Contact printing   Printing with light, the object (typically a negative) being in direct contact with the light-sensitive material.

Contrast (composition)   Photographers who position subjects with different characteristics in the frame together are said to be creating contrast in the composition. Sitting a highly textured object against a smooth and even background creates a visual contrast between the two subjects and emphasizes the main characteristics of each.

Contrast (exposure and tone)   The difference (ratio) between the darkest and brightest parts. In a scene this depends on lighting and the reflecting properties of objects. In a photograph there is also the effect of exposure level, degree of development, printing paper, etc.

Cropping   Cutting out unwanted (edge) parts of a picture, typically at the printing or mounting stage.

Daylight color film   Color film balanced for use with flash, daylight or daylight-matching strip tubes (5500 K).

Depth of field   Distance between nearest and furthest parts of the subject sharply imaged at the same time. Greatest with small lens apertures (high f-number), distant scenes and shortest focal length lenses.

Developer   Chemicals, normally in solution, able to convert the invisible (latent) image on exposed photographic material into visible form.

Developing agents   Chemicals (typically phenidone, metol and hydroquinone) able to change light-struck silver halides into black metallic silver.

Digital image   Stream of electronic data, forms visible image on computer monitor.

Digitize   This is the process by which analog images or signals are sampled and changed into digital form.

Diffuse lighting   Scattered illumination, the visual result of which is gentle modeling of the subject with mild or non-existent shadows.

DIN   Stands for Deutche Industrie Norm (German Industrial Standard). DIN numbers denoted a film's relative sensitivity to light. Halving or doubling speed is shown by decrease or increase of the DIN number by three. Now incorporated in ISO and distinguished by degree symbol.

Dodge tool   For lightening areas in a digital image. See also *Burn*.

Dodging   Local shading in enlarging, usually by means of a piece of opaque material on a thin wire. Has the opposite effect of burning-in.

DPI   Dots per inch, a term used to indicate the resolution of a scanner or printer.

DX coding   Coding printed onto film cassette denoting speed, length, etc. Read by sensors in the film compartment of most 35 mm cameras.

Dynamic range   The measure of the range of brightness levels that can be recorded by a digital sensor.

Emulsion   Suspension of minute silver halide crystals in gelatine that, coated on film or paper, forms the light-sensitive material used in traditional (non-digital) photography.

Enhancement   A term that refers to changes in brightness, color and contrast that are designed to improve the overall look of a digital image.

Enlarger   Optical projector to give enlarged (or reduced) images, which can then be exposed onto light-sensitive paper or film (see page 187).

Enlarging easel (masking frame)   Flat board with adjustable flaps used on the enlarger base board to hold paper flat during exposure.

Exposed   A light-sensitive material that has received exposure to an image. Usually relates to the stage after exposure and before processing.

Exposure   Submitting photographic material to the action of light, usually by means of a camera or enlarger.

Exposure-compensation dial   Camera control overriding film speed (e.g. DX) setting, + or − .

Exposure latitude   The amount by which a photographic emulsion may be under- or overexposed, yet still give an acceptable image when processed.

Exposure meter   Instrument that measures light intensities falling on, or reflected off, the subject, and indicates or sets corresponding camera settings (shutter and aperture).

Extension tubes   Rings or short tubes mounted between camera body and lens to space the lens further away from the film and so allow the sharp focusing of very close subjects.

F-numbers   See *Aperture*.

File format   The way that a digital image is stored. Different formats have different characteristics. Some are cross-platform and can be used on both Macintosh and Windows machines, others have inbuilt compression capabilities.

Fill-in   Illumination to lighten shadows, reducing contrast.

Film speed   Measure of sensitivity of film to light. Usually expressed as an ISO figure.

Filter, digital   A filter is a way of applying a set of image characteristics to the whole or part of an image. Most image editing programs contain a range of filters that can be used for creating special effects.

Filter, lens   Sheet of (usually dyed) gelatin or glass. Used over the camera or enlarger lens mainly to reduce the light (neutral density gray filter) or to absorb particular wavelengths from the light beam.

Fixed focus   Camera lens set for a fixed subject distance. Non-adjustable.

Fixer   Chemical (basically a solution of sodium thiosulfate plus potassium metabisulfite as acidifier). Used after development to make soluble those parts of a photographic image unaffected by the developer. Photographs can thereafter be handled in normal lighting.

Fixing agent   Chemical able to change silver halide into colorless soluble salts.

Flare   Scattered light that dilutes the image, lowering contrast and seeming to reduce sharpness. Mostly occurs when the subject is backlit.

Flash contacts   Electrical contacts, normally within the mechanism of the camera shutter, which come together at the appropriate moment to trigger the flash unit. Older shutters may be fitted with X and M contact sockets. Use X for electronic flash.

Flash (electronic)   Equipment that gives a brief, brilliant flash of light by discharging an electronic capacitor through a small, gas-filled tube. Given time to recharge, a unit gives many thousands of flashes, usually triggered by contacts within the camera shutter.

Flash factor   See *Guide number*.

'Flat' images   Images that are low in tonal contrast, appearing gray and muddy.

Floodlamp   Studio lighting unit consisting of a large reflector containing a photolamp or other pearl glass lamp. Gives diffuse lighting.

Focal length   In a simple lens the distance (typically in millimeters) between the lens and the position of a sharp image for a subject a great distance away. A 'normal' lens has a focal length approximately equivalent to the diagonal of the picture format it covers, i.e. 50 mm for 36 mm × 24 mm.

Focal plane   The plane – normally flat and at right angles to the lens axis – on which a sharp image is formed. In the camera, the emulsion surface of the film must be in the focal plane at the moment of exposure to record a focused image.

Focus priority (trap focus)   Auto-focus camera mode by which you cannot release the shutter until the lens has sharply focused your subject.

Focusing   Changing the lens-to-image (or lens-to-subject) distance, until a sharp image is formed.

Fog   Allowing random light to reach light-sensitive material, as in opening the camera back accidentally or leaving a packet of paper open. Also caused by bad storage or contaminated or over-prolonged development (chemical fog).

Form   An object's three-dimensionality: height, breadth and depth.

Format   Height and width dimensions of the picture area.

Front page   Sometimes called the home or index page, refers to the initial screen that the viewer sees when logging onto a website. Often, the name and spelling of this page file is critical if it is to work on the web server. Consult your ISP staff for the precise name to be used with your site.

Gamma   The contrast of the midtone areas of a digital image.

Gamut   The range of colors or hues that can be printed or displayed by particular devices.

Gaussian Blur   When applied to an image or a selection, this digital filter softens or blurs the image.

GIF   Graphic Interchange Format. This is an indexed color mode that contains a maximum of 256 colors that can be mapped to any palette of actual colors. It is extensively used for web graphics as buttons and logos, and small animated images.

Glossy paper   Photographic paper that can give prints with a shiny, glossy surface.

Grade, of paper   Classification of black and white photographic papers by the gradation they offer between black and white. Soft (Grade 1) paper gives a wider range of gray tones than Hard (Grade 3). See also *Variable contrast paper*.

Grain   Irregularly shaped, microscopically small clumps of black silver making up the processed photographic silver halide image. Detectable on enlargement, particularly if the film emulsion was fast (ISO 1000 or over) and overdeveloped. Hard grade paper also emphasizes film grain.

Grayscale   A monochrome digital image containing tones ranging from white through a range of grays to black.

Guide number (flash factor)   Figure denoting the relative power of a flash source. The GN is the light-to-subject distance (usually in meters) multiplied by the f-number for correct exposure, e.g. GN of 16 = 2 m at f8 or 1 m at f16. (Unless film speed is quoted, factor refers to ISO 100 film.)

'Hard' image   Image with harsh tonal contrasts – mostly blacks and whites with few intermediate gray tones.

'Hard' light sources   Harsh source of illumination, giving strong clear-cut shadows. Tends to dramatize form and texture.

Histogram   A graph that represents the distribution of pixels within a digital image.

Hot linked   This term refers to a piece of text, graphic or picture that has been designed to act as a button on a web page. When the viewer clicks the hot-linked item, they are usually transported to another page or part of a website.

HTML   The Hyper Text Mark Up language is the code used to create web pages. The characteristics of pages are stored in this language and when a page file is downloaded to your computer the machine lays out and displays the text, image and graphics according to what is stated in the HTML file.

Hue   Refers to the color of the image and is separate from how light or dark it is.

Hyperfocal distance   Nearest subject rendered sharp when the lens is focused for infinity. Focused for the hyperfocal distance and without change of f-number, depth of field extends from half this distance to infinity.

Hypo   Abbreviation of hyposulfate of soda, an incorrect early name for sodium thiosulfate. Popular name for fixing bath.

Image layers   Images in programs like Photoshop Elements can be made up of many layers. Each layer will contain part of the picture. When viewed together, all layers appear to make up a single continuous image. Special effects and filters can be applied to layers individually.

Incident light attachment   Diffusing disc or dome (usually of white plastic) placed over the cell of a hand-held exposure meter to make readings towards the light source. Calculator dial is then used in the normal way. Gives results similar to reading off an 'average' subject or gray card.

Infinity   A distance so great that light from a given point reaches the camera as virtually parallel rays. In practice, distances of about 1000 times the focal length or over. Written on lens focusing mounts as 'inf' or a symbol like an '8' on its side.

Infinity lock   Control that sets (auto-focus) lens for distant subjects only. Useful if shooting through windows.

Inkjet printer   Digital printer, forms images using a very fine jet of one or more inks.

Interpolation   This is the process used by image editing programs to increase the resolution of a digital image. Using fuzzy logic the program makes up the extra pixels that are placed between the original ones that were generated at the time of scanning.

Inverse square law   'When a surface is illuminated by a point source of light the intensity of light at the surface is inversely proportional to the square of its distance from the source.' In other words, if you double the lamp distance, light spreads over a larger area and illumination drops to $1/2 \times 1/2 = 1/4$ of its previous value. Forms the basis of flash guide numbers and close-up exposure increases. Does not apply to large diffuse sources or, in practice, the (extremely distant) sun.

ISO   International Standards Organization. In the ISO film speed system, halving or doubling of speed is denoted by halving or doubling number. Also incorporates DIN figure, e.g. ISO 400/27° film is twice as sensitive as ISO 200/24°.

ISP   The Internet Service Provider is the company that hosts or stores web pages. If you access the web via a dial-up account, then you will usually have a portion of free space allocated for use for your own site; others can obtain free (with a small banner advert attached) space from companies like www.tripod.com.

JPEG A file format designed by the Joint Photographic Experts Group that has inbuilt lossy compression that enables a massive reduction in file sizes for digital images. Used extensively on the web and by press professionals for transmitting images back to newsdesks worldwide.

Juxtaposition Juxtaposing is the act of placing two objects side by side so that they are compared. In photographs, unlike subjects are often placed next to each other, or 'juxtaposed', so that their differences are exaggerated.

K (Kelvin) Measurement unit of lighting and color temperature.

Large-format cameras Normally refers to cameras taking negatives larger than 120 rollfilm size.

Latent image The invisible image contained by the photographic material after exposure but before development. Stored protected from light, damp and chemical fumes, a latent image can persist for years.

Layer opacity The opacity or transparency of each image layer in a digital photograph can be changed independently. Depending on the level of opacity, the parts of the layer beneath will become visible. You can change the opacity of each layer by moving the Opacity slider in the Layers palette.

LCD Liquid Crystal Display. A display screen type used in preview screens on the back of digital cameras and in most laptop computers.

Line (composition) Line is one of the strongest visual elements that photographers can use to help compose their pictures. Often, line is used to direct the attention of the viewer towards a certain part of the frame or at a specific focal point. The lines used in photographs may be actual, such as a power cable in a landscape, or may be created by changes of tone or texture, such as the edge between a shaft of sunlight and the dark background.

Liquify A digital filter that uses brushes to perform distortions upon selections or the whole of an image.

Long focal length lens Lens with focal length longer than considered 'normal' for picture format. Gives larger detail and narrower angle of view. Almost all such lenses are telephoto types.

Macro lens Lens intended for close-up photography, able to focus well forward from its infinity position for subjects a few inches away, gives highest quality image at such distances.

Macrophotography Photography at very close subject range.

Marquee A rectangular selection used to isolate a portion of a digital photograph made by clicking and dragging to an opposite corner.

Masking frame See *Enlarging easel*.

Mat or overmat Card with cut-out opening, placed over print to isolate finished picture.

Megapixel One million pixels. Used to describe the resolution of digital camera sensors.

Monochrome image Single colored. Usually implies a black image, but also applies to one which is toned, i.e. sepia.

Montage An image constructed by combining what were originally several separate images.

Mood The mood of a photograph refers to the emotional content of the picture.

Multigrade Multi-contrast printing paper. See *Variable contrast paper*.

Negative image Image in which blacks, whites and tones are reversed, relative to the original subject. Color negatives have subject colors represented by their complementaries.

'Normal' lens   The lens regarded as standard for the picture format, i.e. having a focal length approximately equal to its diagonal.

Optical resolution   The resolution that a scanner uses to sample the original image. This is often different from the highest resolution quoted for the scanner, as this is scaled up by interpolating the optically scanned file.

Options bar   Long bar beneath the menu bar in an image editing program, which immediately displays the various settings for whichever tool is currently selected. Can be moved to other parts of the screen if preferred.

Overdevelopment   Giving too long or too much agitation in the developer, or having too high a temperature, or developer too concentrated. This results in excessive density and exaggerated grain structure in the developed material.

Overexposure   Exposing photographic material to too much light because the image is too bright or exposure time too long. Results in excessive density in the final image.

Palette   A window in the image editing program that is used for the alteration of the characteristics of a digital photograph.

Panchromatic   Photographic materials sensitive to all visible colors, recording them in various shades of gray. Should be processed in total darkness or an exceedingly dark safe light. All general-purpose films are of this kind.

Panning   Rotating or swinging the camera about a vertical axis.

Parallax error   Viewpoint difference between the picture seen in the viewfinder and as seen by the camera lens (see page 30).

Pattern (composition)   Repeating subjects that have similar characteristics such as color, shape and texture create a strong visual element that is often referred to as pattern. Pattern can be used in a similar way to tone, line and color as a way to balance compositions and direct the viewer's eye throughout the frame.

Photo CD   CD format for storing photographs as digital files. Disc typically holds up to 100 images, stored in various levels of resolution.

Photographic lamps   Generalized term now often applied to both 3200 K studio lamps (floods and spots) and the brighter, short-life 3400 K photoflood lamps.

Pixel   Short for picture element, refers to the smallest image part of a digital photograph.

Polarizer   Gray-looking polarizing filter, able to darken blue sky at right angles to sunlight, and suppress reflections from (non-metallic) surfaces at angles of about 30°.

Polycontrast   See Variable contrast paper.

Printing-in   See Burning-in.

'Pushing'   Slang term for uprating film speed.

Rapid fixer   Fixing bath using ammonium thiosulfate or thiocyanate instead of the normal sodium thiosulfate. Enables fixing time to be greatly reduced, but is more expensive.

Reciprocity law failure   Normally the effect of dim light, or small lens aperture, can be counteracted by giving a long exposure time. But this reciprocal relationship (half the brightness = double the exposure time) increasingly breaks down with exposure times beyond 1 second. The film then behaves as if having a lower speed rating. Color films may also show incorrect balance.

'Red eye'   The iris of each eye in portraits shows red instead of black. Caused by using flash directed from close to the lens.

Reflex camera   Camera with viewfinder system using a mirror and focusing screen.

Refraction   Change of direction of a ray of light passing obliquely from one transparent medium into another of different density, e.g. from air into glass. The basic reason why lenses bend light rays and so form images.

Resin-coated (RC) bromide paper   Bromide paper having a water-repellent plastic base. RC papers require less washing, dry more rapidly and generally process faster than fiber-based papers.

Reversal film   Film that can be processed to give a positive image direct. Color slide films are of this type. Some black and white films can be reversal processed.

RGB   All colors in a digital image are made up of a mixture of Red, Green and Blue colors. This is the typical mode used for desktop scanners, painting programs and digital cameras.

Rollfilm   Photographic film, usually 6.2 cm wide (known as 120), attached to a numbered backing paper and rolled on a flanged spool.

Safe light   Darkroom light source filtered to illuminate only in a color to which photographic material is insensitive. The correct color varies with type of emulsion, e.g. orange for bromide papers.

Selective focusing   Using a shallow depth of field (i.e. by means of a wide lens aperture) and focusing so that only one selected zone of the subject is sharply recorded.

Shading, in printing   Preventing the image light from acting on a selected area of the picture for a time during the exposure.

Sheet film   Film supplied as individual sheets, usually 10 or 25 to a box.

Shutter   Mechanical device to control the time the light is allowed to act on the film. Usually consists of metal blades within the lens, or two blinds passing one after another just in front of the film, the exposure occurring in the gap between them (focal plane shutter).

Silver halides   Light-sensitive compounds of silver with the halogens (iodine, bromide, etc.). Normally white or creamy yellow in color. Used as the main sensitive constituent of photographic emulsions.

Single lens reflex (SLR)   Camera in which the viewfinder image is formed by the picture-taking lens.

Soft focus   Image in which outlines are slightly spread or diffused.

'Soft' light sources   See *Diffuse lighting*.

Sponge tool   Used for saturating or desaturating part of a digital photograph that is exaggerating or lessening the color component as opposed to the lightness or darkness.

Spotlight   A compact filament lamp, reflector and lens forming one light unit. Gives hard direct illumination, variable from narrow to broad beam.

Stop-bath   Stage in processing that arrests the action of the previous solution (e.g. a weak solution of acetic acid used between development and fixation).

Subject   The person, scene, situation, etc. being photographed. (Tends to be used interchangeably with object.)

'T' setting   Setting found on some large-format camera shutters for time exposures. Pressing the release opens the shutter, which then remains open until pressed for a second time.

Target audience   The group of people whose experience, understanding and appreciation are catered for when creating a picture, or taking a photograph. The content or style of picture may change depending on the nature of the target audience who will be viewing the work.

Telephoto lens   Long focus lens of compact design (lens is physically closer to the film than its focal length).

Test strip   One of a series of test exposures on a piece of printing paper, then processed to see which gives the most satisfactory result.

Texture   Surface qualities such as roughness, smoothness, hairiness, etc. Like line, pattern and color, texture is a compositional element that can be used to help balance a photograph.

Through-the-lens (TTL) metering   Measuring exposure by a meter built into the camera body, which measures the intensity of light passing through the picture-taking lens.

Thumbnail   A low-resolution preview version of larger digital image files used to check before opening the full version.

Time exposure   General term for a long duration exposure.

Tones, tonal values   Areas of uniform density in a positive or negative image that can be distinguished from darker or lighter parts.

Tone (subject matter)   Tone can also refer to the mood of a picture. When the tone of a photograph is said to be 'dark', then the subject matter and/or the way that the content is depicted can be emotional, complex, sometimes sad, confronting and generally thought-provoking.

Translucent   Transmitting but at the same time also diffusing light, e.g. tracing paper.

Transparency   Positive image film.

Tungsten lamps   Lamps that generate light when electric current is passed through a fine tungsten wire. Household lamps, photofloods, studio lamps, etc. are all of this type.

Tungsten light film   Also known as 'Type B' or 'Artificial light'. Color film balanced for use with 3200 K studio lighting.

Tv   Time value. AE camera metering mode by which you choose shutter speed and the metering system sets aperture (also called shutter priority).

Twin lens reflex   Camera with two linked lenses – one forming an image onto film, the other giving an image on a focusing screen (see page 263).

Underdevelopment   Giving too short a developing time, using too low a temperature, too great a dilution or old or exhausted solutions. This results in insufficient density being built up.

Underexposure   Exposing photographic material to too little light, because the image is too dim or exposure time too short. Results in insufficient density and shadow detail in the final image.

Uprating   Shooting film at more than the manufacturer's suggested speed rating, e.g. exposing 400 ISO film as if 800 ISO. The film is then given extra development.

Variable contrast (multigrade) paper   Black and white printing paper that changes its contrast characteristics with the color of the exposing light. Controlled by enlarger filters typically ranging from yellow to purple.

Viewpoint   The position from which camera, and photographer, view the subject.

Wetting agent   Chemical (e.g. weak detergent) that reduces the surface tension of water. Facilitates even action of developer or final wash water.

Wide-angle lens   Lens with a focal length much shorter than the diagonal of the format for which it is designed to be used. Gives a wide angle of view and considerable depth of field.

Zoom lens   A lens that offers continuous variation of focal length over a set range, maintaining the same focus setting.

Additional technical details on the pictures in this book

Apart from those images supplied by www.ablestock.com and unless otherwise stated, all photographs were exposed on 400 ISO black and white, 64 ISO color slide or 100 ISO color neg. 35 mm film.

Figure 21.1   Exposure measured by a general reading (keeping out of direct sunlight), 50 mm lens, no extension tube, 1/125 second at f4.

Figure 21.13   1/60 second at f16 using ISO 200 film.

Figures 26.9 and 26.10   Exposure read for the lit (side) of the dancer's body, then twice the amount indicated given, 5 seconds at f16.

Figure 37.6   1/125 second at f11 left-hand picture, 1/125 second at f 8 other version.

Figure 37.7   30 seconds at f 8, slide film.

Figure 38.1   Exposure measured entirely from the projected image on the hand, 1/4 second at f4. The wrist was firmly supported.

Figures 38.3 and 38.4   Two strips of black card hung vertically halfway between projector and bottle limited the slide image to bottle shape alone, 1 second at f 5.6.

Figure 38.10   Exposure measured off the ground. The horizontal axis tilt between part-exposures is made easier with a tilting head tripod.

Index

Basic Photography
Michael Langford

'I found this book to be the best that I have ever seen on the subject of photography not only for "basic" knowledge but for far more advanced subjects. It is clear, precise, easy to read and more important, easy to understand and apply.'
Robert A. Freson, Professional Travel and Nature Photographer

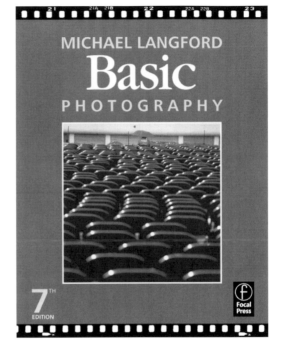

- A clear and concise approach to essential photographic principles, assuming no prior knowledge
- Comprehensive coverage of black and white photography, processing and printing; colour photography, digital manipulation and film processing
- Suitable for students of all ages and all photographic courses

Basic Photography is a longstanding international bestseller and continues to be the introductory textbook for photography courses throughout the world. This new edition now includes:

- Extended coverage of digital imaging techniques, from capturing images digitally, to scanning and using manipulation software and the ethics involved
- Updated and restructured contents to suit the new Art (Photography) A Level
- Hundreds of stunning full colour photographs throughout including inspirational images from world famous photographers including Bill Brandt, Henri Cartier-Bresson, Edward Weston and David Hockney

The late Michael Langford formerly taught at the Royal College of Art for many years, becoming Course Director. He was intimately involved with photography courses and examination syllabuses at all levels and as a result fully understood what a student needed.

September 2000: 189 × 246 mm: 250 Colour images: Paperback:
0 240 51592 7

To order your copy call +44 (0)1865 474010 (UK) or +1 800 545 2522 (USA) or visit the
Focal Press website: www.focalpress.com

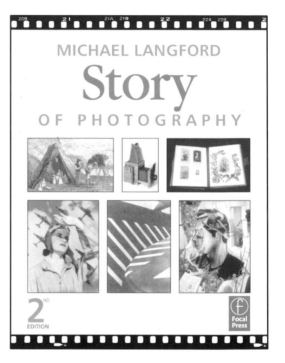